Foundation

OXFORD
GCSE
Maths
for OCR

SPECIFICATION A

Teacher Guide

Neil Tully

OCR
RECOGNISING ACHIEVEMENT

OXFORD
UNIVERSITY PRESS

Official Publisher Partnership

OxBox

UNIVERSITY PRESS

Great Clarendon Street, Oxford OX2 6DP

Oxford University Press is a department of the University of Oxford.

It furthers the University's objective of excellence in research, scholarship, and education by publishing worldwide in

Oxford   New York

Auckland   Cape Town   Dar es Salaam   Hong Kong   Karachi
Kuala Lumpur   Madrid   Melbourne   Mexico City   Nairobi
New Delhi   Shanghai   Taipei   Toronto

With offices in

Argentina   Austria   Brazil   Chile   Czech Republic   France   Greece
Guatemala   Hungary   Italy   Japan   Poland   Portugal   Singapore
South Korea   Switzerland   Thailand   Turkey   Ukraine   Vietnam

© Oxford University Press

The moral rights of the authors have been asserted

Database right Oxford University Press (maker)

First published 2010

British Library Cataloguing in Publication Data

Data available

ISBN: 978-0-19-912728-3
10 9 8 7 6 5 4 3 2 1

Printed in Great Britain by Synergie Basingstoke

Paper used in the production of this book is a natural, recyclable product made from wood grown in sustainable forests. The manufacturing process conforms to the environmental regulations to the country of origin.

About this book

In official partnership with OCR, this Teacher Guide has been specifically written to provide essential support for delivering GCSE in Mathematics A (J562). Part of the series *Oxford GCSE Maths for OCR*, it is designed for teachers of cohorts who are expecting to enter for the Foundation tier.

The author is an experienced teacher who has an excellent understanding of the OCR specifications grounded in practical classroom technique, and so is well qualified to help you successfully meet your objectives.

The Guide is made up of lesson plans that conform to the specification for Mathematics A, and accompanies the associated Foundation Student's Book. The Guide is organised clearly into the three units that will make up your students' assessment:

Unit A501/01: Mathematics Unit A	pages 2 - 63
Unit A502/01: Mathematics Unit B	pages 64 - 118
Unit A503/01: Mathematics Unit C	pages 119 - 175

As well as **lesson plans** giving you lots of ideas for delivering an effective multi-part lesson, the Guide contains:

- Chapter **introductions** comprising specification objectives, prerequisite knowledge, rich task commentary and useful ICT resources from the accompanying OxBox CD-ROMS

- **Assessment commentary** for each chapter, focusing on the new assessment objectives

- **Case study** teacher notes, with ideas for delivering the functional maths case study scenarios inside the Students' Book

- **Answers** to the exercises in the Students' Book, with guidance on the rich tasks and activities

- Free **CD-ROM** containing all lesson plans in customisable Word format.

There are also links and references to other helpful resources, such as Autograph, TI-*n*Spire and Cabri software, as well as OCR's AO3 Guide and problem-solving support pack (SMP).

Note regarding the levels of demand in the student books

The levels of demand attached to the exercises are used by examiners and roughly correspond to the following grades:

Grade G/F	Low demand
Grade E	Medium low demand
Grade D/C	Medium demand (overlap Foundation and Higher)
Grade B	Medium high demand
Grade A/A*	High demand

Contents

Finding your way around this course

NUMBER

ALGEBRA

GEOMETRY

DATA

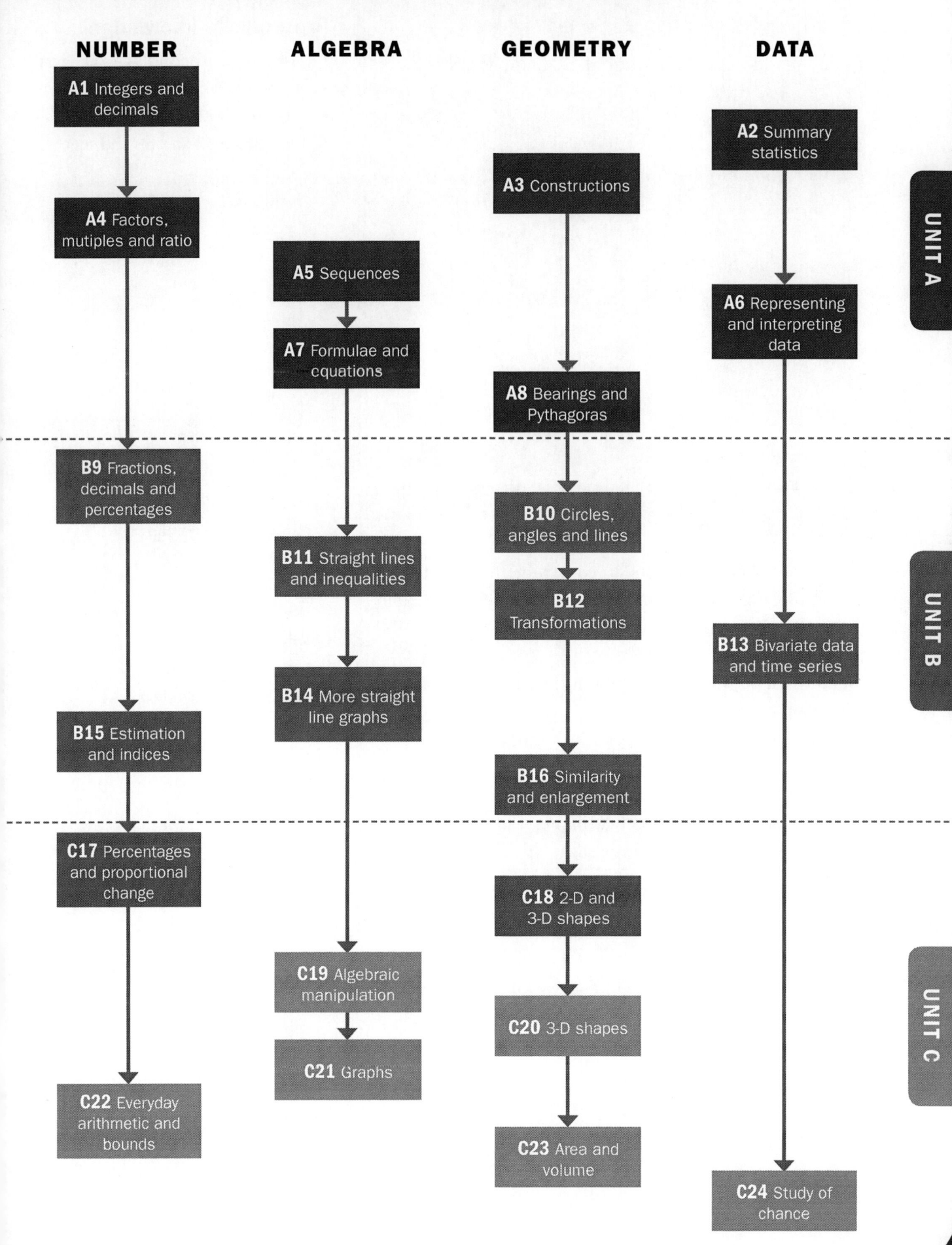

A1 Integers and decimals

A4 Factors, mutiples and ratio

A5 Sequences

A7 Formulae and cquations

A3 Constructions

A8 Bearings and Pythagoras

A2 Summary statistics

A6 Representing and interpreting data

B9 Fractions, decimals and percentages

B11 Straight lines and inequalities

B14 More straight line graphs

B10 Circles, angles and lines

B12 Transformations

B16 Similarity and enlargement

B13 Bivariate data and time series

B15 Estimation and indices

C17 Percentages and proportional change

C19 Algebraic manipulation

C21 Graphs

C18 2-D and 3-D shapes

C20 3-D shapes

C23 Area and volume

C22 Everyday arithmetic and bounds

C24 Study of chance

UNIT A

UNIT B

UNIT C

1

Integers and decimals

Objectives covered in this chapter are:

FA2.1b add, subtract, multiply and divide integers

FA2.2a use their previous understanding of integers and place value to deal with arbitrarily large positive numbers

FA2.2c round to the nearest integer, to a given number of decimal places and to one significant figure

FA2.3b know how to enter complex calculations and use function keys for reciprocals, squares and powers

Prerequisite knowledge

- Place value in decimals and integers
- Arithmetic with directed numbers
- Familiarity with order of operations
- Recognition of squares and square roots

RICH TASK COMMENTARY

Students could be encouraged to construct an accurate number line marked off from −20 to +20 in Centigrade and −4 to +68 in Fahrenheit. They should then be able to read off their answer.

It might then be worth talking about the mathematical connection between them.

Why do we use Fahrenheit when it is hot but Centigrade when it is cold?

Could they construct similar number lines for other mathematical conversions such as inches and centimetres, pounds and kg, gallons and litres etc.

Could they draw some conversion graphs?

Could they invent their own set of units?

Useful ICT resources

Introductory powerpoint	A1
Starter activity	A1.2(x3)
Animation	A1.1
Consolidation	A1
Chapter test	A1
Formative on-screen test	A1
Summative on-screen test	A1

- Use their previous understanding of integers and place value to deal with arbitrarily large positive numbers (FA2.2)

Starter

Ask students to 'Give me an example of:
a 3-digit even number;
a 3-digit number less than 50;
a 2-digit number between 5 and 7;
a 3-digit number between 0.4 and 0.6.'
Students respond using number fans or mini whiteboards. Select a group of students to the front of the class with their 3-digit numbers and ask them to put themselves in order. Involve the whole class in advising.

Resources

Number fans or mini whiteboards

Teaching notes

Begin with a mental maths warm up. They should have developed basic number bonds in earlier work but it does need constant reinforcement. The rich task on bar codes in the text is an interesting context in which the students can practise their basic arithmetic skills. The meaning of digit, odd and even and sum may need revising.

The concept of place value is always worth reviewing through quizzing the group about a number such as 33333. The ability to write numbers in words and in digits can be reviewed through a short quiz. Students often enjoy reading and writing very large numbers and the definition of a billion is worth checking.

Exercise commentary

Question 1 Writing numbers in words.

Question 2 Translating words into digits.

Question 3 Testing place value.

Question 4 This is an AO3 task which, with suitable students, can be taken as far as algebraic justification. The introduction of the idea of writing a general two digit number AB as 10A+B enable the more able students to approach a more general approach to this sort of work.

Plenary

The investigation presented in question 4 provides a lot of discussion material. For the ambitious the same task could be attempted in a different number base and further generalisations made.

- Understand and use positive numbers and negative integers, both as positions and translations on a number line (FA2.1)
- Add, subtract, multiply and divide integers and then any number (FA2.1)
- Multiply and divide by a negative number (FA2.1)
- Use brackets and the hierarchy of operations (FA3.1)

Starter

Give students three digit cards: −7, −2, 3, and three operation cards (+ − ×). By either rearranging the cards or using mini whiteboards ask the students to make the largest number and the smallest number possible. Give the students two minutes for this and then discuss the results.

Now challenge students to find a sentence giving a result nearest to 9. Discuss the resulting sentences here, modelling any on a number line as appropriate.

Resources

Digit and operation cards, mini whiteboards, number line with positive and negative scale

Teaching notes

Students will have met this subject before and the associated rules. A good starter would be to quiz the group about where they have met directed numbers previously and hopefully come to the temperature scale, number line and debt. A number line provides a good picture of calculating, for example, $3 - 6$, $-5 - 3$ or $-5 + 7$. The less intuitive double negative rule is well illustrated by the task presented in the text and students should work through this task in pairs.

Moving onto multiplication and division can be approached by viewing multiplication as repeated addition and then using the number pattern approach suggested in the text.

The students should attempt to summarise the general rules for combining these numbers before the teacher draws together and summarises all the rules from the group.

A mental quiz could help consolidate these basic rules before setting out on the exercise.

Exercise commentary

Question 1 Addition and subtraction including double negatives.

Question 2 Multiplication and division including double negatives.

Question 3 This is set within the context of temperature. Some students may need reminding that finding the difference is equivalent to subtracting.

Question 4 This question about a quiz requires careful reading and reasoning. The last part requires some investigation.

Plenary

There is considerable history about directed numbers to be researched on the web; for example, the Nrich site has an excellent article. The multicultural development of mathematics can once again be highlighted.

The use of a calculator to evaluate expressions involving directed numbers could be investigated by redoing some or all of the exercise with a calculator. Pupils should be enabled to discover the importance of brackets when using a calculator. Powers of negative numbers could be investigated and general rules noticed for $(-1)^n$ and similar expressions.

- Round numbers to a given power of 10
- Round to the nearest integer, to a given number of decimal places and to one significant figure (FA2.2)

Starter

Display some numbers and ask students to use these to give them to: the nearest 10; nearest whole number; one decimal point, and so on.

Also 'Give me a number which to the nearest 10 is ...' and so on, exploring the range of answers offered and the range possible.

Resources

Mini whiteboards

Teaching notes

The starter will make clear how much revision of this mode of rounding is required before moving onto decimal places and significant figures.

Give them some calculations to do on their calculators like converting fractions to decimals or $\sqrt{7}$. As a group discuss how to round the answers to a specified number of decimal places and provide some practice for the class as a whole to try.

The concept of significant figures can be approached via a number like 333554 which could provide the launching point for spotting that some digits are more significant for the overall value of the number than others. Discuss rounding this number to 1, 2, 3… significant figures. A common error for the above number to, for example, 3 s.f. is to see 334 rather than 334000.

Encourage the students to ask themselves: "Is the answer sensible?" "Is it of the same order of magnitude as the original number?"

Allow the students to work through the rich task and observe that both temperatures are the same to 2 s.f. The reverse of this could be emphasised, for example that 180 to 2 s.f. represents a range of possible numbers.

Exercise commentary

Questions 1–3 These are revision of nearest 10 and 100 rounding. Encourage students to ask themselves if their answers make sense compared to the original number.

Question 4 Rounding to 1 s.f.

Question 5 Decimal place rounding.

Question 6 Significant figure rounding. Remind students to check if their answer is of the right order of magnitude compared to the original number.

Question 7 These have many possible answers and help to develop the idea of a rounded number representing a range of values.

Plenary

More awkward and unusual numbers could be considered, for example rounding 0.003477 to 2 d.p. and then 2 s.f.

Students could investigate the Fix mode on a calculator.

The dangers of repeated rounding during a calculation should be considered in a topic area such as area or volume.

- Use brackets and the hierarchy of operations (FA3.1)
- Use calculators effectively and efficiently (FA2.3)
- Know how to enter complex calculations and use function keys for reciprocals, squares and powers (FA2.3)

Starter

Show a calculation with its answer: $4.2 \times 17 = 71.4$. Ask the students to write a calculation on whiteboards that follows from this statement, for example $2.1 \times 17 = 35.7$ or $0.42 \times 17 = 7.14$ Select some to display to the whole group, asking the student to explain the equivalence.

Encourage using related fact strategies such as doubling, halving and links to powers of 10 to work out other calculations such as 42×170.

Resources

Scientific calculators; OCR AO3 Guide section 3.4

Teaching notes

You may want to arrange to have all calculators set up so that they show the same default display; either fractions or decimals.

Review BIDMAS. Focus on the use of a calculator and note that most calculators follow BIDMAS automatically. Set a couple of suitable problems and ask the class to work out their answers which will provide a basis for discussion.

For example $\dfrac{3.3}{2.1 + 5.2}$ will very likely result in at least two different answers enabling a focus on the importance of brackets in this work. Other examples should provoke use of roots and powers. The ANS button which appears on most calculators is a very useful tool which acts as the short term memory of the calculator.

The idea of a reciprocal can be reviewed and some examples both with and without a calculator can be tried.

The powerful fraction button should be demonstrated and also the use of the change sign button which should be distinguished from the subtraction operation.

Exercise commentary

Question 1 This provides basic drill in calculator use. The irrelevant bracket in part **h** could be discussed.

Question 2 This question requires rounding and this process may need a little revision from the previous sections.

Question 3 This question about reciprocals can be done with or without a calculator depending on the ability level of the group.

Question 4 This gives students practice using the power keys on their calculator. Make students aware that these keys vary on different calculators.

Question 5 This question encourages students to explore the keys on their calculator.

Plenary

Other buttons on the calculator could be investigated such as factorial and the standard index form button.

The use of the ANS button in iterative formulae could be looked at in a simple way and related to sequence work elsewhere (e.g. in Chapter A5).

Exam-style question commentary

Worked solution	Commentary
1) a) 2.71828 b) 2.72	1) Some students may confuse the rules for rounding. If 5 dp are required, they should look first to the 6th digit after the point (not the 5th). Don't let students be put off by the letter *e*!

2) a) $\dfrac{7.2 + 9.3}{3.1^2} = \dfrac{16.5}{9.61}$
 	
      $= 1.71696$
 	
  b) 2
	2) a) The order of operations may not be easily apparent here – emphasise that the fraction bar acts as a divide sign.
	
	  b) Students will often confuse dp and sf because the rules are similar – stress the importance of reading the question carefully.

3)	3) This is an AO3-type problem that requires inverse operations and links nicely to algebra. Students may have seen these types of pyramid problem before – you can use an addition rule as an alternative to multiplication. Some students may need reminding about arithmetic with directed numbers.

Summary statistics

A2

Objectives covered in this chapter are:

FA13.1a carry out each of the four aspects of the handling data cycle to solve problems (specify the problem and plan; collect data from a variety of suitable sources; process and represent the data; interpret and discuss the data)

FA13.2a discuss how data relate to a problem, identify possible sources of bias and plan to minimise it

FA13.2c design an experiment or survey and decide what primary and secondary data to use

FA13.2f design and use two-way tables for discrete data

FA13.3a draw and produce stem and leaf diagrams

FA13.3b calculate mean, range and median of small data sets with discrete data

FA13.3c identify the modal class for grouped data

FA13.3d calculate an estimate of the mean for large data sets with grouped data

FA13.4d compare distributions and make inferences, using the shape of distributions and measures of average and range

FA13.4e understand that increasing sample size generally leads to better population characteristics

Prerequisite knowledge

- Familiarity with data collection sheets
- Recognition of inequality notation
- Ability to order numbers

Useful ICT resources

Introductory powerpoint	A2
Starter activity	A2.3 (x2)
Powerpoint worked solution	A2.3 (x2)
Animation	A2.1
Interactive activity	A2.3 (AG), A2.3 (TI)
Consolidation	A2
Chapter test	A2
Formative on-screen test	A2
Summative on-screen test	A2

RICH TASK COMMENTARY

The students will need to gather some data on travel times for your school, and they should be involved in the design of an appropriate data collection sheet. Students should be encouraged to choose a random sample of about 20 boys and a similar size sample of girls, and identify journey time and distance from school or name of town in which they live.

They should produce a grouped frequency table for journey times for boys and girls. They can look at distance from school or the town/village they live in and see what the journey times are from each place. They could use frequency diagrams/bar charts to present their results and show the distribution, and write an analysis comparing the distribution for boys compared to girls. Students should be encouraged to ask and investigate their own questions and design an appropriate questionnaire.

- Specify the problem and plan: formulate questions in terms of the data needed, and consider what inferences can be drawn from the data
- Decide what data to collect (including sample size and data format) and what statistical analysis is needed
- Collect data from a variety of suitable sources, including experiments and surveys, and primary and secondary sources
- Process and represent the data: turn the raw data into usable information that gives insight into the problem
- Interpret and discuss the data: answer the initial question by drawing conclusions from the data   (FA13.1)
- Design and use two-way tables for discrete and grouped data   (FA13.2)

Starter

Collect data from the class to complete a two-way table; for example, Girls/Boys; or family has or has not got a pet.

Resources

Mini whiteboards

Teaching notes

This section is centred on Thao and her memory test. It is worth focusing on using this example since it also provides the context for discussion in some of the later statistical sections.

Once you have explained the problem given, questions can be asked to encourage the group to think up their own hypotheses that can be used with the questions in the text to discuss the data handling cycle. The students could then do the test themselves, recording their data in pairs, and then, if time allows, the teacher could collect the data centrally and some hypotheses tested.

There is some unusual vocabulary which may need explaining. For example, collating, processing data and two-way table.

The use of data collection sheets is something students will have met before when they used tally charts and they may wish to use this approach for summarising their data before writing down the final refined two-way table.

Exercise commentary

Question 1 This is practice in making sense of a two-way table.

Question 2 This provides key experience in designing a two-way table for a survey.

Question 3 This table provides data to interpret but extends into asking the students to pose their own questions using the given data. It is advisable that you have some questions ready to help students who might struggle creating their own.

Plenary

This is the first of a large and important section on Statistics. You may want to further illustrate the work with some examples of statistics used in the world of work or the media.

There is plenty of opportunity of addressing the functional mathematics strand of the curriculum using the ideas and tools encountered.

- Identify key questions that can be addressed by statistical methods
- Design an experiment or survey and decide what primary and secondary data to use
- Design and use data-collection sheets for grouped discrete and continuous data
- Gather data from secondary sources, including printed tables and lists from ICT-based sources (FA13.2)

Starter

The table shows information about students in a school.

	Left handed	Right handed
Girls	12	48
Boys	8	28

What fraction of the girls are left handed?
What percentage of the total are boys?

Resources

None required, though the OCR AO3 Guide Section 3.2 (Activity 2) is directly useful

Teaching notes

This section introduces a number of important definitions. Start by discussing different types of data collection that students can think of. Write their suggestions on the board and split them into primary data and secondary data.

Do something similar with discrete and continuous data. Elicit some examples of different kinds of numerical data that could be collected, elicit their responses and divide them up into discrete data and continuous data.

The ideas of bias and sampling can get very complex but this introductory stage requires only a basic grasp of the principles. All the ideas are revisited and further developed in later sections.

Exercise commentary

Question 1 This provides practice in distinguishing discrete from continuous data.

Question 2 This provides practice in distinguishing secondary from primary data.

Question 3 This focuses on taking a sample and on bias. Part (b) asks about how to take a representative sample.

Question 4 This is an AO3 task which could be actually undertaken by the student individually or as part of a pair or group.

Plenary

The problems of bias could be further discussed by considering groups with things to sell, or ideas to spread, that use biased data to mislead people. The students could try and find some examples of bias as a homework task perhaps in advertising or in history.

Sites such as Amazon and Google on the web collect huge amounts of data and use this to predict consumer behaviour. Pupils could look at this 'data mining' industry and see just how much mathematics does impact on everyone who lives in the modern information-driven world.

- Calculate mean, range and median of small data sets with discrete then continuous data (FA13.3)

Starter

Challenge students to decide which group of five students did best in a test.

Group 1: 2, 3, 5, 7, 8
Group 2: 4, 4, 5, 5, 7
Group 3: 5, 6, 6, 6, 7

Ask students to justify their choice.

Resources

None required, though the OCR AO3 Guide Section 3.2 could be useful

Teaching notes

The students will have met these ideas before so it should be possible to draw the ideas out from the group through suitable questioning.

You could present a list of raw data possibly heights or weights which have not been organised in any way. Then the group could be asked to make some observations. In discussion it should emerge with a little guidance that ordering and summarising the data could help.

The fact that we have three averages in mathematics compared to the one in everyday usage should be made clear and then, using a list of data, the three averages can be calculated. The idea of spread can be introduced and the range of the data under consideration calculated.

The median needs to be considered both with an odd and an even number of data elements.

It can be demonstrated that data sets can be bi-modal, tri-modal etc.

It should be observed that the mean and median can have values which are not part of the original data.

Exercise commentary

Questions 1–3 These are AO1 practice.

Question 4 This provides some more practice in the context of house prices but also asks the student to begin deciding which measure is the optimal for a given situation. Here the mode is a poor summary of the data. The question could be extended at this stage, or later, by asking which measure would be best.

Question 5 This is a more open-ended problem. Students may need some hints to get started.

Plenary

You could bring together the findings from the attempts at question 5 and get the group to formulate general conclusions.

The ease with which outliers can distort calculations of the mean could be investigated.

Stem and leaf diagrams

- Produce stem and leaf diagrams   (FA13.3)

Starter

Ask students to respond on whiteboards to questions such as:
Give four numbers which have a mean of 8;
Give four different numbers with a mean of 8.

Explore and share the responses with the group.

Resources

Mini whiteboards

Teaching notes

Stem and leaf diagrams provide a way of summarising data in a diagram whilst still retaining the original numerical data. Using the example in the book or another prepared example, the key points to demonstrate and emphasise are:

1. To decide on a stem and leaf and write down the key so others know what is going on.
2. Go through the original data set systematically putting it onto the stem and leaf diagram; at this stage it is not necessary to have the leaf data ordered.
3. Have some way of ticking off that the original data has been accounted for. Check all data has been transferred.
4. Once all the data has been transferred rewrite the diagram but this time ordering the leaves in each group.

Then the students can be asked, without guidance, to calculate the central measures and the range. Once they have tried themselves you should go through the processes. Finding the median can be done by counting in from both ends until the fingers meet at the single middle value or two middle values.

Exercise commentary

These provide basic practice in the technique. Though it is fairly clear what a sensible stem and leaf is, it may be noted that with some problems there are several ways of grouping the data. This further emphasises the necessity to show a clear key to the diagram. Do check fairly early on that students are calculating the median and the range correctly; often they will give (very logically but incorrectly) the range as, for example, 40–90 rather than 50.

Plenary

The best use of stem and leaf diagrams is with relatively small data sets as mentioned briefly in the text. It is worth discussing this further.

As an introduction to the next section you could present two sets of data for homework or to be tried in pairs in class and ask students to make some comparisons. This could provide a basis for the next introductory discussion.

- Produce stem and leaf diagrams (FA13.3)
- Compare distributions and make inferences, using the shapes of distributions and measures of average and range (FA13.4)

Starter

Say that you will be showing the students some items of data, one at a time, and their task is to identify whether the data is discrete or continuous.

Ask individuals to remind the group what each term means – establishing that if you can count it, it is discrete and if you can measure it, it is continuous. The students should write DISCRETE on one side of their board and CONTINUOUS on the other.

Display each data item for the students to respond to. Items could include height, number of siblings, age etc.

Resources

Mini whiteboards, cards or smartboard showing discrete and continuous data for the starter

Teaching notes

Using the example in the text or similar, present and discuss with the group a back-to-back diagram. Once again observe the necessity for a clear key and the ordering of the leaves. The phrase 'summary statistics' needs to be explained, and revise, by questioning, how to calculate the various central measures and the range. The phrase 'more varied' may also need clarification and the vocabulary of spread, dispersion and variation can be emphasised. Most students find making comparisons between data quite tricky since there seem to be too many things that can be said. At this stage they should be comparing the various measures of central tendency and the ranges and should write some short, clear sentences.

Exercise commentary

Question 1 This is a decimal stem and leaf and may need to be explained more fully.

Question 2 The units of time are not given and this provides an opportunity to discuss what students think the most likely units are.

Question 3 The teacher may need to explain IQ. Ask students to focus on the three averages and the range.

Plenary

The problems of outliers, and whether or not they should be simply ignored, could be introduced.

Once again the problems of drawing stem and leaf diagrams for large data sets could be noted.

As an introduction to later work the idea of quartiles could be introduced and the general formulae for locating the median and quartiles investigated.

The functional mathematics strand of the curriculum could be addressed by asking the students to collect and compare their own data.

- Calculate mean, range and median of small data sets with discrete then continuous data
- Identify the modal class for grouped data   (FA13.3)

Starter

Offer a hypothesis, for example: Girls own more CDs than boys. Ask students to work in pairs and consider the hypothesis. What data would help investigate the statement, and how would it be gathered? Discuss the students' ideas, drawing out and recording examples illustrating some of the key vocabulary.

Resources

A set of raw data to present to the group; graphical calculators could be used in the plenary; OCR AO3 Guide Section 3.2

Teaching notes

The main ideas of this section are the use of a frequency table and the calculation of the main central measures from such a distribution. A good launching point is to present a set of raw data to the group, and using a tally chart, ask the students to sort the data themselves into a frequency table. Make the distinction between the quantity and the frequency of that quantity very clear. Then using the tables in the text, emphasising that total frequency is the sum of all the frequencies and is not just the number of rows, discuss the procedure for calculation of each of the central measures. A common calculator error in the calculation of the mean is not to find the resultant total before dividing by the total frequency. As mentioned before, ensure they divide by the total frequency not just the number of rows of the table.

The location of the median by $\frac{n+1}{2}$ may have been investigated in the earlier sections but it is worth re-emphasising. Rewriting a simple example as a list can help students to understand.

Exercise commentary

Question 1 These provide basic AO1 practice and you should watch for the common errors of not totalling the numerator before dividing by the total frequency. If students are having difficulty locating the median then it can be helpful to introduce the idea of a cumulative frequency column.

Question 2 This question moves beyond just calculation and asks them to justify or refute statements made on the basis of the data. It addresses the AO2 and AO3 strands of the curriculum.

Plenary

Once again discuss the common errors made in calculations. The power of modern calculators such as the TI graphical could be introduced and some of the exercise quickly repeated using hand-held technology. The rapid calculation allows faster consideration of the meaning of the data. Once again the effect of outliers could be considered and discussion of best measure be developed.

- Identify the modal class for grouped data
- Find the median for large data sets and calculate an estimate of the mean for large data sets with grouped data   (FA13.3)

Starter

Write down a set of numbers, for example

    3.2, 9.1, 9.5, 3.7, 5.2

Ask students to find the mean, median and range using a mental method. (6.14, 5.2, 6.3)

Resources

Graphical calculators could be used in the plenary; OCR AO3 Guide Section 3.2

Teaching notes

Using the data in the text discuss the key elements of a grouped data table. Ask students in which group 14.4 minutes, 14.9 minutes or 20 minutes and 20 seconds would fit. The calculation of the midpoint is often obvious but it is worth giving a technique for less obvious cases. It is important to highlight that the answer is an estimate because the detailed data is not known. Some in the group may ask about the median of the data and mention can be made about cumulative frequency curves which arise later in the course. The calculation of the range is a little more involved than previously and the set of possibilities needs to be discussed.

Exercise commentary

Questions 1–2 Focus on basic techniques that require some interpretation as well. Part **1d** brings out the need for a more flexible approach to the calculation of the range.

Question 3 This question involves calculation and consideration of a comparison statement. Ask the students to make their comments clear and concise. Comments and arguments must be based only on the data given and should not stray into speculation not grounded on the data.

Plenary

Reiterate the key points of this approach to data representation and calculation. Graphical calculators could once again be used.

- Collect data from a variety of suitable sources, including experiments and surveys, and primary and secondary sources   (FA13.1)

Starter

Prepare a short questionnaire with about five questions, some of which are 'leading', for example: *Male/Female; How old are you?*; *How much television do you watch?; Are you a disgusting smoker?* Distribute the questionnaires and ask each student to complete one, saying that it is not named so will not be traced back to individuals. Allow 2–3 minutes for completion.

Teaching notes

Using the rich task in the text, introduce the idea of data collection and bring out the issues that need to be considered.

Ask students to produce their own questionnaire to collect data on musical preferences of either the group or a more general population. These can be discussed in pairs or small groups. The pitfalls given in the text should be avoided. The questionnaires can be brought together and good examples emphasised.

Exercise commentary

Questions 1 Provides a questionnaire and asks students to improve and develop it.

Question 2 This question asks students to design their own questionnaires. These can be then discussed in pairs or in small groups.

Plenary

This is a good point at which to review the whole section and to perhaps get the students to do a functional maths project that will use the whole data handling cycle, from designing a questionnaire, collecting and summarising data, performing calculations to making conclusions. The ideas for the mini-project could be their own or you could provide a small list of possible tasks to choose from. Such a project will address all three assessments strands of the curriculum.

Exam-style question commentary

Worked solution	Commentary
1) a) Charlie b) Charlie leaves, Ellen joins	1) The mode is the easiest average to work with, and students can pick up valuable marks with these types of question.
2) a) total time = 2.5 × 7 + 3.5 × 40 + 4.5 × 38 + 5.5 × 13 + 6.5 × 2 = 413 Total number of tracks = 7 + 40 + 38 + 13 + 2 = 100 Mean length = 413 ÷ 100 = 4.13 mins b) 100 items, so the median is the 50th This is in the class $4 < m < 5$	2) a) Students are often prompted in this type of question to complete a midpoint x frequency column in the table. You may need to recap how to estimate the mean of a continuous distribution. b) Some students may give the answer $4 < m < 5$ just because this is the middle interval. Encourage students to justify their responses.
3) 7 boys, 9 girls Median boys 66% Median girls 62% Range boys = 86 − 42 = 44% Range girls = 89 − 43 = 46% On average the boys performed better than the girls, and showed slightly greater consistency.	3) In distribution comparisons, encourage students to compare both an average and also a measure of dispersion (in this case the range but at higher level could be the IQR). Encourage students to comment on the shape of the diagrams.

Constructions

Objectives covered in this chapter are:

FA9.1a interpret scales on a range of measuring instruments, including those for time and mass

FA9.1d make sensible estimates of a range of measures in everyday settings

FA9.1e convert measurements from one unit to another

FA9.1f know rough metric equivalents of pounds, feet, miles, pints and gallons

FA10.1a measure and draw lines to the nearest millimetre, and angles to the nearest degree

FA10.1b draw triangles using a ruler and protractor, given information about their side lengths and angles

FA10.2a use straight edge and a pair of compasses to do standard constructions

FA10.3a find loci, by reasoning to produce shapes and paths

Prerequisite knowledge

- Measure and draw lengths and angles accurately
- Construct circles accurately using compasses
- Draw triangles using a protractor
- Use a scale

Useful ICT resources

Introductory powerpoint	A3
Starter activity	A3.2
Powerpoint worked solution	A3.4
Animation	A3.4(x2), A3.5(x2)
Interactive activity	A3.3(AG), A3.4(TI)
Consolidation	A3
Chapter test	A3
Formative on-screen test	A3
Summative on-screen test	A3

RICH TASK COMMENTARY

Some students will attempt this task by starting with the square and working inwards; others will start with the triangle and work outwards.

Encourage students to use accurate instruments in constructing these shapes.

Emphasise the importance of finding the centre—if they start with the square, the centre is easily obtained by finding the intersection of the diagonals.

• Interpret scales on a range of measuring instruments, including those for time and mass (FA9.1)

Starter

Show a TV schedule for the day. Look at start and end times of programmes and ask how long the programme lasts. With confidence build up to include hours and minutes. Discuss strategies – calculating how much time until the next hour, then how many minutes after the hour. Demonstrate use of a jotted time line to illustrate this (as in the student book). Ensure students understand that there are 60 minutes in an hour, **not** 100.

Resources

Weighing scales, thermometers, stopwatches, TV schedule.

Teaching notes

This lesson could begin with asking group a variety of questions. What time is it? What is the temperature? How tall do you think I am? How tall is the person sitting nearest you? How much does this bag of sweets weigh? To answer these, or similar, questions accurately will require measurement and, if the appropriate instruments are available in class, some of the above queries can be answered. This will involve reading a scale which is something students will have done many times before, both in the everyday world and across the curriculum.

What has to be emphasised is the importance of using relevant units of measurement and of understanding the meaning of a subdivided interval.

Using appropriate units can be discussed in response to a variety contexts provided by you.

Estimating measurements requires the development of some touchstones by reference to some standard measures like a metre rule, an area of 1 m^2 or a volume of 1 litre which they can then use to compare mentally with what they are trying to estimate.

Exercise commentary

Question 1 You may want to discuss electric, gas and water meters and their purpose. There is a functional mathematics tag here.

Question 2 These are straightforward examples where the scale needs to deduced from the numbers actually given.

Questions 3–4 Revision of the twenty four hour clock may be necessary here, with a reminder about the status of midnight and midday in this time system.

Question 5 In this question the pointer on the scale is between marked divisions and will require careful thought at this level.

Plenary

There is opportunity here for cross-curricular work. The students could consider very small masses or lengths in chemistry or physics.

- Convert measurements from one unit to another
- Know rough metric equivalents of pounds, feet, miles, pints and gallons (FA9.1)

Starter

A normal dice used in board games has a volume of about 2 cm^3. A normal dose of medicine given on a plastic spoon or teaspoon is 5 ml.
If you melted some dice down to a liquid, how many would you need to fill the medicine spoon? (2.5, since 1 cm^3 = 1 ml.)

Resources

Dice, medicine spoon (to illustrate Starter), the internet; OCR AO3 Guide Section 3.9

Teaching notes

Students will have met units work many times before since Year 3. It should be possible to coax out the various units in the two systems by quizzing the class.

Ask them how tall they think you (or a keen member of the group) are and how much you weigh. It is likely you will get answers expressed in both metric and imperial measurements. This can be used as a focus for revising length and weight measurements in the two systems.

Similar approaches can be use for petrol usage and for distances between two cities.

Converting between the two systems can be practised both with and without a calculator.

Students should be encouraged to remember some of the key conversions and these could form the basis of a mental test at a later date.

Exercise commentary

Question 1 This problem uses the man as a touchstone to estimate other heights so reinforces the approach introduced in the previous section.

Question 2 This is similar to the above but is about length.

Question 3 There are two main ways of doing the calculation here and the equivalence of division and multiplication in BIDMAS could be highlighted.

Question 4 The size system for paper could be looked at though A0 may be hard to find. A1 would be available in the Art dept.

Question 5 This is practice of conversions and could usefully be done in pairs.

Question 6 Some may need a reminder about what an integer is.

Question 7 This question requires access to the internet.

Plenary

The work can be extended into different number-base arithmetic e.g. 4 gallons 5 pints + 3 gallons 4 pints etc. There are plenty of very unusual non-metric measures to be found on the web, for example Nibble, Furman, Galactic Year ....

- Use and interpret maps and scale drawings   (FA11.1)

Starter

Display the information: 1 : 50 000 and ask pairs of students to discuss the information: What could it mean? Where is it found? What is it for?

After 2 minutes select some pairs to share the information, and develop the discussion. Explore further questions if the points have not arisen, for example, why are there no units? Summarise using a table with columns labelled map and actual, and show the multiplicative relations with arrows (×50 000; ÷ 50 000; ×1/50 000).

Resources

The internet (e.g. Google Image), Cabri

Teaching notes

There are many good examples of scale drawings ranging from the straightforward to the complex available on the internet (e.g. Google Image). Some examples from architecture or aircraft design should emphasise the importance of this area to the students.

Pose a suitable problem, either the example given or your own, and ask students to attempt a scale drawing either individually or in pairs. Once the whole group has attempted the problem bring the class together into a discussion of what they did and what factors need to be considered. The idea of an appropriate scale will have emerged and this can be emphasised by asking about the problems of using, for example, 1 mm to 1 km in the example. The rich task in the text shows how scale drawing can be used to problem solve, and could be set as a problem directly to the group which can then be discussed after all the students have attempted it.

In both cases it is possible to set these problems up accurately or approximately on software such as Cabri so you can discuss the problem with the whole group very easily.

Exercise commentary

The questions in the exercise are self-explanatory. Diagrams are given which should help the students to plan their use of space in their books more easily. In question 4 they need to choose their own scale. Question 5 may require a quick revision of the word 'elevation'.

Plenary

As an extension for students is a problem in which they have to draw the diagram from only written information. The usefulness of doing a rough sketch of the problem before attempting an accurate drawing can be suggested as a good starting point for this sort of problem.

As a functional mathematics exercise students could draw a plan of their school or house.

- Draw triangles and other 2D shapes using a ruler and protractor, given information about their side lengths and angles.
- Use a ruler and a pair of compasses to construct a triangle. (FA10.1)

Starter

What is wrong with each of these triangles?

(i) Sides of 10 cm, 3 cm and 6 cm (the longest side must be shorter than the sum of the other two sides)
(ii) Two obtuse angles and one acute angle (angles will not sum to 180°)
(iii) An isosceles triangle with two of the angles being 110° and 50° (angles would sum to either 220° or 270° not 180°)

Resources

Board compass, board ruler, ruler, protractor, pair of compasses, the internet, Cabri

Teaching notes

Construction work really needs to be done by demonstration. This can be the teacher using traditional board compasses and ruler at the front or one of the many short demos available on YouTube, some of which focus closely in on the physical process of construction. Constructions can also be done fairly easily using Cabri. If none of the above options are available then students should follow the instructions in the book with the teacher moving around to remedy any lack of understanding or misunderstanding.

Emphasise the necessity of leaving the construction arcs on the diagram since these will be looked for in any assessment of this work.

Exercise commentary

Question 1 There are four triangles to be constructed here. The students are asked to measure their constructions to see how accurate their diagrams are.

Questions 2–5 These provide information which enables a construction to be made and then using the diagram formed a missing length or distance needs to be found. Students may need to be encouraged to label their diagrams carefully.

Questions 6–7 These AO3 challenges could be worked on in pairs.

Plenary

Cabri can be used to construct triangles and some of the above questions could be attempted by the students using this or a similar package.

- Use straight edge and a pair of compasses to do standard constructions, including;
    - an equilateral triangle with a given side,
    - the midpoint and perpendicular bisector of a line segment,
    - the perpendicular from a point to a line,
    - the perpendicular from a point on a line, and
    - the bisector of an angle. (FA10.2)

Starter

A snail crosses a railway track as fast as possible. It can move at a speed of 2 feet every 3 min. The track is 4 feet 8 inches wide. (12 inches in a foot.)

How long will it take to cross the track? (7 min)

What assumption must you make about the way the snail crosses the track?

(The rails are parallel and to cross at the shortest distance you must cross the rails at 90°)

Resources

Board compass, board ruler, ruler, protractor, pair of compasses, the internet, Cabri

Teaching notes

These constructions provide the tools necessary for the Loci section which comes next. If possible a teacher demonstration using board compasses (Cabri) or YouTube or all three should start the lesson. Otherwise the students can follow the instructions in the text with you providing support and advice.

The constructions are based on the basic properties of a rhombus which provides their justification.

With the constructions a few points are worth mentioning. Firstly, when bisecting the lines the compasses must be set to more than half way along the line being bisected. In the third and fourth constructions sometimes the line may have to be extended or produced to enable the construction required.

The vocabulary of *arc* and *bisect* may need to be explained again as well as reminding the students that construction lines need to be shown.

Exercise commentary

Questions 1–3 provide basic practice in the core constructions.

Question 4 This question is set in a context and is also a locus problem. That the shortest distance between a point and line is the perpendicular line may need to be discussed and justified. Similarly the idea of equidistance from two lines is not always obvious and that, once again, it is the perpendicular distance from each line will need emphasising and justifying.

Question 5 Students find angle bisectors in a graphical context. This could lead into a simple proof either for this particular case or a generalisation to any point in this quadrant.

Question 6 This is a good question for students with technical drawing skills.

Plenary

All these constructions can be done on Cabri using a software package and can enable quite complex constructions to be attempted such as the incircle and circumcircle. The really brave may wish to try a nine-point circle.

Loci

- Find loci to produce shapes and paths (FA10.3)

Starter

An empty cube has dimensions 5 m by 5 m by 5 m. You have two sizes of smaller cubes, some with sides of 2 m and some with sides of 3 m. You want to fit as many as possible of the smaller cubes into the empty one, but you have to use at least one of each size.

How can you do it? (Only solution is one with sides of 3 m and seven with sides of 2 m.)

What volume of space is not filled?

($125 - 27 - 7 \times 8 = 42$ m³.)

Resources

Board pair of compasses, board ruler, ruler, pair of compasses, the internet, coins, boxes

Teaching notes

Ask the group what path a football follows if it is kicked toward a goal. Using two students as fixed points ask the group to decide how a third student should walk so that they are always equidistant from the points. Where can they walk if they need to be closer to one student than the other? This should awaken some thoughts from the last section on constructions and enable the introduction of the necessary vocabulary of this topic.

You could then demonstrate the three basic loci constructions and discuss them with the group or let the class attempt question 1 of the exercise and use their responses to those problems to introduce the fundamental loci constructions. You may want to break up these questions to take a slower pace and focus on each different kind of locus with some students.

Exercise commentary

Question 1 See teaching notes. This question contains all the core loci constructions they need.

Questions 2–8 cover in various contexts the core loci and associated regions. They require scale drawing and some revision of earlier techniques may be needed here. The challenge is made easier if the students have access to real coins and boxes and to the web if they are to research hypocycloids and the rotary car engine.

Plenary

This is an area very rich in tasks and problems. The construction of an ellipse is easy and interesting using one of the foci properties of the ellipse. The path that various fixed points on a moving bicycle follow can provide an alternative context to a coin. The famous tethered goat problem can be varied in many ways. The Wankel engine is demonstrated on the web in pictures and video. Following a fixed point on a ladder sliding down a vertical wall can lead into some interesting and difficult mathematics.

Exam-style question commentary

Worked solution	Commentary
1) 4.5 cm 50° 3 cm 3.4 cm, 42°, 88°	1) Encourage students to start with a simple sketch – this will ensure that they can gauge whether their construction looks right.
2) 2.2 lb = 1 kg 20 kg = 2.2 × 20 = 44 lb	2) This question requires students to read a scale – it could however simply ask them to use their knowledge of pounds to kilograms conversion.
3) 4 cm	3) This AO3-type problem requires geometrical reasoning – that a regular hexagon is composed of six equilateral triangles. Alternatively students could use an inscribed circle method.

Aim

- To show how mathematics can be used to accurately record and compare the results of a sporting event

Useful resources

- Sports starter   Presentation
- Sports results   Presentation
- Sports reaction times   Presentation
- Sports measurement   Worksheet

Teaching notes

Introduce the theme by asking if students know what the current 100 m world record is for men and for women. Do they know what degree of accuracy is usually used to report these results?

Let students discuss the results of the 100 m men's final shown in the case study before they answer the related questions. Focus on the first three columns of the tables for now (not the reaction times). You could use the *Sports results presentation* to illustrate this.

Ensure that students know how to round and order numbers and to calculate with decimals as well as how to convert the data into a stem-and-leaf diagram.

Ask students if they know what happens at the start of the race. What is a false start? Do they know how this is judged? If possible, show them a recording of a false start, or a graphic from a TV recording of a race that shows reaction times.

Let students discuss the reaction times shown in the tables and ensure that they understand the limit of 0.1s before they answer the related questions. The *Sports reaction times presentation* could help with this. Ensure that students are comfortable with converting the data to a scatter diagram; recalculating the results as described; and using their diagrams and statistics to draw conclusions.

Extension

Students could look up other, more recent, results and use the data to compare the results and the reaction times.

How do the results compare?

Has there been any change in the way reaction times are recorded? Is there any noticeable difference in the reaction times?

Students could look at the results and reaction times for other race lengths at these championships.

How do the reaction times compare?

How do they think the effect of reaction times on the result of the race differs for different length races?

Is the false start limit the same for each race?

Simplification

Students could research the world record for the Men's 100 m over the last 30 years, plot their findings as a bar graph or a line graph and comment on the trend. Can they predict, with any accuracy, what the world record will be in 2025? Why not?

Factors, multiples and ratio

Objectives covered in this chapter are:

FA4.1a   use ratio notation, including reduction to its simplest form

FA4.1b   know its various links to fraction notation

FA4.2a   divide a quantity in a given ratio

FA5.1a   use the concepts and vocabulary of factor (divisor), multiple, common factor, highest common factor, least common multiple, prime number and prime factor decomposition

FA5.1b   find the prime factor decomposition of positive integers

Prerequisite knowledge

- Understand factors and multiples
- Understand ratio notation

Useful ICT resources

Introductory powerpoint	A4
Starter activity	A4.3
Powerpoint worked solution	A4.2, A4.4
Animation	A4.1, A4.3 (x2)
Consolidation	A4
Chapter test	A4
Formative on-screen test	A4
Summative on-screen test	A4

RICH TASK COMMENTARY

Students could investigate this task by measuring heights and head circumference of different people in the class, plotting a scatter diagram and seeing if it modelled the graph of $y = 3x$.

There are plenty of other parts of the human body (hand span, length of arm, foot size etc) which are worthy of further investigation.

What about head to height ratios for babies and adults?

It might be interesting to compare the proportions of height and head size with other creatures. How big would a human's head be if we were in the same proportion as say a cat?

Which measurements come from the human body e.g. a fathom?

- Use the concepts and vocabulary of factor (divisor), multiple, common factor, prime number   (FA2.1)

Starter

Using only the numbers 2, 3, 5, 7, 11 and 13, and the operation ×, make all the integers from 2 to 16. You may use one or more numbers in your answer (for example, just use 7 to make 7). You may use each number once or more than once. Set this challenge to be completed in 90 seconds. Ask what type of numbers have been used (prime). Can any integer be written as the product of prime numbers? (Yes.)

Resources

List of prime numbers up to 30 (OHP or Smartboard)

Teaching notes

The words *factor* and *multiple* can be reviewed by quizzing the group. It is common for students to get the ideas the wrong way around.

Once clear of these words let them play the game in the text either in pairs or small groups. Once the students have familiarised themselves with the game emphasise the questions posed in the text and let them play a few more times. Bring the group together to discuss responses, especially highlighting the meaning of prime and square numbers.

The idea of common factors can be illustrated using Venn diagrams as in the example. The idea of a common multiple is more difficult and a couple of suitable examples similar to the questions in the exercise should be discussed.

Exercise commentary

Question 1 Mixed set of questions to ensure they grasp the vocabulary of this section.

Questions 2–3 Basic practice in factors. Some may need reminding that 1 and the number itself are always factors.

Question 4 This requires a multiple to be found within a specified range.

Question 5 This requires testing numbers between 30 and 40. It is not unusual for students to think 39 is a prime perhaps because tables are learnt only as far as 12×3.

Question 6 Part (b) requires some reasoned argument which students of all abilities find difficult.

Question 7 Common factors practice.

Question 8 Once again some reasoning is required here.

Question 9 Practice in finding common multiples.

Question 10 This AO3 puzzle provokes some simple deductive thinking and could be supplemented by some more difficult examples.

Plenary

Students could try and create their own puzzles as in question 10 and try them out on their partners.

The ideas of HCF and LCM could be introduced as preparation for the next section.

- Use the concepts and vocabulary of factor (divisor), multiple, common factor, highest common factor, least common multiple, prime number and prime factor decomposition
- Find the prime factor decomposition of positive integers   (FA5.1)

Starter

Elle runs round a 400 m running track in consistent lap times of 60 seconds. Hayley takes 72 seconds. If they both start at the same point and at the same time, how many seconds will pass before Elle overtakes Hayley? At what point on the track will the overtaking take place? How many laps will each of them have completed at that moment?

(360 sec; overtakes at the start point; Elle 6 laps, Hayley 5 laps.)

Resources

Blank factor trees and Venn diagrams

Teaching notes

Review the vocabulary introduced in the last section and explain the game in the text. Let students play the game in pairs or small groups and once they are comfortable with the rules draw their attention to the questions in the text. Bring together their conclusions as a group at a suitable juncture.

Introduce the fact that numbers can be expressed as a product of prime factors. This can be done systematically either by using a factor tree or by repeated division. A couple of examples set to the group and checked should ensure understanding.

The ideas of HCF and LCM can be defined. These can be found in simple cases using a Venn diagram or by inspection of the factors directly. Some may wish to introduce index notation into their answers if they have experienced this subject before. The LCM is usually the more difficult of the two numbers for groups to find at this stage.

Exercise commentary

Question 1 This is basic practice finding the product of prime factors either by a factor tree or by repeated division. A clear method needs to be shown.

Question 2 Provides basic practice in finding the HCF and LCM.

Question 3 This problem solving question provides clues to numbers that need to be found.

Question 4 Returns to the definition of a prime number and presents a statement requiring explanation. The idea of proof could come in here in a simple way.

Plenary

The question as to why 1 is not a prime number could be answered here in terms of reference to the unique factorisation theorem. The HCF and LCM of large numbers could be investigated where the prime factorisation makes use of index notation.

The principles behind the use of prime factorisations in internet security could be researched by students.

- Use ratio notation, including reduction to its simplest form; know its various links to fraction notation   (FA4.1)
- Divide a quantity in a given ratio   (FA4.2)
- Determine the original quantity by knowing the size of one part of the divided quantity   (FA4.2)
- Solve word problems about ratio, including using informal strategies and the unitary method of solution   (FA4.2)

Starter

Use a spider diagram display with a randomly drawn set of 24 black and 6 red dots in the centre. Ask students to suggest equivalent ratios to put on the legs. Does one of the legs give the ratio in its lowest terms? Which is it? (Add it to the diagram if it is not there.)

Resources

Spider diagram for Smartboard or OHP

Teaching notes

Both the notation and concept of ratio have been encountered before. It is worth emphasising that the direction which the ratio is written is determined by the wording of the given information. The vocabulary of simplest form and unitary form will need to be emphasised.

A couple of examples involving simplifying ratios and using ratio in a practical money context could also be attempted by the group.

The rich task in the text concerning the Fibonacci sequence can be attempted in class or as homework and provides a launching point for students if they have access to the internet.

Exercise commentary

Question 1 The key phrase here is 'simplest form'.

Question 2 The phrase 'unitary form' will need emphasising again.

Question 3 These questions all involve applying ratios in simple financial contexts.

Question 4 This substantial AO3 task may need some guidance to get the students started. The idea of writing a two digit number AB as 10A + B could be introduced to more able students to allow an attempt at mathematical explanation. There are a lot of patterns in this task and even those who cannot get to a symbolic explanation of what is going on can derive benefit.

Plenary

The investigation of the Golden Ratio, if not already done, could become a mini-project involving mathematics, history and art.

- Use ratio notation, including reduction to its simplest form; know its various links to fraction notation (FA4.1)
- Divide a quantity in a given ratio (FA4.2)
- Determine the original quantity by knowing the size of one part of the divided quantity (FA4.2)
- Solve word problems about ratio, including using informal strategies and the unitary method of solution (FA4.2)

Starter

Two people buy a lottery ticket; one contributed 75p to the ticket and the other paid the remaining 25p. In what ratio were the payments? What if the amounts were 70p and 30p? 60p and 40p? Take the last combination, if the ticket won £255 000, what would be a fair way of dividing the winnings between the two? Discuss the responses to this, being ready for some students to suggest half the winnings as fair, and explore the reasoning behind the use of the ratio 3 : 2.

Resources

OS Explorer series map(s)

Teaching notes

This probably needs a fairly traditional approach and a focus on the given examples which can be discussed as the group.

After a quick recap of the previous section pose the problem of the brothers from the rich task and give the group some time to think before collecting together their responses. Then go through some archetypal problems with them as in the text. Putting the problem in personal terms, like if they work 4 hours and their friend works 1 hour and they get £60 for the whole job, how should the money be shared?

A triple ratio is introduced in this section and should be highlighted.

The relationship with fractions can be enlightening for students though some will find the idea tricky. Several examples will be required.

Exercise commentary

Question 1 A traditional set of problems about sharing money. Emphasise the phraseology of 'equal parts'.

Questions 2–5 The students must be careful to interpret the order of the ratio as stated by the question. The method then follows the example in the text.

Questions 6–7 These are slightly more substantial questions set in context and students at this level will have to think clearly about them. Encourage a clear method to be set out.

Plenary

Use a scale of 1 : 25 000 to calculate actual distances between places on an OS Explorer map.

Exam-style question commentary

Worked solution	Commentary
1) a) i) 24 ii) 25 iii) 23 b) 28 = 7 × 4 = 7 × 2 × 2	1) a) Ensure that students don't get confused between these terms (multiple, prime, factor). This is an opportunity to gain valuable marks in the exam. b) Some students may need reassuring that it's okay to have a different starting point (eg 14 × 2) and that they will arrive at the same answer. Encourage the correct use of indices.
2) Factors of 30: 1, 2, 5, 10, 15, 30 Multiples of 30: 30, 60, 90, … 45	2) This is an AO3-type problem where some students may struggle to find a strategy. You could suggest they focus on each criterion separately, then look at the overlap.
3) a) $\frac{3}{5}$ b) 5 : 3	3) a) A common misconception is to write $\frac{3}{2}$. Prompt students by asking them how many altogether in the basic pattern. b) The relationship between fractions and ratios is an important one: a fraction compares a part to a whole; a ratio compares a part to another part.

Sequences

Objectives covered in this chapter are:

FA7.2a generate terms of a sequence using term-to-term and position-to-term definitions of the sequence

FA7.2b generate common integer sequences (including sequences of odd and even integers, squared integers, powers of 2, powers of 10, triangular numbers)

FA7.3a use linear expressions to describe the nth term of an arithmetic sequence, justifying its form by referring to the activity or context from which it was generated

Prerequisite knowledge

- Generate terms of a sequence
- Describe a sequence in words
- Substitute values into an expression

Useful ICT resources

Introductory powerpoint	A5
Starter activity	A5.4
Powerpoint worked solution	A5.2
Animation	A5.3 (x4), A5.4 (x3)
Interactive activity	A5.4 (TI)
Consolidation	A5
Chapter test	A5
Formative on-screen test	A5
Summative on-screen test	A5

RICH TASK COMMENTARY

Students should arrive at 4,5,6; 3,5,7; 2,5,8 and 1,5,9 (illustrated).

Extending to algebra, these can be written as $n + 3$; $2n + 1$; $3n - 1$ and $4n - 3$ respectively.

As students investigate their own numbers of circles they should come across some quadratic sequences as well.

The nth term of these could be derived by looking at the geometric structure, as in a real suspension cable where the cables make tightly packed hexagons, giving 1, 7, 19, leading to $3n^2 - 3n + 1$.

Generating sequences

- Generate common integer sequences　　　(FA7.2)

Starter

Challenge students to do some rapid arithmetic, going up in 3s and recording each result on mini whiteboards as quickly as possible in a set time limit. Tell them that the time limit will be one minute. Start from 38 – go!

See who got the furthest and ask students to check with a neighbour that each sequence is correct. Repeat, this time going down in 4s starting from 29. Again check results.

Resources

Mini whiteboards, the internet; OCR AO3 Guide Section 3.5

Teaching notes

The rich task can provide the starting point for this section. Let the students try the task and after a short time bring together their conclusions and define clearly what is meant by a numerical sequence. This is a geometric sequence which can lead to awareness of the rapidity of growth in such sequences. If access to the internet is available then students should be encouraged to find out about exponential growth.

Using the example in the text introduces them to an arithmetic sequence with a common difference of 6. Emphasise the language of adding on 'lots' of six to the starting term 20 as this will help when seeking general rules for the sequence. Ask them to work out how much Ben will have after a large number of weeks and this should lead to an effective shortcut to calculating terms in an arithmetic sequence. It could be worth showing them an arithmetic sequence with a negative common difference as well.

Exercise commentary

Question 1 This is a decreasing arithmetic sequence. Part **b** requires clear explanation as well as the correct numerical answer.

Question 2 Students should be noticing the structure of the sequence as adding on 'lots' of four to the starting number 5.

Question 3 Once again a clear explanation of how they calculate the answer quickly is required, not just numerical answers.

Question 4 Using the pattern $10 + (n - 1)^2$ should be their method though for most this will be not expressed algebraically at this stage.

Plenary

The famous story of placing a grain of rice on the first square of a chessboard then two grains on the second square and so on usually surprises people. Mentioned elsewhere in the course is the problem of repeatedly folding a piece of paper in half and calculating the thickness of the resulting folded paper. This is only possible physically for about six folds but the theoretical thicknesses achieved are mind-boggling.

- Generate terms of a sequence using term-to-term definitions (FA7.2)

Starter

Challenge students to do some rapid arithmetic, doubling and recording each result on whiteboards as quickly as possible in a set time limit. See who got the furthest and ask students to check with a neighbour that each sequence is correct.

Repeat, this time halving, starting from 32. Again check results. Repeat, halving from a more challenging starting point: 14.

Resources

Mini whiteboards; OCR AO3 Guide Section 3.5

Teaching notes

This section can be started with the rich task set in the text. The structure of the sequence should be clear from the diagram and the term-to-term rule easy to write down.

The flow chart supplied with the example is more complex and involves two stages. The vocabulary of 'consecutive' will need explaining and the formation of an algebraic description using x can be reinforced by using the rule for a couple of the terms given.

Exercise commentary

Question 1 Using matchsticks or straws may help some to see the underlying structure of the sequence though some will notice the pattern very quickly. The rule needs to be written down clearly.

Question 2 This question provides practice in generating a sequence given the first term and the term-to-term rule.

Question 3 This provides practice in the use of a flow chart.

Question 4 This rich task gets the student to play with permutations of some rules and they need to ensure they cover all the six possibilities.

Question 5 These provide some good challenges in spotting some two stage rules. A number of valid term-to-term rules can be found for some of the sequences and should be valued but students should be encouraged to find the simplest rule possible.

Question 6 Spreadsheets are very powerful tools for generating sequences quickly and at great length. The investigation of sequences can be taken a long way in this challenge.

Plenary

Students could investigate the Collatz conjecture. Take any number, if even divide by two, if odd multiply by three and add one, then repeat. Whatever number you choose you will end up with 1 eventually. This conjecture is also known as Ulam's conjecture or the $3x + 1$ conjecture, and the sequences generated are called hailstone sequences.

- Generate terms of a sequence using position to term definitions

(FA7.2)

Starter

Write these expressions on the board:

$3n - 1$ $12 - 2n$

$2n + 4$ $3n^2 + 1$

For each expression, ask students to substitute the values $n = 0, 1, 2, 3$ and 4.
Students should write the values of the expression as a list of numbers on mini whiteboards.

Resources

Mini whiteboards; OCR AO3 Guide Section 3.5

Teaching notes

Pose Hayley's problem to the group and ask them to find the first few terms and the 100th term and/or the 200th term. Bring the group together to clarify the issues with using the term-to-term approach for finding a term well into the sequence. The table approach can then be introduced. If the students are unclear as to why the three times table is the key then direct their attention to adding lots of three to the original two tiles. It can also be helpful to highlight that the difference between the terms is a constant 3 and this also tells us which table to use. Comparing the times table with the sequence value should make clear what adjustment needs to be made to move from the three times table to the number of tiles used. The rule can be written in words and some may be able to use algebra.

A second sequence set to the group should reinforce the basic ideas.

Exercise commentary

Question 1 The key to this one is the four times table. Students should check their rule carefully before using it for the 50th term

Question 2 The differences between the terms give the clue to the correct times table. More able students may be able to go directly to the correct rule and use it for the 100th term. Part **g** involves a fractional common difference.

Question 3 Terms are missing earlier in the sequence so the common difference needs to be applied earlier in the sequence.

Question 4 The double 00 may put some off the solution. It could be emphasised that it is the differences that matter not the way the number is presented.

Questions 5–6 These AO2 problems may need a little interpreting for some.

Plenary

The (apocryphal) story of Gauss summing the integers from 1 to 100 or a 1000 could be told or searched on the web.

- Use linear expressions to describe the *n*th term of an arithmetic sequence, justifying its form by referring to the activity or context from which it was generated (FA7.3)

Starter

Distribute number cards to each student. Display an *n*th term on the board: $2n - 1$

Ask students to check if their number is in this sequence.

All those whose card is in the sequence should stand up and show their cards.

Display a different *n*th term on the board: $3n - 2$

Ask these students to stand up, and show the numbers.

Resources

Number cards for starter; OCR AO3 Guide Section A3.5

Teaching notes

This section builds on the previous one where a written description of the rule was all that was required. Some students will already have progressed to an algebraic statement of the rule or a flow chart approach. Now all students need to reach that level. The table approach with the times table is a clear way of developing the structure of the *n*th term. Once again the common difference between the terms can be pointed to as the guide to the formula.

The rich task can provide the focal point for the class activity and once the students have attempted the task then the overall approach can be summarised and the *n*th term demonstrated and used. Labelling the *n*th term expression creates a formula/function and the difference between a formula and expression could be noted if it is appropriate at this stage. It is worth demonstrating how the notation works with a couple of examples. It is also worth reversing the problem by using an *n*th term formula to create the first few terms of the sequence.

Exercise commentary

Questions 1–2 These provide practice in forming an *n*th term expression and using it to calculate terms in the sequence. Labelling the expression forms an *n*th term rule.

Question 3 Lots of examples here to reinforce the whole process of finding the *n*th term. Encourage to check their formula works by trying it out on a couple of early terms.

Questions 4–5 These AO2/AO3 problems need careful reading and interpretation by the students.

Plenary

Students could investigate some famous sequences on the web as a preparation for the next section on common sequences.

- Generate common integer sequences (FA7.2)
- Use linear expressions to describe the *n*th term of an arithmetic sequence, justifying its form by referring to the activity or context from which it was generated (FA7.3)

Starter

Ask students to respond to questions using mini whiteboards.
What number is halfway between ...?
Use questions which explore negatives and decimals. Share results after each question.
What value is halfway between $2p$ and $4p$? $5y + 2$? and $9y + 6$?
Explore responses and ask students to share strategies.

Resources

Mini whiteboards, the internet; OCR AO3 Guide Section 3.5

Teaching notes

This section looks at some commonly occurring simple sequences. Some examples should be used to show the constancy of the common difference for linear-rule based sequences; this will provide a basis for further extension in the plenary session. It is worth emphasising that not all sequences can be described by a linear rule and the example in the text is about exponential growth; the general rule for the *n*th term of a geometric sequence could perhaps be introduced here with a suitable group.

Plenary

The second and third row difference method for finding quadratic and cubic formulae could be investigated and proved for a sufficiently able group.

Fibonacci is, of course, always worth looking at.

If access to the web is available then the Encyclopaedia of Integers site could be investigated. The site finds the next terms of a sequence through the TV programme *Lost* (4, 8, 15, 16, 23, 42,....) and provides an interesting response. There are many suggestions for a rule for this sequence to be found on the web including some very difficult mathematics.

Exercise commentary

Question 1 This question looks at odd and even linear sequences and provides practice in the use of the $T(n)$ notation.

Question 2 This question is focused on the sequence of square numbers.

Question 3 This question focuses on the triangle number sequence and revisits the formula for the *n*th triangle number which was justified by diagram earlier.

Question 4 This is the famous handshake problem which leads to a simple rule; the structure of which underlies a number of areas to do with various things being connected. A variant of the problem is to draw several mystic rose diagrams using points on the circumference of a circle. Encourage the students to specify how many dots are required and count diagonals, enabling a table of values to be built up quickly and the pattern to be investigated.

Question 5 This puzzle involves comparison of differing ways of getting money. The students could extend the question themselves by investigating increasing the number of days the money is doubled before this approach exceeds the lump sum given.

Exam-style question commentary

Worked solution	Commentary
1) a) 16, 19 b) start with 3 and double c) $1^2 + 1 = 2$ $2^2 + 1 = 5$ $3^2 + 1 = 10$	1) Students often find it easy to describe sequences and identify subsequent terms. Remind them to state the first term when a full description is required. Order of operations is needed for (c).

2) a) central tile + 4 × (shape number – 1)
   i) shape 6: $1 + 4 \times 5 = 21$
   ii) shape 16: $1 + 4 \times 15 = 61$
 	
b) $t = 1 + 4(n - 1)$
t = number of tiles
n = shape number
	2) Students will need a rule which could be in words to answer a) ii) – discourage attempting to draw the pattern.
	In b) students may need more practice in writing formulae using algebra.

3) 37, 34, 31, 28 $28 - 9 \times 3 = 1$ $28 - 10 \times 3 = -2$ 10 minutes more	3) This AO2/3-type problem can be tackled in a number of ways, including simply counting down from 28.

Objectives covered in this chapter are:

FA13.3a draw and produce pie charts for categorical data, and diagrams for continuous data, frequency diagrams and stem and leaf diagrams

FA13.3c identify the modal class for grouped data

FA13.4b interpret a wide range of graphs and diagrams and draw conclusions

FA13.4d compare distributions and make inferences, using the shapes of distributions and measures of averages and range

Prerequisite knowledge

- Label axes and plot coordinates in the first quadrant
- Calculate a fraction or a percentage of an amount
- Find the midpoint of two values

RICH TASK COMMENTARY

You will need to gather some data on the times that goals are scored during football matches. There are ready sources of such data both in newspapers and on the internet.

Students should be encouraged to choose a sample of matches and construct frequency tables of when goals are scored. They can represent these using a variety of diagrams, to find the time of the median and mean goal, the modal time period for goals, what percentage of goals are scored in the last 10 mins etc (where injury time may need to be brought into their thinking), etc They may wish to look at the interval between a goal scored and a goal conceded and maybe look at this in relation to the final result. Comparisons could be made between home teams and away teams, premier and championship teams, top four teams and everyone else, etc.

Football can be substituted for a different sport depending on the class interests!

Useful ICT resources

Introductory powerpoint	A6
Powerpoint worked solution	A6.1, A6.3
Animation	A6.1 (x2), A6.2, A6.5
Consolidation	A6
Chapter test	A6
Formative on-screen test	A6
Summative on-screen test	A6

- Produce bar charts for categorical data   (FA13.3)

Starter

Sketch a bar chart, a pictogram and a pie chart on the board and ask questions relating to the sketches. For example:
Which is easier to read? What sorts of data could you display using these types of diagram? Where do you see similar diagrams?

Resources

Topical statistical diagrams from web or newspapers, unlabelled bar chart, Excel

Teaching notes

Statistics is an important branch of mathematics used in many areas of everyday life. Information presented pictorially is often easier to understand and interpret. Clearly this whole section on statistical diagrams nicely fits in with the functional mathematics dimension of the new specification.

Question the group about what diagrams they have studied and present some examples of statistical diagrams gathered from the web and/or newspapers.

Bring focus to bar charts and to a discussion about what is meant by discrete data. Have a list of data types and go through it asking the students to give their thoughts about the nature of the data and their reasons why it is discrete or not. Reinforce the idea that discrete data can be counted and comes in chunks that cannot be meaningfully broken down, for example, you cannot have 0.35 of a medal.

Using the examples in the textbook, emphasise the importance of a good scale for the axis and that labelling is essential if the diagram is to be meaningful. You could present an unlabelled bar chart and ask them to answer questions about it to bring out the need for labelling.

Diagrams should fit the page and not be microscopically small just to fit the squares in their books.

Exercise commentary

Questions 1–2 These questions reinforce basic skills. Ensure axes are clearly drawn and labelled.

Question 3 All reasonable responses need to be valued but questions must be based entirely on the information presented.

Question 4 This is at a higher level and involves using the data to extrapolate into the future. A reminder about how to work out a scale factor change might be required. The dangers of extrapolation from data like this could be made a point of class discussion. Reference to the recent financial collapse in the banking sector could be made.

Plenary

Summarise key points by questioning the group. There could be further consideration of the problems of extrapolation. Demonstrate use of Excel to quickly draw bar charts. Get them to repeat a couple of the questions using Excel.

Histograms for continuous data

A6.2

- Draw and produce histograms for continuous data

(FA13.3)

Starter

Discuss the timing of the 100 metre sprint. How long does it take to run a 100 m? 10 s, 9.9 s, 9.85 s? It all depends on how accurate they want to be or what timing equipment they have. Ask students for examples from other areas of the curriculum like science or CDT and from everyday life.

Resources

Prepared example showing horizontal axis not starting at zero; if available Autograph can be used to draw histograms quickly.

Teaching notes

A quick re-cap on the differences between continuous and discrete data. You may wish to discuss a list of different types of data again.

Students have represented discrete data on bar charts and the focus now is on continuous data grouped into equal-sized intervals. This means no gaps on the horizontal axis and bars of equal width. The vertical axis still shows frequency. Use examples to discuss scales and drawing axes and discuss carefully the different meanings of $5 < t \leq 10$ and $5 \leq t < 10$. Ask students to express this in words to ensure understanding.

The horizontal axis does not have to start at zero and you could emphasise this with a prepared example. Data can be put in groups of different sizes, depending on context, discuss why too few or too many groups could be ineffective.

You may need to revise mean, mode and median.

Exercise commentary

Question 1 An AO1 task reinforcing basic technique.

Question 2 A more stretching question requiring knowledge of modal class and median which may need revising. Get students to test their sentence and reasoning on a partner.

Question 3 This can be discussed and tested in pairs though do check with the whole class on the reasons and comparisons given.

Plenary

Key points can be summarised by questioning the group. If available Autograph can be used to draw histograms quickly. Diagrams can be exported into Powerpoint and students could then be asked to do a short presentation as a homework. There is plenty of opportunity here for setting tasks that sit within the functional mathematics strand of the course.

42

- Draw and produce pie charts for categorical
  data   (FA13.3)

Starter

What is the median of the numbers 1 to 10? (5.5)
What is the mean of the numbers 1 to 10? (5.5)
What is the median of the numbers 1 to 100? (50.5)
What is the mean of the numbers 1 to 100? (50.5)
This can be continued for other ranges of numbers, for example
1 – 1000, 1 – 50, even numbers to 100.

Resources

Schedule of school day for question **1b**, some examples of pie
charts from the web and the media, Excel in the plenary would
be useful; also protractors and compasses.

Teaching notes

Recap on diagrams encountered so far. The focus in this
section is pie charts and you may want to show a variety of
examples you have found on the web and in the news
media.

Using the first example in the book ask the class to draw
the pie chart accurately.

The second example will require more input from the
teacher. Calculating the size of the angle required by a
category is a tough challenge for many at this level and it is
safest not to make too many assumptions about what they
can do. Get some ideas for how to calculate angle from
students but demonstrate the calculation process for the
whole group. Ensure they are clear on how to evaluate an
expression like $\frac{12}{40} \times 360$ either by use of the fraction button
or division. It is probably worth doing a couple of these as
a group to be confident that they know how to do the
calculation.

Drawing pie charts is a challenge for many and needs both
compasses and protractor skills. Remind them about
drawing angles. Is the angle acute or obtuse? Is what I am
drawing sensible?

Calculation leads to valid angles like 7.2° but drawing will
involve approximation.

Exercise commentary

These questions address the AO1
AO2 strands of the specification; AO3
is addressed in the next section.

Question 1 Be prepared with a
timetable of your school day.

Question 2 Careful distinction needs
to be drawn between the number of
farms and the size of those farms.
You may need to explain the nature
of the units being used and the
degree of accuracy which is sensible
when calculating the percentage of
farmland in England. Revision of how
to calculate a percentage may also
be required.

Question 3 Students may need
reminding about how to calculate the
percentage of a given quantity.

Plenary

Summarise key points. Demonstrate how
Excel can be used to draw artistically-
sophisticated pie charts very quickly.
They could repeat a couple of questions
using Excel. If doing a functional maths
task or project by using Excel they can
focus on AO2 and AO3 strands and this
can certainly help in the next section on
problem solving.

- Interpret a wide range of graphs and diagrams and draw conclusions (FA13.4)

Starter

Write these values on the board:

23   26   29   31   34   25   39

42   43   64   71

Ask students to find the mean, the median and the range.

Resources

Excel would be useful; protractor and compasses (question 3).

Teaching notes

This section follows on from A6.3 but extends the work into the AO3 domain.

Recap, by questioning, the key facts associated with pie charts and then the examples in the textbook provide good launch points for discussion in small groups or in pairs.

What must be emphasised is that conclusions made must be based on the information the diagrams provide and expressed in numerical terms from the diagrams. Stories not based on the evidence provided have to be discounted.

The teacher could provoke awareness of this need by making a spurious comment such as 'The same number of girls as boys recalled the iPod.' and refine the understanding of the group using the responses given to this statement.

Since the basic skills of calculating the angles and drawing a pie chart have already been practised in the previous section the use of Excel could again allow quicker access to the AO3 aspect of this work.

The teacher should have some questions ready for question 3 (for example, Which continent has the greatest population/land area? Does the continent with the greatest population correspond to the one with the greatest land area?), just in case the group experiences difficulty finding three clear questions.

Exercise commentary

Questions 1–2 These make use of real data; the meaning of the information and the units used may have to be clarified for some.

Question 3 Can be done effectively using Excel to draw the charts, enabling focus on the interpretation and problem solving aspects of the question. The questions asked of the data must be clear and can be tested amongst the students themselves.

Plenary

Students in pairs or small groups can give a presentation of their answers to the whole group for a specified question.

The teacher can perhaps summarise the questions formulated, in particular for question 3, and hopefully will have a good set of questions produced by the students to use as a summary at the end of the lesson.

- Draw and produce frequency polygons for continuous data
- Identify the modal class for grouped data   (FA13.3)

Starter

Ask students to respond to questions using whiteboards.

Write three values which have: a mode of 4; a mode of 4 and a range of 1; a mode of 4 and a range of 5.

Write four values which have a mean of 5; a mean of 5 and a range of 3; a mean of 5 and a range of 6; a mean of 5 and a mode of 6.

Explore the answers given and share them with the students. Ask students what strategies they are using to find solutions.

Resources

Mini whiteboards, Autograph

Teaching notes

By questioning the class recap on diagrams met already.

Histograms lead easily into polygons simply by taking the midpoint of the top of a bar of the histogram and demonstration can be made of this using previous work. Finding the midpoint of an interval is not always obvious to a student at this level and it is worth going through a couple of examples to demonstrate how to find it either didactically or by questioning the group.

Once again it is probably worth reminding everyone about the modal class and the range.

The first example in the book can be used to demonstrate the basic mechanics of drawing a frequency polygon.

The second example is about interpreting the diagrams and clear statements are required. You should help students refine their initial raw comments into more exact and clear statements. It is worth having a few comments prepared.

Later in the lesson demonstrate how Autograph can quickly draw frequency polygons. This can enable greater focus on the AO2/AO3 aspects of this topic.

Exercise commentary

Question 1 Both graphs may be drawn on the same axes. Emphasise the need for good clear scales and labelling. A reminder about modal class and range may be needed. Suitable responses include 'Office workers take longer to get to work than teachers because the modal class of teachers times is 20–30 whilst that of office workers is 30–40' and 'the spread of travelling times is the same.' Reasons why this is the case are interesting, but emphasise these are just hypotheses and would need further investigation.

Question 2 The two data sets have the same modal classes but different ranges.

Question 3 This might be a good stage to allow students to draw frequency polygons on Autograph.

Question 4 This question requires interpretation and clear statements and reasons, not simply the year. The aim is to be able to convince another person using the data supplied.

Question 5 This question asks students to compare two graphs. Encourage them to discuss their answers, which may differ.

Plenary

Summarise key points. Demonstrate use of Autograph for this work and get them to to repeat question 3 again using the package or a similar one. The 'view statistics' box provides ready-calculated central measures, quartiles and standard deviation for the data; this could enable a more sophisticated discussion of the data for some students.

Exam-style question commentary

Worked solution	Commentary
1)	1) Ensure that axes are labelled, and the scales are linear. Ensure that the bars have no gaps (you might like to discuss why). The bars should be of equal width.
2) a) $\frac{1}{4}$, so 15 girls b) £0–10 c) The actual amounts are not given in the diagram, only the class intervals.	2) Ensure that students appreciate that you cannot find the actual mode, only the interval in which it lies.
3) a) b) The modal time interval is the same $(5 < m \le 10)$. The range in times is greater in August.	3) a) Ensure that axes are labelled, and the scales are linear. Ensure that the crosses are placed at the midpoint of each class interval. In comparisons, encourage students to look for an average (modal class) and a measure of spread (range).

Aim

- To demonstrate how statistics can be used by catering professionals to understand their customers' behaviour and to run their service accordingly
- To show how the manager of a catering business can use mathematics to control stock levels and to plan for the future

Useful resources

- Sandwich starter   Presentation
- Sandwich customers   Presentation
- Sandwich stock   Presentation
- Catering   Worksheet

Teaching notes

Ask students how they think the manager of a sandwich shop could collect data about customer numbers before leading into the example on the case study page.

Make sure that students understand the data and the bar chart and that they can extract the values from the bar chart in order to compare the two data sets. Encourage them to use statistics vocabulary such as range, mode, mean, etc.

Encourage students to think about the open-ended question. Prompt them to think about unusual weeks when the customer behaviour might be different from normal, for example during the Christmas period. You could use the *Sandwich customers presentation* to illustrate this.

Use the introductory text to start a discussion about stock levels and orders. What restraints do students think can affect the stock levels? How do they think a manager can monitor this and ensure that they do not run out of stock?

Students could then work through the stock-take example. The *Sandwich stock presentation* could help with this. Encourage them to consider each ingredient and the current stock levels to decide if the previous week's order had been appropriate.

Extension

Students could consider the effect of changes to the weekly routine.

For example, the shop only opens for 5 days a week; or another sandwich type was added to the product list.

Students could create a data table, bar chart and stock data for such changes and compare the data sets against each other and the original diagrams.

Using the worksheet, students could invent their own catering business scenario.

They could use, for example, the product of a pair of numbers chosen from a bag to create the data values.

Alternatively, students could consider real data from local businesses or the school canteen.

Simplification

Students could use the data from the case study to create a bar chart showing the number of sandwiches sold each day in one week.

Objectives covered in this chapter are:

FA6.2a distinguish between the words 'equation', 'formula' and 'expression'

FA6.3a use the conventions for coordinates in a plane; plot points in all four quadrants

FA6.3b understand that one coordinate identifies a point on a number line, two coordinates identify a point in a plane using the terms '1D' and '2D'

FA6.3e find the coordinates of the midpoint of the line segment AB, given points A and B

FA7.1a use formulae expressed initially in words and then using letters and symbols

FA7.1b substitute numbers into a formula; derive a formula and change its subject

FA8.1b manipulate algebraic expressions by collecting like terms, by multiplying a single term over a bracket, and by taking out common factors

FA8.2a set up simple equations

FA8.2b solve simple equations by using inverse operations or by transforming both sides

FA8.2c solve linear equations, with integer coefficients, in which the unknown appears on either side or on both sides of the equation

FA8.2d solve linear equations that require prior simplification of brackets

Prerequisite knowledge

- Substitute values into an expression
- Combine like terms in a simple expression
- Understand inverse operations
- Write coordinates in the first quadrant

Useful ICT resources

Introductory powerpoint	A7
Starter activity	A7.2, A7.3, A7.4, A7.6, A7.7, A7.8
Powerpoint worked solution	A7.2, A7.3, A7.5, A7.6, A7.9
Animation	A7.2, A7.3 (x3), A7.4, A7.5, A7.6, A7.7 (x4), A7.8 (x4)
Interactive activity	
Consolidation	A7
Chapter test	A7
Formative on-screen test	A7
Summative on-screen test	A7

RICH TASK COMMENTARY

Students should enjoy trying to spot magic squares and will be solving lots of intuitive mathematical equations along the way. You might need to give the students some partially completed magic squares to get them going.

They should spot that the number 5 appears in the middle and that the different magic squares are essentially rotations and reflections of the one given. They could investigate a 4 x 4 magic square and see if they could identify the magic number.

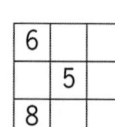

- Distinguish in meaning between the words 'equation', 'formula' and 'expression' (FA6.2)

Starter

Display a spider diagram with $5a$ at the centre. Ask students to write expressions equivalent to this on whiteboards. Select some to be added as legs to the diagram.

Encourage further expressions by saying, for example, 'write one with a divide in it'.

Repeat the activity with another expression at the centre: $12p + 8w$

Discuss some of the expressions offered and why they are equivalent.

Resources

None required

Teaching notes

This section focuses on some key algebraic tools. At this level a rigorous definition of function is not required. Definitions are given in the text and looking at examples should develop the students' 'feel' for which tool is which. It is particularly important to emphasise the distinction between an expression and a formula or an equation, as this does help with the later parts of this algebra section. The use of three lines for identities can be mentioned but does not have to become part of the student's written work at this stage.

Once a number of examples have been considered with the class, and you feel that the students are getting a sense of the categories, then proceed into the exercise.

Exercise commentary

Questions 1–2 These questions go together; question **2** reinforces the answers in question **1** and provides further guidance toward the correct category if the student is unsure.

Question 3 This question requires a one-to-one matching and in itself is a type of function.

Question 4 This asks a similar question to question **1** but uses an alternative way of posing the question.

Question 5 This further reinforces the definitions given.

Question 6 This demands a little creativity from the students and they could try their ideas out on partners before contributing to an end of class plenary.

Plenary

Bring together the results of the class work noting any common worries or errors.

• Manipulate algebraic expressions by collecting like terms, by multiplying a single term over a bracket, and by taking out common factors   (FA8.1)

Starter

Write 6–8 student names on the board and give a scenario about items in each student's pencil case.

Begin with the first student and say that there are t items in this case. Now ask students to listen and record expressions for the next number of items on whiteboards.

Give descriptions, one at a time, such as: Gary has 3 more items than May; David has 4 items less than May; Helen has twice as many items as May, and so on.

Show responses, discuss as necessary and add to the board display.

Now continue using descriptors based on the other students' numbers of items until every named student has a correct expression recorded on the board.

Resources

Mini whiteboards

Teaching notes

Students will have had some experience of this before. It is best taught by demonstration; do some examples with the class as a whole before letting them attempt the exercise individually. The key phrase in the first part of the section is 'like terms' and, unless students are very fluent and confident in this area already, they should be encouraged to rearrange the terms in their written answers before simplifying. The presence of a negative sign can cause problems and it should be emphasised that when collecting together 'like terms' that the sign immediately preceding the term stays with the term.

Expanding brackets should be illustrated using 'think-lines' emphasising that everything inside the bracket is being scaled up by the number outside.

Most students find the inverse operation of factorising more difficult and it needs to be emphasised that the highest common factor is to be taken out. They can be encouraged to multiply out the bracket again as a check.

Exercise commentary

Question 1 Count carefully and remind some that writing $4x$ is clearer than $x4$.

Question 2 Some students may be confident enough to group these directly by observation but most at this level should be encouraged to write down the like terms together before combination.

Question 3 Some may need reminding that expanding and multiplying out mean the same thing. Think-lines can help those who are still a little uncertain.

Question 4 This question requires both expansion and collection of like terms. The directed number rules are useful here though there are no double negatives to worry about yet.

Question 5 Once again emphasise that the terms must be factorised completely using the highest common factor.

Question 6 This involves collection of like terms and then factorisation.

Question 7 Once again a potentially infinite number of dissections of the expression is possible which should refine the students' feel for the creation of an expression.

Question 8 This is a similar problem to the previous one but its discrete structure gives a finite number of solutions.

Plenary

The students may be served well by summarising for themselves some of the main errors possible in this work.

Students could build their own expressions for their partners to simplify or factorise.

- Substitute numbers into a formula   (FA7.1)

Starter

Write the statement $3x^2 = (3x)^2$ on the board.
Ask students to decide if this statement is
always/sometimes/never true, showing the result on
whiteboards.

Discuss the results, sharing some of the students' reasoning.
Suggest that the students may show that the statement is not
always true by using a particular value for x.

If x is 2, what is the value of the LHS? What is the value of the
RHS? Now discuss whether this also shows if the statement is
never true.

Resources

Mini whiteboards, the internet, famous formulae from physics,
mathematics and other areas to share with the group

Teaching notes

Present on the whiteboard a number of famous formulae
from physics, mathematics and other areas. Using formulae
is an essential skill in many subject areas, and cross-
curricular references are useful in motivating the interest of
the students. The concept of a variable should be
introduced and once again reference to the sciences or
other areas could be helpful. Encourage the students to read
a given formula to themselves to understand its structure
better.

Using the examples given in the text, and perhaps some
others, work through some examples of substitution into
formulae with the class as a joint group exercise.

Plenary

Question 7 could provide the starting point for a functional
mathematics mini-project, though if they decide they wish to collect
data themselves, students should be made aware of the sensitivity of
some to enquiries about weight.

More complex and interesting formulae can easily be found on the
web and students could investigate the use of some of these.

Exercise commentary

Questions 1–2 These formulae are
expressed fully in words and some
students may wish to condense them
further by letting single letters
represent the quantities involved.

Question 3 Some students may
need reminding to enclose the
numerator in a bracket, or to use the
ANS button, when using their
calculator to evaluate the answer.
The teacher should be prepared to
suggest some ideas for part **b** of this
question.

Question 4 The students should be
encouraged to say the formula to
themselves, for example, e add R
times i: and think about what
BIDMAS says about the order of
calculation.

Question 5 Some students may
need guidance on entering fractions
and negative numbers into the
calculator.

Question 6 This formula can be used
by multiplying by one half or dividing
by two. The equivalence of the
processes needs pointing out to some
students. You could ask the students
to write down the formulae in at least
two equivalent forms.

Question 7 This AO3 question
shows the use of a formula in a
medical context. Access to a
computer enables the student to
create their own table of values for a
variety of adults.

- Substitute numbers into a formula, derive a formula and change its subject (FA7.1)

Starter

Give out sets of expression cards, one per student. Ask the students to match the expression to the description and check with a neighbour for agreement.

Resources

Set of equivalent expression cards include equivalent pairs such as $4x$ and $2 \times 2x$; also $3y$ and $5y - 2y$; also $6z$ and $\frac{12z}{2}$.

Teaching notes

The rich task in the text provides a good starting point to get the students working and thinking. They need to use their skills in collecting like terms to get the required expression for the perimeter. This can be labelled to give a formula for the perimeter hence emphasising the distinction between an expression and formula recently encountered. This formula can then be used to find the perimeter and also, given the perimeter, be used to find the width of a gate. The arrangement can be done by a balancing approach or flow chart method.

A couple of further examples set to the group as a whole and then the solution demonstrated should provide the necessary tools for the exercise to be attempted.

Exercise commentary

Questions 1–3 These provide basic practice in substitution and rearrangement. Students need to write the formula, the substitution and then show the stages of rearrangement carefully in a logically presented fashion.

Question 4 This rich task is an interesting error-checking question which helps refine the students' skills.

Plenary

There are plenty of much more difficult and interesting formulae which could be used as an extension in this work.

Look on the web or in a physics textbook.

- Use formulae from mathematics and other subjects expressed initially in words and then using letters and symbol   (FA7.1)
- Set up simple equations   (FA8.2)

Starter

Show a display of a rectangle with a length of $2x$ and ask students to use whiteboards to respond to:

If the width is 3 more than the length, write an expression for the width.
What expression would represent the area of this rectangle?
Allow sufficient thinking and working time, and ask students to check with a neighbour before sharing responses. Make sure that the stages are checked. Share and discuss the different, but equivalent, ways of writing the expression.

Resources

Mini whiteboards, Excel

Teaching notes

The rich task can be explained to the class and then they can try it. A number of approaches to calculating the area are possible; some more efficient than others but all valid approaches should be valued. If access to Excel is available than some may wish to set the problem up on a spreadsheet. They should try to write down a formula for their approach to calculating the area.

At a suitable point you can bring the class back together and summarise what has been attempted and found. At this stage the most efficient formula could be highlighted and the equivalence of different dissections indicated if not demonstrated.

The example in the text uses a flow chart to highlight the structure of the formula and students may find this a useful precursor to the exercise.

Exercise commentary

Question 1 The expression 'one for the pot' may need explaining to some students.

Question 2 The students may need reminding to label their expressions for the area of the shape to make a proper formula.

Questions 3–4 All these questions require careful definition and labelling of the terms involved.

Question 5 After following the sequence of instructions for some specific ages the students eventually need to give a symbol to the starting integer and turn the set of instructions into a formula which can be simplified to reveal the underlying structure of the process.

Plenary

On the web there are a lot of magic trick puzzles similar to question 5, and some students may wish to try them out on the group or on their partners.

- Solve simple equations by using inverse operations or by transforming both sides in the same way (FA8.1)

Starter

Ask the students to use whiteboards to record expressions based on verbal descriptions.

'I am thinking of a number.' Say that the students may use any letter to represent this variable.

'I double it and add 4.'

Share results, prompting and recording the most efficient expressions. Repeat for others.

'I multiply by 5 and subtract 4'; 'I add 6 then multiply by 3'; 'I square it and add 7.' and so on.

Resources

Mini whiteboards, the internet would be useful

Teaching notes

Students will have some experience of solving equations from KS3. Begin by discussing inverse operations pairs, add/subtract, multiply/divide. Set the rich task to the group and at a suitable moment bring all findings together. The problem provides revision in setting up an equation and the solution should be done by a balancing method. The final answer can be checked by substitution and this can be emphasised as good practice when solving equations.

It is worth doing a number of examples in this very important area with the whole group, demonstrating the need for a logical presentation laid out vertically. That the sides of an equation can be swopped around is a useful technique if the initial equation is presented with the unknowns on the RHS.

There are some excellent demonstrations of the balance method on beam balances on YouTube.

The best way of gaining fluency in this area is by experience, so get the group working through the examples set as soon as possible.

Exercise commentary

Question 1 This question could be done orally as a warm up for the rest of the exercise.

Question 2 Get students to visualise the balance moving up and down as the sides are changed and rebalanced.

Question 3 Students need to be reminded to show their working logically and set out vertically. Some of these questions bring out the useful operation of swapping the left and right hand sides of the equation.

Questions 4–6 These questions require the student to set up their own equation which makes them more difficult for most. They are translating information into algebraic form which is an important problem-solving skill.

Question 7 This rich task demands considerable thought by students at this level. You could simplify it by setting a couple of smaller three-tier arithmagons

Plenary

The students could try building their own equations, starting with a solution, labelling it x and then multiplying or dividing it by suitable numbers and adding or subtracting numbers to give a result. These could be tested on their neighbours.

- Solve linear equations, with integer coefficients, in which the unknown appears on either side or on both sides of the equation
- Solve linear equations that require prior simplification of brackets, including those that have negative signs occurring anywhere in the equation, and those with a negative solution   (FA8.2)

Starter

Use a spider diagram display with an equation at the centre: $4x + 5 = 19$. Add three legs to the diagram and ask the students to notice what you are adding. They will need to respond using whiteboards later.

On one leg write $8x + 10 = 38$. Ask what you have done to get this. What would the next leg look like if this continued? Add that leg to the previous leg and repeat with an additional leg.

Now on a new leg, write $4x + 6 = 20$. Ask what has happened here. What would the next be, and the next?

On the third leg, write $4x + 4 = 18$ and repeat the procedure, asking for the next. Continue with this leg to get to $4x = 14$. Prompt halving, and again, to give the equivalent statement as an answer.

Resources

Mini whiteboards

Teaching notes

Set the rich task to the group and allow them to work on it for a short while before bringing the class together to consider its solution.

Demonstrate the solution of an equation with unknowns on both sides and then do a couple more examples with the input of the group.

Do a couple of examples with the group involving the expansion of brackets, paying close attention to the directed number rules for multiplication which so often catch students out with these questions. Once again whole number solutions can easily be checked for correctness though it is worth setting a question which has a more awkward answer so that students do not get conditioned to always expect nice whole number answers. Awkward fractional answers can still be checked with the aid of a calculator.

Exercise commentary

Questions 1–4 These provide plenty of basic practice in technique. Encourage the students to set their work out logically and show their method. They should get in the habit of checking their answers. In question **1** some students may choose to divide both sides first rather than expand the brackets. Both approaches should be valued and the fact that there are sometimes a number of routes to the solution noted.

Questions 5-7 Require students to set up the equation first.

Question 8 This rich task may need a little help from the teacher to help students to start.

Plenary

The history of algebra provides a good insight into the multi-cultural development of the subject and students might wish to research the contributions of the Islamic civilisation, for example Al-Khwarizmi, as well as the further development of the subject in the West.

A mixture of equations

- Solve simple equations by using inverse operations or by transforming both sides in the same way $\qquad$ (FA8.1)
- Solve linear equations, with integer coefficients, in which the unknown appears on either side or on both sides of the equation
- Solve linear equations that require prior simplification of brackets, including those that have negative signs occurring anywhere in the equation, and those with a negative solution $\qquad$ (FA8.2)

Starter

Use a spider diagram with the expression $2n^2 + 4n + 6$ at the centre. Add a leg showing $n^2 + n^2 + 3n + n + 6$. Ask students to use whiteboards and write another equivalent expression. Select some to be added to the diagram as legs. Encourage more diverse versions if necessary, including use of brackets. Ask selected students to explain how they know that these are equivalent.

Resources

Mini whiteboards

Teaching notes

This section introduces a range of other types of equation for solution, including reciprocal equations and simple quadratics. Once again the rules for directed numbers need emphasising in some of the more complex problems.

A couple of examples of the new types should be demonstrated. The balance method is still the guiding strategy and if the students grasp this idea then they should cope with these more difficult challenges.

Exercise commentary

Question 1 This focuses on reciprocal equations and the strategy is to get rid of the fractions and turn the equation into a type students are already familiar with.

Questions 2–4 These questions are very much extensions of types they have met before though the negative number rules are used a lot more.

Questions 5–6 These questions provide practice in setting up and solving an equation from information provided.

Plenary

This is probably a good place to correct any recurrent errors in these more difficult problems and to consolidate all the algebraic work so far.

- Use the conventions for coordinates in the plane; plot points in all four quadrants
- Understand that one coordinate identifies a point on a number line, two coordinates identify a point in a plane using the terms '1D' and '2D'
- Use axes and coordinates to specify points in all four quadrants
- Locate points with given coordinates
- Find the coordinates of the midpoint of the line segment AB, given points A and B, then calculate the length AB   (FA6.3)

Starter

Begin by chanting a sequence of numbers, starting from 6 and going up in steps of 0.5. You could use a count stick or number line. Repeat the activity going up in steps of 0.4.

Challenge students to individually record these sequences (perhaps on a mini whiteboard) as quickly as possible, this time going up in steps of 0.3, beginning at 4.1. Give students exactly one minute for this activity, and then compare results.

Repeat with 0.3s but this time going back from 12.5.

Resources

Mini whiteboards, Autograph

Teaching notes

Students will have met the idea of plotting coordinates before, at least in the first quadrant. A quick test of plotting points using Autograph should both revise basic ideas and indicate the knowledge base of the students. Extend the axes into four quadrants and indicate how negative numbers are interpreted in a pair of coordinates. Using Autograph invite students to come up individually and plot specified points, perhaps to produce shapes. The order (x, y) needs to be emphasised and that brackets need to be drawn around the numbers. It is worth plotting points like $(0, 3)$ $(-6, 0)$ etc since these can cause confusion.

It worth highlighting the coordinates of the origin and the vocabulary 'origin' as well.

Once they are familiar with the idea of plotting points then set a task of finding the midpoint of a line segment joining two points. They can investigate this and hopefully come up with some conclusions on a general method. The results can be collected together at a suitable point and the method summarised and its use reinforced with a further example.

Exercise commentary

These questions can be done on squared paper or on screen using Autograph.

Question 1 The coordinates need to be enclosed in brackets and be in the correct order.

Question 2 This problem-solving question does require calculation of the coordinates of the midpoints and not just observation from the coordinates-axes.

Question 3 This question involves more calculation of midpoints, which could be done by drawing or calculation.

Question 4 This question requires knowledge of the properties of the diagonals of some quadrilaterals, or can be solved by plotting the points on axes scaled in tens.

Question 5 This question can be answered by reasoning alone or by plotting and observation.

Plenary

Fractional/decimal coordinates can be introduced as a simple extension.

The historical development of the system of coordinates and why they are called Cartesian coordinates can be investigated.

Some students may wish to look at other coordinate systems such as map references or polar coordinates.

3D coordinates could be investigated as a precursor to later work.

Exam-style question commentary

Worked solution	Commentary

1) a) $3a + 4b$
 	
  b) i) $5(x - 3)$
    ii) $x(x + 4)$
 	
  c) $5x = 23$
    $x = \frac{23}{5} = 4\frac{3}{5}$
	1) Students may need more practice in the factorising in b). Remind them that the common factor can be a letter as well as a number. The equation in c) gives a non-integer solution. Encourage students to give their answer as a mixed number.

2) $e = \frac{5}{4}b + 32$
 	
  $e - 32 = \frac{5}{4}b$
 	
  $b = \frac{4}{5}(e - 32)$
	2) Some students will lack confidence in rearranging the fraction. Encourage them to think of this in two steps rather than one. A common mistake is to forget the bracket.

3) a) No – $n + 2$ only works for (5, 7)
    $3 + 2 = 5$ not 3
 	
  b) $3 \rightarrow 3$
    $5 \rightarrow 7$
    $8 \rightarrow 13$
 	
    Rule is $\times 2 - 3$
    Or $2n - 3$ (n is the input)
	3) Students should ensure that they give some justification to their response, in order to satisfy QWC.
	In b), students should try to articulate the rule in words before attempting to use algebra.

Bearings and Pythagoras

Objectives covered in this chapter are:

FA11.1a   use and interpret maps and scale drawings

FA11.1b   use bearings to specify direction and to solve problems

FA12.1a   understand, recall and use Pythagoras' theorem to solve simple cases in 2D

Prerequisite knowledge

- Know the sum of angles on a straight line, around a circle, and in a triangle
- Calculate square roots
- Give answers to a specified degree of accuracy
- Construct a scale drawing

Useful ICT resources

Introductory powerpoint	A8
Starter activity	A8.2
Powerpoint worked solution	A8.1
Animation	A8.3
Interactive activity	A8.1 (AG), A8.2 (TI), A8.1 (CA)
Consolidation	A8
Chapter test	A8
Formative on-screen test	A8
Summative on-screen test	A8

RICH TASK COMMENTARY

Students should construct accurate scale drawings for each change of 10° in the bearing.

What is interesting about the locus of the points where the boats meet?

They could investigate if the ships were moving at different speeds, if the ships started at different bearings, if they both increased their bearing by 10° etc.

A practical demonstration of this would be to use two torches and ask two students to point the torches in given directions whilst a third student tries to stand where the two beams cross.

- Use and interpret maps and scale drawings.
- Use bearings to specify direction and to solve problems. (FA11.1)

Starter

Ask students to think about what they remember of bearings and write three important facts about them on their boards. Ask student to share these with a neighbour, discuss and agree a final set of three facts. Share and agree these as a group.

Give students a North reference, and ask them to stand up and turn through given bearings.

Resources

Mini whiteboards, projection or poster of a compass showing eight main directions; map of UK showing major cities, protractors, 360° measurers (if possible), the internet, tracing paper.

Teaching notes

There are many skills needed in this section so, as the lesson progresses, you should use feedback from the group to check if any basic skills need to be revised in more detail.

From the web or elsewhere have a projection of the eight main compass directions.

The North line is usually set vertically up the page. Bearings are always measured clockwise from North and need to be three digits. Throughout the lesson emphasise in what is said and done that A <u>FROM</u> B means B is the point where the North line is drawn. Students can take some time to spot the difference between A from B and B from A.

There are some excellent simple programs available which enable bearing estimations to be made.

If students have 360° measurers then this will make things easier. If they only have conventional 180° protractors then some guidance for drawing bearings greater than 180° will be required.

Revision of map scales will be needed. Converting 30 000 cm to km may need two stages at this level: first divide by 100 to get m then by 1000 to get km.

Exercise commentary

Questions 1–2 These questions are basic skills practice. Students may find tracing paper useful for question 1.

Questions 3–4 A rough sketch drawn first can help avoid the inevitable running-out-of-space problems that arise in this work. This approach should become a good strategy in all scale drawing problems. It may be necessary to check on scale conversions.

Question 5 Students need to be clear what the point of reference is. A UK map showing these cities may well help make the question more real.

Question 6 This question is a short revision on scales and ratios. Tracing paper may be useful here.

Questions 7–8 These need rough sketches first before doing the accurate scale drawing.

Question 9 The challenge provides AO3 opportunities and the potential for some interesting project work on nautical miles and knots. Basic definitions of all these nautical measures are on the web via Google.

Plenary

Summarise all the main skills and points. Collaboration with the geography department could provide some interesting cross-curricula work or approaches. There is potential here for a functional maths project based on the challenge or extension of the challenge. A slightly easier option might be to plan a multi-stage journey around Europe or the world. Mention could be made of the effect of the curvature of the earth as distances increase.

• Understand, recall and use Pythagoras' theorem to solve simple cases in 2D. (FA12.1)

Starter

A right-angled triangle has an area of 6 cm^2 and a perimeter of 12 cm. What are the lengths of the sides of the triangle? (3, 4, 5 cm.)

Can you find a right-angled triangle that has the same value for the perimeter and area? (Simplest solution, 6, 8, 10 cm.)

Resources

Triangular grid paper; copies of the diagram for the activity; OCR AO3 Guide Section 3.3

Teaching notes

If using the rich task then a supply of triangular paper will be required. The students will need to record their results systematically in a table and will hopefully observe the emerging pattern. At a suitable moment you can intervene and draw a conclusion using what the students have discovered.

The activity can be speeded up if you provide copies of the relevant diagram, though drawing it themselves does provide some good practice in following instructions. The diagram could also have been drawn for a previous homework. The students should attempt the activity and try to write down in their own words what the solution of the activity suggests. A class discussion can then bring out the formal statement of the theorem.

You could finish with a clear statement of the theorem and demonstrate with the help of the example how to solve a missing hypotenuse problem.

Exercise commentary

Students will probably need reminding about rounding answers only at the last stage and always to write down the units of length with the final answer.

Question 1 Working needs to be set out clearly. The final answer needs to be given to 1 d.p. and units should be given with the final answer.

Questions 2–5 These AO2 problems need the students to draw a suitable context-free triangle and then proceed as in question **1**.

Question 6 This requires error location by the student. The errors demonstrated are among the most common.

Plenary

There is a great deal of history which can be researched in this area and the fact that the theorem was known well before Pythagoras' time may be of interest to the students.

In preparation for the next section students could try problems in which one of the shorter sides is missing.

- Understand, recall and use Pythagoras' theorem to solve simple cases in 2D. (FA12.1)

Starter

In how many ways can you arrange 4 dots on square dotty paper to make a square or rectangle (there should be no spaces between the dots)? (2)
How many ways for 8 dots? (2) And 16 dots? (3) And 32 dots? (3) And 64 dots? (4) And 128 dots? (4) What is the rule? [For 2^n dots, one solution is that the number of ways $= \frac{1}{2} \times (n+1)$ if n is odd, and $\frac{1}{2}(n+2)$ if n is even.]

Resources

None required, though the OCR AO3 Guide Section 3.3 is directly useful

Teaching notes

Begin with a resumé of the previous section and make a clear statement of the theorem. Present the group with a problem with one of the shorter sides missing and ask them to solve it; perhaps discussing the problem in pairs. After a short time bring the group together and collect together what has been found. It is likely the method of solution will come from the group. Once again emphasise the necessity for clear working as shown in the examples.

The two archetypal Pythagoras problems can then be demonstrated. The students can be encouraged to decide at the outset if it is the hypotenuse or one of the shorter sides that is missing. They should come to associate subtraction being involved with the calculation of a missing shorter side.

Exercise commentary

Question 1 This question gives practice of calculating a missing side length of a triangle using Pythagoras' theorem.

Question 2 These provide plenty of practice of calculating a missing shorter side. As always encourage the full method to be shown and remind students to round their answers only at the final stage and to put units with the final answer.

Questions 3–5 These AO2 problems need to be redrawn as context-free right-angled triangles and then solved as in question **1**.

Plenary

Some of the more able students may like to research a proof of the theorem and present their findings the group as a whole. The rich task could be covered if it has not been done already.

Exam-style question commentary

Worked solution	Commentary
1) $3^2 + 9^2 = 90$ $AC = \sqrt{90} = 9.49$ cm	1) Remind students to square root their answer. They should give correct units in their answer.
2) **a** Using a ruler, 2.2 cm 1 cm = 50 km 2.2 × 50 = 110 km Bearing = 098° (using a protractor) **b** 3.3 cm × 50 = 165 km Bearing = 071° **c** 1.9 cm × 50 = 95 km Bearing = 245°	2) Students will need to use tracing paper – they only need to trace the positions of the six towns, not the whole map. Emphasise that in their assessment they will have any maps or diagrams drawn out for them, and they can draw lines on them directly. Remind students that bearings have three digits; also be careful with the 'back-bearing' in part c.
3) 24 m 5 m $24^2 + 5^2 = 4121$ $\sqrt{4121} = 24.5$ $24.5 \div 0.8 = 30.6$ The builder will need 31 tubes.	3) This AO2-type problem really needs a sketch, so that students can see the right-angled triangle. They will need to round their answer up to interpret it properly in the context of the problem.

Objectives covered in this chapter are:

FB2.1d   add and subtract mentally numbers with up to two decimal places

FB2.1e   multiply and divide numbers with no more than one decimal place

FB3.1c   add and subtract fractions

FB3.1d   perform short division to convert a simple fraction to a decimal

FB3.1e   multiply and divide a fraction by an integer and by a unit fraction

FB3.1g   use efficient methods to calculate with fractions

FB3.2b   order fractions

FB3.2c   order decimals

FB3.3a   understand equivalent fractions and simplify a fraction by cancelling all common factors

FB3.4a   use decimal notation and recognise that each terminating decimal is a fraction

FB3.4b   recognise that recurring decimals are exact fractions

FB3.4c   know that some exact fractions are recurring decimals

FB3.5b   know the fraction-to-percentage (or decimal) conversion of familiar simple fractions

FB3.6b   convert simple fractions of a whole to percentages of the whole, and vice versa

FB3.6c   understand the multiplicative nature of percentages as operators

Prerequisite knowledge

- Know basic equivalances between fractions, decimals and percentages
- Multiply and divide integers using a method or written method
- Understand decimal place value

Useful ICT resources

Introductory powerpoint	B9
Starter activity	B9.2, B9.6
Powerpoint worked solution	B9.1 (x2), B9.2, B9.4, B9.6
Animation	B9.1, B9.2 (x3), B9.5
Interactive activity	B9.5 (TI)
Consolidation	B9
Chapter test	B9
Formative on-screen test	B9
Summative on-screen test	B9

RICH TASK COMMENTARY

Encourage the students to use a range of strategies to solve this problem. For example for piece A

-   finding area of A and express as a fraction of area of square, so $\frac{8}{64} = \frac{1}{8}$
-   divide the square into smaller equal sized pieces so that $\frac{1}{16} + \frac{1}{16} = \frac{1}{8}$
-   express the sides as fractions and use the formula for area of a triangle (base × height ÷ 2) so that $\frac{1}{2} \times \frac{1}{2} \div 2 = \frac{1}{8}$

- Order fractions by rewriting them with a common denominator (FB3.2)
- Understand equivalent fractions and simplify a fraction by cancelling all common factors. (FB3.3)

Starter

Ask students to respond on whiteboards. Ask questions such as: Give me a fraction larger than $\frac{1}{2}$ but smaller than 1; larger than $\frac{4}{5}$ and smaller than 1.

Continue by asking for more fractions between two given fractions, select some of the values given to each question, record them and ask students to order these.

Look at responses and explore the reasoning behind some of the answers.

Resources

Mini whiteboards, fraction diagrams showing shapes divided into various fractions.

Teaching notes

A quick review of the meaning of factors and multiples may be needed, and perhaps also a brief mental arithmetic test on multiplication tables.

The concept of an equivalent fraction will have been encountered a number of times before. You should present a number of fractions to the students and ask them to write three or so equivalent fractions. After a short while the responses can be collected together and the reason for their equivalence, or non-equivalence if they are incorrect, can be discussed.

A fraction diagram can be presented on the whiteboard and the fractions shaded noted. If simplification is possible then this can be done in discussion with the class.

Ordering fractions is a common test of students' understanding. At a suitable time you can collect together the answers and methods used; highlighting how converting the fractions into the same common denominator is an effective and easy way to proceed.

Exercise commentary

Question 1 Fractions for simplification. Sometimes students may arrive at the simplest fraction after several stages rather than directly.

Questions 2–3 These require the students to interpret shaded/unshaded parts of given diagrams.

Questions 4–5 These require simplification.

Question 6 This more substantial question requires students to provide clear explanation for which fraction is closest. Answers alone are not acceptable.

Question 7 The fractions should be converted to ones over a common denominator to enable ordering.

Plenary

One possibility is a mental test which either:

- asks for fractions to be simplified as much as possible, or
- asks for an equivalent fraction to be expressed over a specified denominator.

- Know the fraction-to-percentage (or decimal) conversion of familiar simple fractions   (FB3.5)
- Convert simple fractions of a whole to percentages of the whole, and vice versa   (FB3.6)

Starter

Show the statement: $\frac{1}{2} \equiv 0.5 \equiv 50\%$.

This is a familiar and well-known set of equivalent fractions, decimals and percentages.

Ask students to list as many other equivalent fractions, decimals and percentages that they know on mini whiteboards. Allow 2 minutes. Give 1 minute for comparison with a neighbour. Then show and share some of the most important equivalents.

Resources

Mini whiteboards

Teaching notes

This section focuses on a number of important skills which can only be developed through practice. It is therefore likely that you will be demonstrating techniques in a fairly traditional way and then getting the students to practice the skill themselves. The key skills in this section are to be able to convert between a fraction, a percentage and a decimal. Some decimals are well known, such as 0.25, and should be recalled almost immediately but some like 0.48 will need some work.

Converting a fraction into a decimal can be difficult for some, though the examples encountered tend to be relatively straightforward at this level and dealing with halves, quarters and eighths should be sufficient.

Exercise commentary

Question 1 This requires interpretation of the shading of a diagram.

Question 2 This table needs be completed since it provides a thorough grounding in basic conversion processes.

Question 3 Converting all the numbers into decimal form is probably the most effective strategy here.

Question 4 This is a more awkward fraction to convert but if they have met one eighth before they could see this as one half plus one eighth.

Question 5 Students need to show their method.

Question 6 Again they need to show their method.

Question 7 These require conversion to percentages and the students could focus on how they change the denominator to 100 using the idea of equivalent fractions encountered in the previous section.

Questions 8–9 There are a number of possible methods for these so encourage the students to write their method clearly.

Plenary

Various mental tests could be tried here. A short test to ensure familiar percentages such as 25%, 20%, 30%, 65% can be written down in their simplest form. Alternatively a short test on converting decimals to fractions and/or vice versa could be attempted.

- Add and subtract mentally numbers with up to two decimal places
- Multiply and divide numbers with no more than one decimal place, using place value adjustments
- Use a variety of methods for addition and subtraction of integers and decimals, understanding where to position the decimal point
- Perform a calculation involving division by a decimal (up to two decimal places) by transforming it to a calculation involving division by an integer   (FB2.1)

Starter

Roll three dice. Challenge students to write a number using these three digits and a decimal point on a mini whiteboard, for example, 8, 3, 1 can make 83.1. How many different numbers can be made? What is the largest and smallest number possible?

Resources

Three dice, mini whiteboards

Teaching notes

This should be revision of skills students have used before. There are a number of problems to look out for. With addition and subtraction it is vital to get the columns lined up correctly and some students may need reminding about borrowing from columns.

With multiplying, the text uses the method of ignoring the decimal point, doing long multiplication and then placing the decimal point by counting the total numbers are after the decimal point in the original. A justification for the answer can be seen if the decimals are converted into fractions and multiplied, or by estimation. Be aware that students sometimes come armed with a variety of ways of doing long multiplication from their younger days.

Division can be seen in the same way as equivalent fractions with the strategy being to change the number denominator into a whole number and changing the numerator in the same way to maintain equivalence.

It is worth bringing to the students' attention the value of 0.1^2, 0.2^2.....etc.

Exercise commentary

Question 1 This question revises how to compare the size of decimals.

Questions 2–5 These provide basic drill in the core arithmetic operations.

Question 6 This investigation problem requires some careful thought.

Question 7 This question invites the students to find errors which are common in this sort of work.

Plenary

As an extension of question 7, you could encourage students to correct one another's work, looking for any common errors in groups or as a class.

- Know the fraction-to-percentage (or decimal) conversion of familiar simple fractions (FB3.5)
- Interpret percentage as the operator 'so many hundredths of' (FB3.6)
- Understand the multiplicative nature of percentages as operators (FB3.6)

Starter

Display a fraction, decimal and percentage spider diagram with 240 kg as the centre, and various proportions as the legs (for example, $\frac{1}{10}$, 25%, 0.4). Ask students to find the values one at a time.

Resources

Spider diagram for IWB or OHP

Teaching notes

This section is all about developing strategies for finding percentages without the aid of a calculator.

Finding 10% and then doubling or halving is a key method which can be developed for any multiple of 10. Finding 1% is also easy and can be used to find 49%, 39% etc. The VAT rate of 17.5% needs a multiple halving process.

Once some of these basic ideas have been discussed with the class then the activity in the text provides an interesting way of developing and practising the various tactics they have encountered.

Exercise commentary

Questions 1–3 These provide good experience of using the methods students have developed in the previous phase of the lesson.

Questions 5–6 Similar problems involving comparisons. Question **6** requires students to give an explanation, so students can practise QWC.

Question 7 This requires the inverse operation of finding the original number.

Plenary

Simple percentages can be practised mentally up, to and including 17.5% of simple amounts such as 60 etc.

- Add and subtract fractions by writing them with a common denominator

(FB3.1)

Starter

Write sets of four fractions on the board, three of which are equivalent and an odd one out. Ask students to identify the odd one out.

For example, $\frac{9}{21}$, $\frac{3}{7}$, $\frac{12}{14}$, $\frac{15}{35}$

Resources

Mini whiteboards

Teaching notes

The activity provides a good introduction to this section and leads easily into the core idea of a common denominator.

Recap equivalent fractions and simplest form. Start with a few simple examples of adding and subtracting fractions where the denominators are the same, then progress to examples where the denominators are different. Emphasise the necessity of the common denominator being the lowest possible.

Discuss simple fractions of amounts – this will lead into multiplying factions (the topic of the next lesson). To find $\frac{5}{8}$ of 32, start with $\frac{1}{8}$ of 32 and literally read this as '32 divided by 8' (4). Then multiply by 5.

Once students gain some practice in this, they will start to develop their own rules like 'multiply by the numerator, and divide by the denominator'.

Exercise commentary

Students may need help in identifying a common denominator – recap the idea of the least common multiple (LCM) from unit A.

Questions 1 and 2 These focus on fractions of amounts. All units are in pounds sterling.

Question 3 Focuses on adding fractions – parts **b** to **d** have different denominators. Remind students to simplify their answer.

Question 4 Focuses on subtracting fractions.

Plenary

Discuss how to add and subtract fractions using a calculator – most scientific calculators have this facility. Emphasise that calculators cannot be used in the unit B examination.

- Multiply and divide a fraction by an integer and by a unit fraction

(FB3.1)

Starter

Try comparison-type questions: 'Which one's bigger?'

$\frac{1}{2}$ of 45 or $\frac{2}{3}$ of 30

$\frac{3}{4}$ of 90 or $\frac{1}{2}$ of 140

$\frac{1}{3}$ of 53 or $\frac{1}{4}$ of 70 (harder)

Students can respond using mini whiteboards.

Resources

Mini whiteboards

Teaching notes

Multiplying fractions is easier to do, but harder to understand than adding or subtracting. A simple multiplication like $\frac{1}{2} \times \frac{1}{3}$ can be explained as one half **of** one third and the method seen to extend to more difficult fractions. It is worth highlighting the fact that a whole number can be written as a "top-heavy" fraction with denominator 1. Depending on the sophistication and previous experiences of the group, cancelling the fraction down to its simplest form can be performed either at the final stage or prior to the actual multiplication.

Division is harder to justify; start with simple questions with unitary divisors like $6 \div \frac{1}{8}$ which can be understood as: 'how many eighths can be fitted into 6?' The same can be done with other simple divisions and then the 'reciprocal and multiply' algorithm may become clearer for extension to less obvious problems.

Exercise commentary

Many students like to be given a clear simple algorithm that they can apply to all cases. The techniques of multiplying and dividing fractions provide this – more practice can be found in the accompanying practice books.

Question 1 Provides practice in multiplying fractions. Some students may try to apply the techniques of adding and subtracting (by finding a common denominator). Emphasise that they just multiply the numerators, then multiply the denominators.

Question 2 Provides practice in dividing fractions. Parts **a-d** provide fractions divided by an integer – students can turn this into a fraction with denominator 1, then apply the division algorithm. Parts **e-h** offer a fraction divided by a fraction.

Question 3 This AO3-style problem relies on students' ability to be able to select appropriate fractions using a strategy, rather than randomly selecting and seeing what they add up to. The word 'product' may need explaining.

Plenary

Ask how you might multiply fractions containing algebra terms: $\frac{a}{b} \times \frac{c}{d}$.

Then try $\frac{a}{b} \div \frac{c}{d}$.

- Add and subtract fractions by writing them with a common denominator
- Perform short division to convert a simple fraction to a decimal
- Multiply and divide a fraction by an integer and by a unit fraction
- Use efficient methods to calculate with fractions (FB3.1)
- Understand equivalent fractions and simplify a fraction by cancelling all common factors (FB3.3)

Starter

Say to the students that they are going to chant 'times tables', and the first table is the $1\frac{1}{2}$ times table: $1\frac{1}{2}$ times 1 is ..., $1\frac{1}{2}$ times 2 is ... and so on, writing the answers as improper fractions on the board. Establish that these can be written as mixed numbers.

Now repeat with the $\frac{3}{4}$ times table, again establishing the equivalence of improper and mixed fractions.

Resources

None required

Teaching notes

Begin by defining what a mixed number is. Provide three or so examples of mixed numbers and three or so top-heavy (improper) fractions and ask the group to convert them into top-heavy or mixed numbers. After they have had a go at this collect the responses and lead a discussion to produce refined algorithms to convert both ways between mixed numbers and top-heavy fractions.

Adding mixed numbers can be done in a number of ways. The method in the text is a good standard approach though if some students deal with the whole number parts and fraction parts separately then this is an equally valid method if it works for them.

Multiplication or division involving mixed numbers <u>has</u> to be started by converting the numbers into improper form. The fact that whole numbers can be written as fractions as indicated in the last section should be re-emphasised.

Exercise commentary

Question 1 This provides good practice in multiplying fractions involving mixed numbers. Once again it may need highlighting that whole numbers can be written as fractions with denominator 1.

Question 2 Students need to choose the correct operation to use here.

Question 3 This asks for a mixed number to be converted into a top-heavy fraction.

Question 4 This is a good mixture of adding and subtracting. Part **h** results in a negative answer which may catch some out.

Plenary

A simple mental test could help reinforce the ideas here both converting from a mixed number to a top-heavy fraction or vice versa.

Converting mixed numbers into decimal form could also be considered.

Recurring decimals and exact fractions

- Use decimal notation and recognise that each terminating decimal is a fraction
- Recognise that recurring decimals are exact fractions
- Know that some exact fractions are recurring decimals   (FB3.4)

Starter

Ask students to convert simple decimals to fractions: 0.25, 0.1, 0.5, 0.75, 1.75

Then ask for conversion from fractions to decimals, starting with terminating decimals, for example, $\frac{1}{2}$, $\frac{3}{4}$, $\frac{7}{10}$ and then introduce $\frac{1}{3}$, $\frac{2}{3}$, $\frac{5}{6}$. This could usefully be done using calculators.

Resources

Calculators

Teaching notes

The rich task will provide a good basis for discussion. There are a lot of patterns in the decimals, with the structure of the recurrence related to the remainders after division by 11.

The students are probably familiar with thirds and two-thirds as decimals but a look at ninths and sixths will extend their awareness of these recurring type decimals. The correct dot notation used should be introduced paying particular attention to cases such as 0.293293293...........

Exercise commentary

Question 1 This question looks at ninths; it might be interesting to note that 0.99999999......is actually 1 and that the pattern in the digits does in a sense carry on for $\frac{9}{9}$.

Questions 2–3 These look at some more recurring decimals as well as needing rounded answers. Some may need reminding about how to round to a specified number of decimal places.

Question 4 This question brings out why it is sometimes more accurate to work with fractions rather than decimals.

Question 5 The student has to consider where to show the number specified. Some may appreciate that the decimal expansion is approaching the upper bound which is the exact value of the infinite

Plenary

The technique for converting a recurring decimal into its fractional equivalent is a higher-level task but some students may be ready to investigate it at this early stage.

That some numbers cannot be expressed as fractions and hence recurring decimals may lead to some discussion of irrational numbers.

Exam-style question commentary

Worked solution	Commentary
1) a) $6\frac{1}{2} = \frac{12+1}{2} = \frac{13}{2}$ 13 halves b) 20% of £400 $= \frac{20}{100} \times 400$ $= 20 \times 4$ $= £80$	1) a) Some students like to recall rules eg multiply the whole number by the bottom then add the top. Others may prefer jottings or a sketch. b) Students should read 'of' as 'multiply' in these contexts. Encourage correct units in the answer.
2) Lowest common multiple is 120 $\frac{1}{4} = \frac{30}{120}$ $\frac{4}{20} = \frac{24}{120}$ $\frac{7}{30} = \frac{28}{120}$ $\frac{9}{40} = \frac{27}{120}$ $\frac{7}{30}$ is closest to $\frac{1}{4}$	2) This AO3-type question looks simple, but students will need to develop a clear strategy that does not involve calculators. Encourage the use of equivalent fractions – you could refer to some simpler questions from the chapter.

3) a) i) $\frac{50}{400} = \frac{1}{8}$
     ii) $\frac{250}{400} = \frac{5}{8}$
 	
 b) i) $\frac{1}{8} = 0.125$
     ii) $\frac{5}{8} = 0.625$
	3) a) Students should be encouraged to simplify fractions where possible.
	
	 b) It will help students considerably if they add eighths to their itinerary of learned equivalences.

Aim

- To introduce students to some of the ways that mathematics can be used in business
- To emphasise the importance of mathematics in financial situations

Useful resources

- Business starter   Presentation
- Breakeven analysis   Presentation
- Business   Worksheet

Extension

Using the *Business worksheet* students could apply what they have learned in this case study to a business of their own choosing.

Encourage students to think about the costs involved.

They could use the breakeven analysis to determine if their business would make a profit or a loss.

Teaching notes

Ask if any of the students' families have their own business. Show an example of a balance sheet template and invite volunteers to explain what it means to the rest of the class.

Introduce the scenario of Annie's cards as outlined in the student book (you could use the *Business starter presentation*) and ask students to complete the cash flow data (ensure that they understand the information!) They could then work through the example, including the further questions at the bottom of the page. If students have ICT access, this is an ideal opportunity to show the benefits of using a spreadsheet.

Ask students if they know what 'breakeven' means. Discuss why it is important for a business to know their 'breakeven' point, and talk students through the method for creating the 'breakeven chart' using the PowerPoint presentation. Ensure that they understand how the lines are drawn from the data (the *Breakeven analysis presentation* might be helpful with this*)*. Also, discuss the relevance of the gradient and *y*-intercept of each line, again linking these values back to the data.

Students could then use the questions below the graph to create their own 'breakeven charts' for the new conditions described. This is a good opportunity to reinforce how to draw straight-line graphs.

This case study is also good for introducing or reinforcing formulae – you could ask how many formulae are presented on the case study pages.

Students may be unfamiliar with the term 'direct proportion' as this is outside the GCSE Foundation specification, although it is referred to in the student book.

Students could use the worksheet to plan another new business.

Simplification

Students could investigate some simple mobile phone tariffs and draw graphs to compare the merits of "pay-as-you-go" against monthly contract.

Objectives covered in this chapter are:

FB9.1a recall and use properties of angles at a point, angles at a point on a straight line, perpendicular lines, and opposite angles at a vertex

FB9.1b distinguish between acute, obtuse, reflex and right angles; estimate the size of an angle in degrees

FB9.1c distinguish between lines and line segments

FB9.1d use parallel lines, alternate angles and corresponding angles

FB9.1e understand the consequent properties of parallelograms

FB9.1f understand a proof that the angle sum of a triangle is 180°

FB9.1g understand a proof that an exterior angle of a triangle is equal to the sum of the interior angles at the other two vertices

FB9.2a use angle properties of triangles

FB9.2b explain why the angle sum of a quadrilaterial is 360°

FB9.2c recall the essential properties and definitions of special types of quadrilateral

FB9.2d classify quadrilaterals by their geometric properties

FB9.2e recall the definition of a circle and the meaning of related terms, including centre, radius, chord, diameter, circumference, tangent, arc, sector and segment

FB9.2f understand that inscribed regular polygons can be constructed by equal division of a circle

FB9.3a calculate and use the sums of the interior and exterior angles of quadrilaterals, pentagons and hexagons

FB9.3b calculate and use the angles of regular polygons

Prerequisite knowledge

- Know that the angles in a triangle add to 180°
- Recognise language associated with lines and angles – parallel, perpendicular, polygon

Useful ICT resources

Introductory powerpoint	B10
Starter activity	B10.3
Powerpoint worked solution	B10.3, B10.4
Animation	B10.2, B10.3 (x2), B10.8 (x2)
Interactive activity	B10.3 (AG)
Consolidation	B10
Chapter test	B10
Formative on-screen test	B10
Summative on-screen test	B10

RICH TASK COMMENTARY

Students should be encouraged to start with simple cases of polygons with 3, 4, 5, etc sides and look for patterns.

For a 12-sided polygon there are 54 lines required.

For an n-sided polygon there are $\frac{1}{2}(n-3)$ diagonals

Students might benefit from the practise of constructing regular polygons accurately with a ruler and protractor. (Another worthy investigation would be to construct as many regular polygons as possible using just compasses and a ruler!)

Extending the task further, students could try to work out the number of regions inside each polygon, the number of cross-overs etc.

- Recall the definition of a circle and the meaning of related terms, including centre, radius, chord, diameter, circumference, tangent, arc, sector and segment. (FB9.2)

Starter

Challenge students to sketch and name as many 2D shapes as they can in a timed interval.

Resources

Both Cabri and the internet would be useful; compasses

Teaching notes

This section is primarily a revision of some basic vocabulary. The students will have met most of the words before and the definitions can be drawn from the group through questioning. The words *chord*, *sector*, *segment* and *tangent* will probably need description and defining and emphasis should be placed on the distinction between a sector and segment. The idea of a tangent can be developed by slowly moving a line from intersecting a circle in two points, to touching, to non-intersection on a program such as Cabri.

The extra detail of major and minor arcs, sectors and segments can also be introduced. The common notation of O for the centre of a circle and using letters to describe sectors should be demonstrated.

Exercise commentary

Question 1 This looks at the vocabulary of describing fractions of circles.

Question 2 This could be done on Cabri as a dynamic image makes the result clearer. You may need to help the students explain the result.

Question 3 This question leads to the circle theorem about angles in a semicircle. Again the result can be easily observed using drawing or Cabri.

Question 4 This question needs the student to cut out the sector and construct a cone.

Question 5 This question requires some simple algebra. It may be worth discussing the equivalence of writing $x \div 2$ and $\frac{x}{2}$.

Question 6 This question will be helped if the student can access the web to research this topic.

Plenary

Question 5 can be extended into a search for a general formula. The more difficult problem of joining points on the circumference together and counting the regions could be introduced.

- Distinguish between acute, obtuse, reflex and right angles; estimate the size of an angle in degrees.   (FB9.1)

Starter

Ask students to work in pairs and write as many facts about triangles as possible in 2 minutes.

Which pair has the most? Prompt further by asking if students can remember the special names, or have they remembered about symmetry, and so on.

Resources

The internet would be useful

Teaching notes

This is revision of work which students have met before at KS2 and KS3. The idea of angle as a measure of turning should be emphasised and then by quizzing the group revise the names of the different sorts of angles. There are a number of angle estimation programs on the web, and these can be a fun way of getting the students to improve their estimation skills. Strategies should be discussed, especially for angles greater than 90°.

A couple of missing-angle problems should be set to the group. The manner of setting out the solution as demonstrated in the text should be highlighted.

It is worth reminding students about the box notation for a right angle on diagrams.

Exercise commentary

Questions 1–2 These estimation problems practice the use of appropriate vocabulary.

Question 3 This may require revision of compass directions (see Section A8.1).

Question 4 This is practice in finding missing angles, and once again emphasise the correct way of setting out a clear solution.

Question 5 Allow a number of degrees of accuracy here. It may be necessary to discuss the structure of the year and number of days in these months.

Question 6 This rich task will require careful recording or listing of the angles.

Plenary

Ask students to consider if an angle of 400° or 720° has any meaning. A look at the history of angle measure could be started, possibly with a look at other angle measures such as gradians or radians.

- Recall and use properties of angles at a point, angles at a point on a straight line (including right angles), perpendicular lines, and opposite angles at a vertex.   (FB9.1)

Starter

Using mini whiteboards and working in pairs, ask students to consider the truth or otherwise of one of the statements 'a square is a rectangle' or 'a rhombus is a parallelogram'. After 2 minutes thinking time, get feedback from the group and explore reasons.

Resources

Mini whiteboards, a program such as Cabri would be useful

Teaching notes

Review angles as a measure of turning and then quiz the group on the size of a quarter, half and three-quarter turn. Review the language of 'straight-line angle' and 'right-angle'.

Review the idea of vertically opposite angles. Cabri can demonstrate the equality of opposite angles dynamically.

Set the group to work through the examples in the text in pairs and then go through these, once again highlighting the need for clearly set out solutions with simple reasoning. If necessary set more problems to reinforce the approach otherwise get the group working on the exercise.

Exercise commentary

Questions 1–2 provide practice in finding missing angles. Expect the students to provide reasoning and working for their answers and not simply supply numerical answers.

Question 3 Consolidates the skills learned within a context. Encourage students to give justifications for their responses, thereby practising QWC.

Plenary

If it is necessary to extend some of the group, then introducing algebra into the missing-angle problems can raise the level of difficulty.

- Use parallel lines, alternate angles and corresponding angles.
- Understand the consequent properties of parallelograms and a proof that the angle sum of a triangle is 180°. (FB9.1)

Starter

Display a geometric design, and ask students to examine it carefully, pick out and name any shapes noticed. Allow students 2 minutes to look at the design and make any notes necessary. Select individuals to name a shape and identify it on the design. Encourage some greater detail from each student: Why is it a ... ? How do you know?
Encourage looking for some less obvious shapes, perhaps crossing or linking in the design. Again, select a few students to share the findings.

Resources

Geometric design for starter, a program such as Cabri would be useful

Teaching notes

This is revision of work from KS3 but the formal language of alternate and corresponding may be new as this work is often introduced using the language of F and Z angles. The definition of alternate and corresponding can easily be shown on Cabri, as can the translation of one parallel line onto another to demonstrate the equality of alternate angles and corresponding angles.

The next stage is to consider a particular quadrilateral, the parallelogram, and to get the students to investigate and summarise its angle properties. Findings can be drawn together for the whole group. It may be necessary to extend the sides of the quadrilateral as a hint of how to apply the initial results to find the angle properties.

The vocabulary of opposite and adjacent angles in a parallelogram may need clarification and the idea of interior angles may be introduced.

Working through the given examples with the group should enable them to progress onto the exercise.

Some students can confuse the arrow notation for parallel lines with the dash notation for equal length sides so it may be worthwhile to clarify the difference.

Exercise commentary

Questions 1–4 provide basic AO1 practice to encourage working and reasoning to be written down clearly.

Questions 5–8 are AO2 problems and once again reasoning must be shown.

Question 9 is a challenge question and requires both an algebraic result and a straight line graph to be drawn. Some guidance may be required here.

Plenary

More complex problems can be provided if necessary. With the idea of alternate and corresponding angles covered, it could be a good time to demonstrate a written proof that the angles of a triangle sum to 180°.

- Recall and use properties of angles at a point, angles at a point on a straight line (including right angles), perpendicular lines, and opposite angles at a vertex
- Distinguish between acute, obtuse, reflex and right angles; estimate the size of an angle in degrees
- Use parallel lines, alternate angles and corresponding angles
- Understand the consequent properties of parallelograms and a proof that the angle sum of a triangle is 180°
- Understand a proof that an exterior angle of a triangle is equal to the sum of the interior angles at the other two vertices   (FB9.1)

Starter

Display a geometric design, and ask students to examine it carefully, pick out and name any shapes noticed. Allow students 2 minutes to look at the design and make any notes necessary.

Select individuals to name a shape and identify it on the design. Encourage some greater detail from each student: Why is it a ... ? How do you know?

Encourage looking for some less obvious shapes, perhaps crossing or linking in the design. Again, select a few students to share the findings.

Resources

Geometric design for starter

Teaching notes

The rich task is a graphical investigation of supplementary angles. This could be done as a class task or as homework. You should work through the formal proof of the angle sum of a triangle, stressing that an algebraic proof means the rule works for all possible triangles. Students should then work through the example before attempting the exercise.

Some students confuse the arrow notation for parallel lines with the dash notation for equal length sides, so it may be worthwhile to clarify the difference.

Exercise commentary

Questions 1–9 These triangles provide basic AO1 practice to encourage working and reasoning to be written down clearly.

Questions 10–11 These questions require careful reading, and then algebra to build and solve an equation.

Plenary

More complex problems can be provided if necessary, or students could devise their own problems for others to solve.

- Calculate and use the sums of the interior and exterior angles of quadrilaterals, pentagons and hexagons

(FB9.3)

Starter

Ask students to listen carefully, and create a 'mind picture' from the instructions that you give them verbally. Choose a type of shape (perhaps an isosceles triangle, or a right trapezium), and describe it using its geometrical properties. They do not need to draw or sketch what they see (this should be a purely mental exercise). After describing the shape, ask students to name the shape. Repeat for different shapes.

Resources

A display of standard quadrilaterals and polygons would be useful; also compasses and protractors

Teaching notes

The starter activity will lead nicely into a consideration of the different types of quadrilateral that students know. It would be useful to have a display of the main types of quadrilateral, either on an interactive whiteboard, or as a poster or an OHT.

Discuss what types of shapes are polygons, and what types aren't (eg circles, 3-D shapes).

Define interior and exterior angles, and set students the problem of finding the sum of the interior angles of a hexagon. You could display a hexagon split into triangles, as in the student book.

Try different polygons and generalise the rule for an n- sided polygon (this forms the basis of question 6). Discuss the sum of the exterior angles of a polygon - what do they always add up to, and why? (ask students to visualise the locus of a point that starts from a vertex on the perimeter of the polygon, then moves all the way around the shape to come back to its start point – what angle has it turned through in total?)
Extend to the interior angles of a regular polygon.

Exercise commentary

Questions 1 The focus here is on regular polygons. Note that 7-sided and 9-sided shapes are missing – you could ask students what these are called. Encourage students to use their results to identify a rule to calculate the interior angles of any regular polygon. Consolidate with a formula.

As an extension to this question, challenge students to construct the regular polygons in the table by using compasses and first constructing a circle. Go through this procedure as a whole group.

Questions 2–4 Students need to use their knowledge of interior and exterior angles of regular and irregular polygons. Ensure that students have a formula for the sum of all the interior angles of an n- sided polygon, and that they understand it.

Plenary

Either discuss the rich task in question 9, or the maths/ art research activity in question 10 – if you have some attractive tessellation images to show, this could be an inspirational end to the lesson.

Summary

Exam-style question commentary

Worked solution	Commentary
1) 66 + 71 + 53 = 190 XYZ will not form a straight line because their angles do not add to 180°.	1) Students will need to use knowledge of angles in a straight line. Emphasise that the question requires them to explain their answer.
2) $\angle DAC = 24°$ (isosceles) ACDE must be a rhombus (AC = CD) So AD bisects $\angle EAC$. And $x = 24°$. $\angle DCA = 180 - 2 \times 24$ $= 132°$ (angles in a triangle) $y = 180 - 132 = 48°$ (angles on a straight line)	2) This problem involves a fair amount of geometrical reasoning that some will find demanding, including knowledge of the geometrical properties of quadrilaterals. Encourage good practice in short justifications of each step, as this addresses QWC.
3) Angles in a triangle add to 180°, so the missing angles in the isosceles triangle are $(180 - 30) \div 2 = 75°$ Exterior angles of a polygon add to 360°, so each exterior angle of a regular pentagon is $360 \div 5 = 72°$ Angles on a straight line add to 180°, so the interior angle of the pentagon is $180 - 72 = 108°$ Angles at a point add to 360°, so $x = 360 - (2 \times 75 + 108) = 102°$	3) This is a substantial multi-step A03-type problem. In the absence of scaffolded parts, encourage students to use their angle facts to find the angles they can deduce, starting with what they know. Even if they don't get to the final answer, students will get method marks. It is very important in this question to show justifications.

Objectives covered in this chapter are:

FB6.1a construct linear functions from real life problems and plot their corresponding graphs

FB6.1b discuss and interpret linear graphs modelling real situations

FB7.1a solve simple linear inequalities in one variable, and represent the solution set on a number line

Prerequisite knowledge

- Substitute values into an expression
- Expand single brackets
- Solve a linear equation
- Draw a straight-line graph from a table of values

Useful ICT resources

Introductory powerpoint	B11
Starter activity	B11.1
Powerpoint worked solution	B11.1
Animation	B11.1 (x2), B11.2
Consolidation	B11
Chapter test	B11
Formative on-screen test	B11
Summative on-screen test	B11

RICH TASK COMMENTARY

A great way to start this activity is to play Connect 4 where students take turns to place a counter on any point visible on the grid. First to make a line of 4 in any direction is the winner.

Students should record the coordinates of any winning lines and try to write in words and in algebra any connections they spot between the x and y coordinates.

They should be able to generate examples such as:

'x-coordinate is always 3' $\qquad x = 3$

'x coordinate and y coordinate add up to 4' $x + y = 4$
    etc

Students could extend the activity by predicting points that will lie on their winning lines which are not on the grid; examining what all the winning lines have in common where the y-coordinate is double the x-coordinate $\pm$ something etc.

- Construct linear functions from real life problems and plot their corresponding graphs.
- Discuss and interpret linear graphs modelling real situations.   (FB6.1)

Starter

There are approximately 2.2 pounds (lb) in 1 kg. Ask students to convert these weights:
10 kg, 11 lb, 8 lb, 7 kg and 3.8 lb.

Pounds	(22)	11	8	(15.4)	3.8
kg	10	(5)	(3.6)	7	(1.7)

What might make this easier, apart from a calculator?
(A graph of the relationship).

Resources

Various thermometers and the internet would be useful; 2 mm or 5 mm graph paper

Teaching notes

Ask the group how temperature is measured. The Celsius scale will be well known but you may have to explain the older Fahrenheit system or may have set research of this as part of a preparatory homework. The conversion from centigrade (Celsius) to Fahrenheit can be done using a flow chart which can also be translated into a formula. The formula can be graphed and this is a good opportunity to discuss how much information is required to plot a straight line graph. Whilst two points is all that is necessary, three points will provide an error check. The example about flight journey time can be done as a group discussion to reinforce the ideas before commencing the exercise.

Exercise commentary

Questions 1–3 These questions provide basic experiences similar to the examples worked in the text.

Question 4 This rich task requires students to choose their own value range and to discuss the validity and reasonableness of the model provided. The idea of a mathematical model may need discussing in simple terms with the group.

Question 5 This rich task involves a more complicated function. The manner in which the RHS is evaluated may need highlighting with the addition of brackets in the numerator perhaps emphasising the order of calculation. The students need to consider the validity of the model. In part **b** students are invited to set up a spreadsheet to give a table of values for m and h. This is a very useful tool in dealing with the investigation of functions since the values inputted can be changed very easily.

Plenary

If the students have access to the web then they could be set the task of finding three functions used in everyday business or work. They may be able to set up a simple functional model of some aspect of their own lives or use some simple experimental data to gain a linear functional relationship between two variables.

- Construct linear functions from real life problems and plot their corresponding graphs.
- Discuss and interpret linear graphs modelling real situations. (FB6.1)

Starter

A robot is given these instructions for running a bath:

1. Turn on the taps.
2. When the bath is $\frac{3}{4}$ full the task is complete.

What will happen if the robot follows these instructions? What is wrong with these instructions? (Did not mention putting in the plug, does not tell you to turn off the taps, does not take any notice of the temperature of the bath.)

Resources

Analogue clock; 2 mm or 5 mm graph paper

Teaching notes

The rich task can be set to the group. At a suitable moment stop the group and collect together what has been found out. The group can then be allowed to finish off the task, ending with a short plenary session to summarise all the necessary techniques.

The examples given of the car windscreen and water tank can be used to reinforce the ideas encountered in the rich task.

Exercise commentary

Question 1 Some students may go straight to the formula so the order in which the question is attempted is flexible.

Questions 2–3 These questions require the graph to be drawn for a simple practical situation, the formula relating the variables written down and the graph to be used to find required values.

Question 4 This rich task is based on the angle sum of any triangle being 180 degrees. The student has to decide on the size of the axes and their scales.

Question 5 This rich task may be easier if there is an analogue clock in the room and students can see the angles that are being referred to. Once again the axes and scales used are to be decided by the students.

Plenary

Students could complete the rich task if not already done.

• Discuss and interpret linear graphs modelling real situations. (FB6.1)

Starter

I cycle to work a distance of 30 miles there and 30 miles back. I travel at 30 mph on the way to work and 15 mph on the way back. What is my average speed? [You could let students know that the answer is not $(30 + 15) / 2 = 22.5$ mph] Remind students that speed = distance ÷ time. In this case distance = 60 miles and time is 3 hours. So speed is $60 ÷ 3 = 20$ mph.

Resources

None required

Teaching notes

The rich task about the business people provides a good entry into this section. The task is self-explanatory and focuses the students' attention on the significance of the gradient of the lines. Some students may have encountered these sorts of graphs in physics already. After students have tried the task, go through what has been deduced from the graph. It is worth focusing on
the meaning of the different steepness of the lines and interpreting the gradient as speed.

The example presented in the text about investment is well worth doing with the students. It brings out the meaning of the gradient of the line without any abstract definitions being required. Students at this level will need reminding how to work out the rate of interest.

Exercise commentary

Question 1 The temperature at the start may be found by looking at where $t = 0$. The meaning of the gradient of the line is required.

Questions 2–3 Both these questions require interpretation of graphs drawn. The last part of question **3** requires some comment and reasoning from the student which should be written down clearly.

Question 4 This question requires the student to construct their own conversion graph by using two given values, though the (0, 0) value is not explicitly stated.

Plenary

Students should use the web to research current currency exchange rates and use them to draw their own conversion graphs, for example GB£ to Euro or US dollar.

- Solve simple linear inequalities in one variable, and represent the solution set on a number line. (FB7.1)

Starter

Ask students to respond to questions using whiteboards. Write on the board $n > 5$. Ask students to write any possible value for n. Share and discuss the responses.

Write $p < 4$ and request possible values for p. Share some of these responses, particularly if negative values are offered. Explore what students think might be the largest possible value of p.

Write a third statement: $m \geq 7$ and ask the same kind of questions.

Share any fraction or decimal responses, and explore what the smallest value here might be.

For each of these, draw the solutions on a number line, showing and discussing the open and closed circle convention.

Resources

Mini whiteboards

Teaching notes

This section begins with a quick look at the distinction between an equation and an identity which should be illustrated with examples.

The students should be familiar with the meaning of the different inequality signs since they first meet them in primary school and then again at KS3. The group can be presented with a simple linear equation to solve which they should solve individually and then the answer checked by going through the problem. The same question but written as an inequality can then be set and the same process repeated but with the final answer being an inequality. This should enable the difference between equations and inequalities to be highlighted and discussed.

The use of number lines to illustrate inequalities will have been encountered before and should be demonstrated.

Exercise commentary

Question 1 Students have to distinguish between identities, equations and inequalities.

Question 2 This ensures understanding of the basic inequality symbols so any core issues will be picked up at this early stage.

Question 3 Students have to interpret given number lines. They may need reminding about the distinction between open and closed circles.

Question 4 Using the same sort of diagrams as in question 3 students need to draw number lines to describe the given inequalities.

Question 5 There are a complete set of problems here which need to be set out vertically and logically. Some students do have a tendency to transform the inequality symbol into an equality symbol and may need to be reminded. The final answer must be clearly stated as an inequality.

Question 6 These can be solved as two separate inequalities or as they are since no x terms appear at the left or right hand ends.

Question 7 Students may need reminding what an integer is.

Question 8 Students may need reminding what an odd number is.

Plenary

Students could write their own inequalities for others to solve, or investigate solutions to "double" inequalities such as $4 < x \leq 10$.

Exam-style question commentary

Worked solution	Commentary
1) a) $2x - 3 \geq 12$ $2x \geq 15$ $x \geq 7\frac{1}{2}$ b) i) ii) 8, 9	1) Emphasise the similarities between solving inequalities and equations. In b) ii) students can be encouraged to check their answers in the inequality.
2) a) Calls up to 1 minute are a fixed rate of 40p. b) Cost = $40 + m \times 30$ $C = 40 + 30m$	2) a) Encourage a clear concise explanation to satisfy QWC. b) Students may need help – ask how many parts there will be to the formula.
3) a) b) 15 swims breakeven, so 16 swims	3) a) Students could be encouraged to start by drawing a table of values. b) Students will need to read the question carefully – the graph gives the breakeven value, not the required answer.

Objectives covered in this chapter are:

FB10.2a recognise and visualise rotations, reflections and translations, including reflection symmetry of 2D and 3D shapes, and rotation symmetry of 2D shapes

FB10.2b understand that rotations are specified by a centre and an (anticlockwise) angle

FB10.2c understand that reflections are specified by a mirror line, at first using a line parallel to an axis, then a mirror line such as $y = x$ or $y = -x$

FB10.2d understand that translations are specified by a column vector

Prerequisite knowledge

- Plot coordinates in all four quadrants
- Know and use angle measure in degrees
- Recognise the equation of straight lines parallel to the coordinate axes

Useful ICT resources

Introductory powerpoint	B12
Starter activity	B12.3
Powerpoint worked solution	B12.1, B12.4
Animation	B12.1, B12.2, B12.3 (x2)
Interactive activity	B12.4 (AG), B12.2 (TI)
Consolidation	B12
Chapter test	B12
Formative on-screen test	B12
Summative on-screen test	B12

RICH TASK COMMENTARY

Students should be systematic in recording the image and object coordinates of any transformations they investigate. Students should focus upon translations, reflections in the x and y axes and rotations of 90°, 180° and 270° around the origin, and try to arrive at rules for each of these transformations.

- Recognise and visualise reflection symmetry of 2D and 3D shapes
- Understand that reflections are specified by a mirror line   (FB10.2)

Starter

Arrange 12 equally spaced dots in a rectangle. You can move between the dots either vertically or horizontally. **What is the minimum number of moves to move between dots at opposite corners?** Experiment for different sized rectangles all with 12 dots.

(Best arrangement is 4 by 3, with 5 moves.)

Resources

Small mirrors, tracing paper, Autograph and Cabri (if available)

Teaching notes

If available, both Autograph and Cabri can be used very effectively as both a teaching aid and investigation tool.

Students have met symmetry before at KS3. A revision of the basic types of symmetry could be done by projecting a suitably symmetric object on the board and questioning the group about its symmetries. Focus on line or mirror symmetry. How can they justify the symmetries. Mirrors, folding, observation....?

Project an object and a vertical mirror line on the board; at this stage the mirror and object should not intersect. Invite a student to draw in the reflected image. Similarly, project an example with a slanting mirror line and then one where the object intersects the mirror line (this will have invariant points). Once again get students to have a go at the front. These can easily be related to the examples in the book.

Discuss the illustrations in the book once again, perhaps with the help of a projection on the board.
The mirror line can be found by measuring for midpoints or if they are familiar with constructions then by construction of a perpendicular bisector.

Exercise commentary

Tracing paper can be a great help with this work.

Questions 1–2 These questions are basic AO1 practice.

Question 3 This question involves problem solving and is more investigative. Mirrors would probably help the students considerably. If literacy levels could be an issue with some at this level then be ready to supply a clearly written set of capital letters for the students to use.

Plenary

The challenge problem can be generalised and students can justify whether or not the same strategy works for all measurements. The problem could also be related to a reflected light ray. The role of reflection in, for example, Islamic art could be a launching point for a project and presentation by the students. It is worth revisiting the lack of line symmetry of a parallelogram and getting the student to justify this. The 12 pentominoes could be drawn and their line symmetries considered. Some quite complicated moving reflection designs can be easily drawn on Cabri.

- Recognise and visualise reflection symmetry of 2D and 3D shapes
- Understand that reflections are specified by a mirror line, at first using a line parallel to an axis, then a mirror line such as $y = x$ or $y = -x$
- Recognise that these transformations preserve length and angle, and hence that any figure is congruent to its image under any of these transformations (FB10.2)

Starter

Ask students to work in pairs, person A and person B. Person A will follow the teacher's directions, but person B will 'mirror' person A's movement. After 2–3 minutes, these roles should be swapped over. The instructions may include: face the front; face your mirror; lift your left knee; raise your right hand; turn 90 degrees clockwise; put your left hand on your right knee; take two paces forward; take two paces to your left; and so on.

Resources

Small mirrors, tracing paper, Autograph and Cabri (if available), squared paper

Teaching notes

Both Autograph and Cabri can be used very effectively as both a teaching aid and investigation tool if available.

This section continues the work of 12.1 to formalise the use of mirror lines on coordinate axes. Use the example in the text, perhaps with the help of a projection on the board, to show how to draw and label the mirror line.

The mirror line can be found by joining the midpoints of the line segments between object points and their images or, if students are familiar with constructions, by construction of perpendicular bisectors.

Exercise commentary

Tracing paper can be a great help with this work.

Question 1 This question practises drawing images including those where the mirror line intersects the object.

Question 2 This question requires students to draw mirror lines from equations before reflecting given objects.

Question 3 This question has a mirror line in the negative quadrants.

Question 4 This question requires the students to do their own diagrams.

Plenary

Students could continue the work of question **5c**, looking for words with either horizontal or vertical line symmetry. They could also try and construct words with both line symmetries or with only rotational symmetry.

- Recognise and visualise rotations, and rotational symmetry of 2D shapes
- Understand that rotations are specified by a centre and an (anticlockwise) angle
- Transform triangles and other 2D shapes by rotation
- Recognise that these transformations preserve length and angle, and hence that any figure is congruent to its image under any of these transformations   (FB10.2)

Starter

A trampolinist can perform 2 full revolutions on each bounce. If he bounces every 2 seconds, how long will it take him to have turned through 108 000 degrees? (5 min.)

Resources

Tracing paper, Autograph, Cabri, squared paper

Teaching notes

Students will have met rotational symmetry at KS3.

Both Autograph and Cabri can make teacher demonstrations and student investigations in this area much quicker and easier.

Project a suitable object with rotational symmetry order 3 and ask the group to describe its rotational symmetry. This should bring out the idea of order of rotation and the need to specify a centre of rotation. Angle of rotation and direction need to be discussed using the same image. The key language at this level includes clockwise and anti-clockwise, though if it is felt appropriate at this stage, the convention of anti-clockwise angles being considered positive can also be mentioned.

Project an object and centre onto the board and ask the group to rotate it 90° clockwise. After discussion of various methods, you may need to describe how to use tracing paper to map a rotation. This involves marking the centre of rotation, tracing the object to be rotated and then rotating the tracing paper through the relevant angle to rotate the shape.

It should be stressed that rotational symmetry order 1 means a shape has no rotational symmetry.

Exercise commentary

Questions 1–4 These questions provide practice of the basic skills in the AO1 strand.

Questions 3 and **4** involve rotation using coordinate axes in all four quadrants.

Plenary

Students could look at rotational symmetries of polyominoes, either drawn previously or now, and look at all symmetries for the individual shapes. Students could be set the task of drawing shapes with a specified number or lines of symmetry and order of rotational symmetry, for example, a shape with rotational symmetry but no reflection symmetry.

- Recognise and visualise translations
- Transform triangles and other 2D shapes by translation
- Understand that translations are specified by a column vector   (FB10.2)

Starter

A parallelogram is made from six congruent rhombuses. The perimeter of each rhombus is 15 cm. What is the perimeter of the parallelogram?
($10 \times 15 / 4 = 37.5$ cm for a 2 by 3 arrangement or $14 \times 15 / 4 = 52.5$ cm for a 6 by 1 arrangement.)

Resources

Autograph would be useful; squared paper

Teaching notes

Pose a problem about how to describe exactly a journey from one place to another. This could be a whole group discussion using the board or on sheets to be discussed in pairs.
From discussion the two main methods of distance and bearing, and distance right and up should emerge. A similar puzzle but this time involving going left and down could be set.

The column vector notation should be introduced as a precise instruction on how to move from one place to another. Stress that a vector is not a fraction and must always have brackets, as these are the most common errors. Note the difference between a row coordinate and a column vector.

When translating a shape make sure students are clear about considering corresponding corners. The problem could be done using Autograph where the students predict the position of the image which is then drawn as a check.

The language needs to be clear. The words object and image need to be defined clearly by reference to a diagram. Translation is a sliding without rotation or flipping.

Exercise commentary

Question 1 Students should begin to spot the relationship between changing the sign of a vector and reversing the direction of the journey. The language image/object may need clarifying in part b.

Question 2 This question emphasises the need to choose corresponding corners. Students should check with a second pair of corners.

Question 3 You could extend this question by asking students to find the vectors which get them back from the image to the object and spotting the general change-sign rule.

Question 4 The challenge may need support for students who are unfamiliar with chess.

Plenary

The challenge could provide a lead into describing other chess moves. There are many games and puzzles which can be played using vectors. One of the most straightforward is describing the journey around an island or a treasure hunt. Islamic tiling is also rich in translations and other transformations and would help as an introduction to combining transformations. The web can provide plenty of illustrations.

Summary

Exam-style question commentary

Worked solution	Commentary

1) a) i) 1 line of symmetry
   ii) no rotational symmetry
 	
b) i) 5 lines of symmetry
   ii) rotational symmetry order 5
	1) Students may need help in describing symmetry concisely in words, particularly order of rotational symmetry.
	
	Note that if a shape has rotational symmetry order 1, it is regarded as having no rotational symmetry.

2)	2) Have tracing paper at hand to help students with rotating shapes. A common error with reflection is to forget to flip the shape over – a small mirror can help.
3)	3) This question is effectively a combined transformation – students will need to ensure they translate the image from the first translation.

Aim

- To demonstrate how mathematics can be applied to create works of art

Useful resources

- Art starter — Presentation
- Art enlargement — Presentation
- Art grid method — Presentation
- Art — Worksheet

Teaching notes

You could start by showing students a picture of some graffiti on a wall and ask them how they think the artist would approach creating such a large design.

Using the *Art enlargement presentation,* let students consider the first slide and answer the related questions. Ensure that they understand the concept of using a scale factor and complete all the questions.

Let students look at the 'TAG' image (*Art grid method presentation*) and work through the accompanying questions. Encourage them to create their own designs based on a coordinate grid and using geometric shapes, which they can then enlarge.

Ensure that students are comfortable with using coordinates and that they understand how different sized grids can be used to enlarge an image while preserving its proportions.

To introduce the theme of crop circles, you could show students the photo of the crop circle shown in the Case study.

Work through the construction method on the Case Study with students to ensure that they understand and follow the steps correctly.

Encourage students to create their own crop circle designs using geometric construction methods. They should be able to write down the steps of their constructions so that others could use them to recreate the design.

Extension

Students could explore examples of real life graffiti and see if they are based on geometric shapes or if they can see a method (such as a grid) used in their creation.

Students could look at more complex crop circles and see if they can determine the construction methods.

Do they think that these designs could be created by people?

What materials/tools could they use to create such large designs?

Students could research the impact of crop circles on the farmers' crops.

What area of corn is damaged?

Simplification

Students could practice drawing simple letters and graffiti patterns on coordinate axes. They could then write down a set of coordinate points so others can reproduce their designs.w

Bivariate data and time series

Objectives covered in this chapter are:

FB10.2a recognise and visualise rotations, reflections and translations, including reflection symmetry of 2D and 3D shapes, and rotation symmetry of 2D shapes

FB10.2b understand that rotations are specified by a centre and an (anticlockwise) angle

FB10.2c understand that reflections are specified by a mirror line, at first using a line parallel to an axis, then a mirror line such as $y = x$ or $y = -x$

FB10.2d understand that translations are specified by a column vector

Prerequisite knowledge

- Plot coordinates in all four quadrants
- Find the mean of a set of numbers

Useful ICT resources

Introductory powerpoint	B13
Powerpoint worked solution	B13.4
Animation	B13.1, B13.4
Interactive activity	B13.3 (AG)
Consolidation	B13
Chapter test	B13
Formative on-screen test	B13
Summative on-screen test	B13

RICH TASK COMMENTARY

You will need to gather some data on people's heights and weights. There are sources of such data on the internet. Students should be encouraged to choose a sample at different age groups, and produce grouped frequency tables for each group. They can then plot scatter diagrams, calculate averages and present their results using box plots to make the necessary comparisons.

Students should be encouraged to ask and investigate their own questions.

- Draw and interpret scatter graphs   (FB11.1)

Starter

Write these values on the board:

28 32 21 53 60 24 37 49 35 44 13

Ask students to find the mean, median and range.

Resources

Mini whiteboards (for the Starter), Autograph and the internet would be useful; graph paper

Teaching notes

This is a move into bivariate statistics after covering single variable work in earlier sections. One approach is to present some paired data to the group and ask them to plot it on a pair of axes. Alternatively they can collect their own data, for example, hand span/thumb length. Some quizzing of the group and discussion should bring out the need to think about scales carefully and that with this work it is not always necessary to begin the axes on (0, 0). Once the group have attempted plotting the data a short review should solve any arising issues.

Depending on the group, the idea of controlled variables could be introduced and that such variables are usually plotted on the horizontal axis. In most of the exercise it doesn't matter which way around the data is plotted.

Exercise commentary

Note that questions 1 and 2 are referred to again in exercise B13.2.

Question 1 This is straightforward practice of plotting points. The axes do not need to start at (0, 0). It may be helpful to plot the data on Autograph using axes staring at (0, 0) to show why.

Question 2 Once again the scale of the axes is the key here. You may need to explain what anthropometric data is and perhaps have some examples from the web.
If students have collected data about their own hand span/thumb length then this automatically provides a context for discussion.

Question 3 This is a substantial question with plenty of potential for discussing associations between measurements. If you are confident the students can plot graphs then Autograph may speed them to the interpretive parts of the question.

Plenary

The collection of data in science could be discussed and begin the discussion about correlation and causation which will ensue in later sections.

Correlation

- Appreciate that correlation is a measure of the strength of the association between two variables
- Distinguish between positive, negative and zero correlation using lines of best fit   (FB11.1)

Starter

The table shows the number of burglaries recorded and the number of dishwashers owned in England and Wales.

Burglaries (millions)	1.39	1.23	1.21	1.17	1	0.9	0.83
Dishwashers owned (millions)	6.9	7.4	7.6	8	10.8	11.2	12
Year	1993	1994	1995	1996	1997	1998	1999

Can you cut the number of burglaries by increasing the sales of dishwashers?

Resources

Graph paper

Teaching notes

This section builds on the last, introducing the more formal language of correlation to describe any association between the variables under consideration. The material encountered in the last section can be used to introduce the basic vocabulary. The example in the text provides further discussion material which could be worked on by the students in pairs before bringing the ideas and responses together as a group.

The starter activity could be used to illustrate the fact that correlation does not always imply causation.

Exercise commentary

Question 1 This requires a straightforward statement involving the type and strength of correlation.

Question 2 This question refers back to the exercise in section 13.1.

Question 3 Some thought will need to be given to appropriate scales on both axes.

Question 4 The students need to pick out the relevant paired data to plot here; some may be tempted to plot the year and another variable.

Plenary

The growth of 'data mining' could be investigated and this should be related to problems of liberty and privacy.

It is worth looking at some false correlations, many examples of which can be found on the web.

- Draw lines of best fit by eye and understand
  what these represent   (FB11.1)

Starter

A butterfly's wings flap between 5 and 20 times a second. On average a butterfly lives for between 1 and 2 weeks once it reaches the winged stage of its evolution.

Estimate the number of beats a butterfly's wings make during its life.

($12.5 \times 60 \times 60 \times 12 \times 10.5$, which rounds to between 5 and 6 million)

Resources

Autograph and graphical calculators could be used for Question 3; graph paper

Teaching notes

This section builds on sections 13.1 and 13.2. When there is correlation then a line of best fit can be drawn; at this level it can be drawn by eye and so there will be variation from person to person. It does not have to pass through the origin. The data in the B13.1 example can be used again, this time drawing a line of best fit. The graph can then be used to predict drop heights or bounce height.

The students could use their hand span/thumb length data to predict similarly. With this example the limitations on the data can be discussed and the dangers of unthinking extrapolation noted.

The final example in the text introduces non-linear correlation and warns that a straight line should not always be assumed.

Exercise commentary

Questions 1–2 These questions provide basic practice in using lines of best fit. Question **2** gets students to consider the limitations of extrapolating from the data.

Question 3 This AO2 problem uses data about animals and requires some interpretation as well as basic plotting.

Plenary

Question 3 could be done on Autograph and this could initiate a discussion about how the software draws a line of best fit. Using the software it will be seen that the equation of the line can also be worked out and this can be related to their straight-line work elsewhere. Alternatively graphical calculators could be used to investigate the data sets.

The computer or a graphical calculator could be used to investigate non-linear correlation.

- Draw line graphs for time series
- Interpret time series   (FB11.1)

Starter

A company's profits for the last 5 years, measured in millions of pounds are 12, 10, 9, 15, 18. **Are things getting better? Discuss**.

(Depends on how you look at it. Looking year to year, profits have gone up twice and down twice. But the overall trend is certainly good.)

Resources

The internet and/or newspapers; graph paper

Teaching notes

Using some examples from the web or newspapers present some examples of time series.

There are no new concepts in this section, it is all about learning the form of presentation of a particular type of information diagram. This means, initially at least, the lesson will be a teacher-led demonstration.

Using the data given in the example demonstrate how to draw a time series graph and the questions asked can be discussed with the group. Emphasise in particular how the horizontal axis is labelled and note that there are alternative labelling which use a mid-point of the group approach. The important thing is that the graph is easily understood by the reader. A legend explaining the situation should be appended to any such graph.

Exercise commentary

These questions are self explanatory. The key points to emphasise are thinking carefully about the axes and any scales used. Each time series should be labelled to make the situation it describes clear.

Plenary

If the students can get some of their own data they could produce their own time series. There are plenty of interesting ones on the web. For example there are some interesting time series on the 100 m world record for men and other athletic events going back over many years and these or related data could form the basis of an interesting functional maths task.

Exam-style question commentary

Worked solution	Commentary
1) 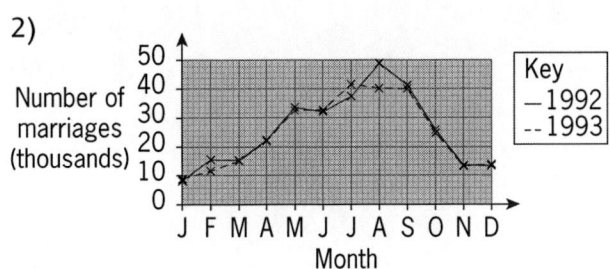 The temperatures vary, although no overall trend is evident.	1) Ensure axes are correctly labelled and the graph is scaled appropriately. You could suggest the use of a false zero in the vertical axis.
2) 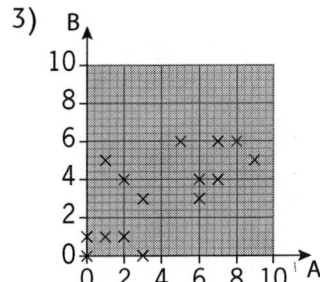 In general less marriages per month in 1992 than 1993, taking into account that more Saturdays mean more marriages	2) Encourage students to describe any trends over time, also any particular anomalies.
3) Mean of A : 60 ÷ 15 = 4 mins Mean of B : 49 ÷ 15 = 3.3 mins Median of A = 3 mins Median of B = 4 mins Neither A nor B have a clear mode Range of A = 9 − 0 = 9 Range of B = 6 − 0 = 6 A and B have similar average queuing times, but B has less variability so it is better.	3) This question provides an opportunity to practise calculating statistics, and to make a reasoned interpretation based on comparison. Although a scatter diagram can be drawn (as shown here), it is of little value in this context as it is not really paired data.

Objectives covered in this chapter are:

FB6.2a understand that the point of intersection of two different lines in the same two variables that simultaneously describe a real situation is the solution to the simultaneous equations represented by the lines

FB6.3a recognise that equations of the form $y = mx+c$ correspond to straight-line graphs in the coordinate plane

FB6.3b find the gradient of lines given by equations of the form $y = mx+c$; investigate the gradients of parallel lines

FB6.3c plot graphs of functions in which y is given explicitly in terms of x, or implicitly, where no tables or axes are given

Prerequisite knowledge

- Complete a table of values
- Plot points on a coordinate grid
- Substitute values into an equation

Useful ICT resources

Introductory powerpoint	B14
Starter activity	B14.1
Powerpoint worked solution	B14.1
Animation	B14.2 (x3), B14.3 (x2)
Interactive activity	B14.1 (AG), B14.2 (TI)
Consolidation	B14
Chapter test	B14
Formative on-screen test	B14
Summative on-screen test	B14

RICH TASK COMMENTARY

Students will need to generate some L-shapes and record the L-number and the total of the numbers in the L-shape. They could plot a graph of L-number against the total of numbers inside the L-shape and see that they lie on a straight line.

Use of algebra will need to be guided depending upon ability. It may well be worth trying to define the L-number as n, and then working back along the shape describing each square using algebra.

For a 10×10 grid Total = $5n - 37$ (where n= L-number)
Extend by working on an 9×9 grid, an 8×8 grid, an $n \times n$ grid?

For a 9×9 grid   Total = $5n - 34$
For an $n \times n$ grid   Total = $5n - 3g - 7$ (where g=grid size)

- Plot graphs of functions in which y is given explicitly in terms of x, where no table or axes are given. (FB6.3)

Starter

Which integers between -10 and 10 are neither even nor prime? (Note, negatives can be odd, even or prime in exactly the same way as positive numbers. 0 is even, 1 is not prime, so list is -1, 1, -9, 9.) What answers can you make by adding two of these numbers? For example, $-1 + 9 = 8$. (-10, -9, -8, -1, 0, 1, 8, 9, 10)

Resources

Spreadsheets, graphical calculators and Autograph could be used in Question 7; also graph paper

Teaching notes

This section begins with a function machine activity which spells out the order of calculation for a straight-line equation. Students should be encouraged to read the function to themselves before calculation so they get the order of operation correct. This is particularly important with non-calculator work. They have already been through the process of plotting straight-line graphs but may need reminding to work out at least 3 points to help avoid error.

The example in the text or a similar one will address any problems which students may have dealing with a negative gradient graph and the associated directed number arithmetic.

Exercise commentary

Question 1 This provides a function machine or flow chart and requires an equivalent equation to be written down. Some may only write down an expression and this will need to be remedied.

Question 2 This provides further practice at plotting straight-line graphs.

Question 3 In this question students need to substitute the given x and y values into the straight-line equation and demonstrate that the LHS and RHS are the same.

Questions 4–6 These AO2 problems require the students to use their graphs to problem solve.

Question 7 Spreadsheets are powerful tools for generating tables of values and graphs, though the same work can also be done on graphical calculators that have a table of values application or on Autograph.

Plenary

As a preparation for later work the intersection of straight-line graphs could be investigated further as providing the solution to simultaneous equations.

- Find the gradient of lines given by equations of the form $y = mx + c$ (when values are given for m and c); investigate the gradients of parallel lines (FB6.3)

Starter

Helen cycles up hill for 2 km. She rises in height by 400 m and the ride takes her 8 min. Fran cycles up hill for 3 km. She rises in height by 300 m and the ride takes her 16 min. Who is the fitter rider? How did you decide?

(Helen. One solution is to look at what each rider can achieve in the same amount of time.)

Resources

Autograph could be used; graph paper; OCR AO3 Guide Section 3.7

Teaching notes

The mathematical definition of gradient should be given and its meaning considered carefully so that students have a clear understanding what the gradient number means. A gradient of 3 means for every one unit we move horizontally we move up 3 vertically. For a gradient of -3 for every one we move across we move three down. Plenty of lines can be looked at using Autograph to make the definition clear. That the gradient of a line can be calculated in many equivalent ways is also worth emphasising; ideally the triangle used to calculate the gradient should use an opposite and an adjacent which are whole numbers.

The gradient of a line segment whose end points are known should be given and it should be emphasised that it is (difference in the y-coordinates) divided by or over (the difference in the x-coordinates) which gives the gradient. The order in which the coordinates are used must be consistent. The equivalence of this approach to the gradient calculations above should be made clear. Negative as well as fractional gradients should be calculated.

The example is key in bringing out that the gradient of a line is the coefficient of the x term in an equation of the form $y = mx + c$.

Exercise commentary

Question 1 Using the line segments given the gradient can be calculated.

Question 2 This provides practice in finding the gradient of a line segment. The question encourages students to plot the segment and get the gradient; some of the more able may use the formula for gradient directly.

Question 3 Students have to write down the gradient of these lines. They may need reminding that gradients can be negative or fractional.

Question 4 This highlights the fact that parallel lines have the same gradient.

Question 5 The rich task further reinforces the gradient of a straight line and invites students to discover the significance of the $+c$ value as well. The use of Autograph speeds the whole process up for the investigation.

Plenary

The key result $y = mx + c$ needs to be revised again and the result made clear for everyone.

The rich task can be tried or revisited.

- Plot graphs of functions in which y is given implicitly, where no table or axes are given   (FB6.3)

Starter

Display a set of axes to the whole group. Ask the students to sketch graphs on whiteboards.

Where would this be? $x = 5$, $x = 12$, $x = -3$, $y = 6$, $y = -2$, $y = x$, $x + y = 4$, $x + y = 9$ and so on.

Resources

Mini whiteboards, Autograph could be useful; graph paper; OCR AO3 Guide Section 3.7

Teaching notes

The rich task provides an excellent entry into this section. Once it has been attempted thoroughly by the students then draw together the findings and discuss the key implicit equation that emerges from the problem. To ensure students have a good idea what the graph looks like you could illustrate the answer on Autograph.

The idea of implicitly defined functions can be illustrated in the simple context of linear equations.

The technique of drawing these implicit straight-line functions is very important and time saving, so a number of examples should be done to ensure the technique is clear.

Exercise commentary

Questions 1–2 These provide plenty of experience in drawing implicitly defined straight-line graphs.

Questions 3–4 These questions take the problems of questions **1** and **2** one step further to finding the gradient of the lines from the graphs. Some students may of course notice they could rearrange the equation and use $y = mx + c$.

Question 5 This question requires students to find solutions to an implicit function.

Question 6 This rich task models a practical situation and requires problem-solving.

Students could check their answers using Autograph which, unlike most graphical calculators, accepts implicitly defined functions.

Plenary

Students could invent their own problems similar to that in the rich task.

- Understand that the point of intersection of two different lines in the same two variables that simultaneously describe a real situation is the solution to the simultaneous equations represented by the lines   (FB6.2))

Starter

Give students simple expressions such as:

$y = 2x - 1$ $y = 3x + 4$

$y = 3 - 2x$ $y = 1 - 3x$

Ask them for the value of y given a value of x. Include negative values.

Resources

Autograph would be useful; graph paper

Teaching notes

The rich task can provide a good launching point for this section.

Autograph can provide an excellent teaching and learning aid in this section. Project two intersecting lines for the group to discuss. The key question to ask is: What is the significance of the intersection? That the values satisfy both equations simultaneously should come out of the discussion fairly rapidly. It is worth getting the students to substitute the variables into the equations to verify they do indeed satisfy both equations.

Students will need to revise drawing straight lines whether they appear in
$y = mx + c$ form or $ax + by = p$.

You can provide visual feedback checks on the exercise questions at suitable moments using Autograph.

Exercise commentary

Question 1 These come with the table of values to complete for each equation. The graphs can then be plotted and the intersections found. Encourage the students to substitute the values into the equations to demonstrate that they work.

Question 2 These are implicitly-defined straight-line equations and students should use the $x = 0$, $y = 0$ approach to drawing the lines. Once again encourage the students to check their answers by substitution.

Question 3 This rich task requires the equations to be built and solved and a decision made on the basis of the solution.

Plenary

Students could check their graphs and solutions using Autograph.

Exam-style question commentary

Worked solution	Commentary
1) a) 2, 5 b)	1) Ensure that the axes are appropriately scaled, and that the points (crosses) are correctly plotted and joined with a straight line.
2) a) $\frac{1}{2}$ b)	2) A common mistake is to mix up the formula for gradient, so that some students may give the answer as 2. You could ask students to think about what gradient means (a measure of steepness).
3) $x = 1.3$, $y = 3.6$ (estimated)	3) Emphasise that the graph will only give an estimated solution. Some students will see that one of the equations doesn't work exactly with these values (actual answer: $x = 1\frac{1}{3}$, $y = 3\frac{2}{3}$).

Estimation and indices

Objectives covered in this chapter are:

FB2.1c develop a range of strategies for mental calculation; derive unknown facts from those they know

FB2.2b estimate answers to problems involving decimals

FB4.1a use the terms 'square', 'positive square root', 'negative square root', 'cube' and 'cube root'

FB4.2b use index notation for simple integer powers

FB4.2c use index laws for multiplication and division of integer powers

FB4.2d use index laws to simplify, and calculate the value of, numerical expressions involving multiplication and division of integer powers

Prerequisite knowledge

- Understand place value
- Know how to multiply and divide by 10 and 100
- Use the order of operations

Useful ICT resources

Introductory powerpoint	B15
Starter activity	B15.4
Animation	B15.2
Consolidation	B15
Chapter test	B15
Formative on-screen test	B15
Summative on-screen test	B15

RICH TASK COMMENTARY

Students need to split 1000 into numbers which add to make 999 and then multiply these together. Students should gradually realise that smaller numbers are better and the question becomes 'What powers of prime numbers work best?' (for example if 9 is one of the numbers to add to make 999, 9 could be written as $4 + 5$, and 4×5 is bigger than 9 so it would be better to use $4 + 5$ rather than 9 and so on). Logically you should arrive at a number made from 2s and 3s.

It might be worth looking systematically at the sums of numbers which make 8 and calculating the product of each of them e.g. 8 can be made as $2 + 2 + 2 + 2$ which gives $2^4 = 16$, compared with $2 + 3 + 3$ which gives $2 \times 3^2 = 18$.

Hopefully you will arrive at $3^{332} \times 2^2$ as your answer.

You might want to compare it with $3^{333} \times 1$ (just to convince yourself).

Students could investigate other numbers...

108 **Estimation and indices**

- Develop a range of strategies for mental calculation
- Derive unknown facts from those they know
- Add and subtract mentally numbers with up to two decimal places
- Multiply and divide numbers with no more than one decimal place, using place value adjustments (FB2.1)

Starter

Display a calculation and answer as the centre of a spider diagram on the board: $32.4 \times 0.35 = 11.34$.

Give one equivalent statement: $3.24 \times 3.5 = 11.34$ as a leg, and ask students to record others using whiteboards. Select some to be added to the display.

Now extend to related statements by adding a leg from an offered equivalent statement, say $3.24 \times 7 = 22.68$.

Ask students for other related calculations and add some of these to the display.

Resources

Spider diagram template, mini whiteboard

Teaching notes

The first type of problem in the text is where a calculation is given and related sums can be worked out by considering the size of the numbers. One approach to this is to give a calculation and show them how it can be used to work out a related calculation and then ask them to work out as many other related problems as they can. These could be collected together at a suitable moment and should provide a good cross-section of possibilities.

The last set of strategies which are introduced are doubling and halving which also make use of the ease of multiplying by 10, 100, 1000 etc.

The meaning of the word *reciprocal* will need to be reviewed.

Exercise commentary

Question 1 This provides a revision of the basic four rules for both whole numbers and decimals. There may be a need to review the methods required.

Question 2 These give a calculation and its answer and then require the students to use it to work out a related calculation.

Question 3 This is an everyday calculation.

Question 4 This revises the use of a simple timetable.

Question 5 This problem requires some investigation and checking. If students work in pairs then they can check on each other's answers.

Plenary

Using a real timetable from their local train or bus station or the internet students could work out the timings of some actual journeys.

- Recall integer squares from 11^2 to 15^2 and the corresponding square roots
- Recall the cubes of 2, 3, 4, 5 and 10
- Use index notation for squares, cubes and powers of 10
- Use index notation for simple integer powers (FB4.2)

Starter

Ask students to work out strings of multiplications:

$2 \times 2 \times 2 \times 2 \times 3$ $2 \times 2 \times 3 \times 3 \times 7$

$3 \times 3 \times 3 \times 5$ $4 \times 4 \times 4 \times 4 \times 5$

Resources

None required

Teaching notes

This section revisits roots and simple indices. Students need to know their square numbers up to 15^2. This could form the basis of a short mental test. Give the students 2 or 3 minutes and then test them.

Once students know these squares they should automatically know their square roots. They need to remember that there are two square roots for each number.

They need to know their cube numbers up to at least 5^3 and also 10^3. The index notation begins to be useful here and can be emphasised. Their knowledge of the cube numbers should also be tested alongside the square numbers until they become second nature to the students.

Some BIDMAS-type questions should be set and their solution discussed before embarking on the exercise.

Exercise commentary

Questions 1–5 These require knowledge of the basic squares and square roots. Remind them if necessary that there are two possible square roots.

Question 6 This tests their understanding of basic index notation.

Question 7 These mixed sums need calculation in stages.

Question 8 Using known square roots enables the students to approximate these more awkward square roots.

Question 9 This investigation reinforces the students' knowledge of square numbers.

Question 10 This introduces the students to the famous result that the sum of the odd numbers gives a square number.

Plenary

Following on from question 10 there are many interesting number patterns like this, for example the sum of the cube numbers, the triangle numbers or the various patterns to be found from Pascal's triangle.

- Round to the nearest integer, to any number of decimal places and to one significant figure
- Estimate answers to problems involving decimals
- Estimate and check answers to problems (FB2.2)

Starter

Give out digit cards 0–9. Ask the class to display in turn the even numbers, the odd numbers, the square numbers, the prime numbers, the multiples of 3 and the factors of 8.

Resources

Digit cards 0–9 for each student

Teaching notes

The activity using the Olympic reports is a good entry discussion for this section and makes clear that sometimes exact answers are not the best. The second example in the text brings out an everyday use of estimation.

Estimation is an important skill and the usual approach is to round the numbers to 1s.f. and then calculate the resultant problem. Some examples can be set for the group which after a short while will provide the material for discussion and the sorting of any problems. The approach to dividing by decimals less than 1 will need emphasis.

Exercise commentary

Question 1 This is a relatively easy estimation question which can be done by rounding to 1s.f.

Question 2 These simple practical problems do ask for working to be shown.

Question 3 These nicely review known square roots since they need to be used to estimate these more awkward roots and squares.

Question 4 These present tougher estimating challenges and need awareness of BIDMAS as well.

Questions 5–7 These estimating problems are set in realistic contexts.

Plenary

A good exercise for students is to try and keep a good estimate tally of the cost of the shopping as their parents do a major shop.

- Use index notation for simple integer powers
- Use index laws for multiplication and division of integer powers
- Use index laws to simplify, and calculate the value of, numerical expressions involving multiplication and division of integer powers   (FB4.2)

Starter

Ask students to write any two terms which will multiply to give $12x^3$ on whiteboards. Select some students to add their versions to a group display. After taking a few suggestions, ask the students to think of more unusual possibilities. Now add these to the display.

Give the students a different expression such as $18a^2b$. Ask them to write on whiteboards, in a given time limit, as many different multiplications as they can which will produce this result. Ask students to compare versions with a neighbour.

Resources

Mini whiteboards

Teaching notes

The rich task provides a nice introduction to a topic area many will have met before.

The index notation can be quickly reviewed and the associated vocabulary reinforced.

The rules for indices can then be investigated as a rich task. The main errors to avoid are students trying to combine different base numbers and the related problem of multiplying the base numbers as well as adding the indices.

Once the idea of an index has been covered and understood then the way of expressing a number in terms of its prime factors can be revisited. There are various valid methods of breaking a number down including a factor tree or repeated division.

The fact that $a^1 = a$ can be emphasised and using the division algorithm in suitable examples should ensure they understand that $x^0 = 1$.

Exercise commentary

Remind the students that this is a non-calculator lesson.

Question 1 This reinforces the basic rules for combining index type terms.

Question 2 These successive multiplications just need care.

Question 3 This requires choices to be made from a given list.

Question 4 Either factor trees or the division algorithm can be used here.

Question 5 These provide more experience of using the rules for indices.

Question 6 Listing the cube and square numbers from memory would be a good exercise and will help with this question.

Question 7 This puzzle needs missing indices to be located.

Plenary

Students could research Franciscus Vieta (1540–1603) who developed the index notation as well as contributing a lot of other ideas to mathematics.

Exam-style question commentary

Worked solution	Commentary
1) $\dfrac{(12.8 + 14.09)}{(32 \times 0.1)}$ $\cong \dfrac{(13 + 14)}{(30 \times 0.1)}$ $= \dfrac{27}{30}$ $= \dfrac{9}{10}$ $= 0.9$	1) This problem gives a neat estimate if numbers are rounded as shown. Division questions of this type can often lead to problems whereby the estimated version is harder to solve than the original – encourage students to 'engineer' the numbers to give an easy estimate (they may need practice!)
2) odd × odd = odd (eg 3^2 = 3 × 3 = 9) So odd × odd 30 times over will also be odd	2) Students at the Foundation tier will need encouragement with these new-style questions that look simple but give no clues as to a strategy. A common mistake might be to say 3 × 30 = 90, so even. Encourage students to try some small powers of 3 (and other odd numbers). Discourage working it out in full, though some may need to make the attempt first to convince themselves it's a bad idea!
3) £11.99 per month $\cong$ £12 £7.99 per month $\cong$ £8 £20 × 12 = £240 per year 195 days $\cong$ 200 £0.80 × 200 = £160 per year £240 + £160 = £400 The librarian will have just enough money	3) This AO2-type problem contains lots of information that students will need to process – encourage the use of jottings. Emphasise the word 'estimate' in the question, and encourage students to consider whether the amounts have been rounded up or down when giving their answer.

Aim

- To demonstrate how statistics can be used by the government to monitor and assess progress, and to set future targets
- To encourage students to think responsibly about recycling and waste and to show how mathematics may be used to help reduce waste as well as to monitor recycling levels

Useful resources

- Recycling starter   Presentation
- Recycling rates   Presentation
- Recycling packaging   Presentation
- Recycling   Worksheet

Extension

Direct students to the government statistics website, http://www.statistics.gov.uk/hub/, to look at further examples of how the government uses statistics.

Simplification

Students could draw plans and elevations of some real examples of packaging.

Teaching notes

Encourage students to discuss recycling in their country or local town.

Example discussion points:

- How does the government/local council encourage recycling?
- How has the approach to recycling changed over recent years?

Encourage students to discuss the trends shown in the bar chart and to answer the questions. Ensure that they understand how the bar chart relates to the actual data.

What explanations can students think of for the trends shown? Are the results what they would have expected? Encourage students to also think about the open-ended questions posed in the case study. Look at the *Recycling rates presentation*.

Show students examples of packaging. Some are shown in the *Recycling packaging presentation*. They could work out the surface area and volume of each package. Students could also compare different packaging used by different brands and for different products. How necessary is the packaging?

Use the note in the case study to illustrate how packaging has changed before students work through the Cola and tomato packet examples.

Encourage students to read the text about product/pack ratio, to answer the open-ended questions and to carry out their own research.

Objectives covered in this chapter are:

FB10.1a understand congruence

FB10.1b understand similarity of plane figures

FB10.2e transform triangles and other 2D shapes by translation, rotation and reflection and by combinations of these transformations

FB10.2f recognise that these transformations preserve length and angle, and hence that any figure is congruent to its image under any of these transformations

FB10.2g understand that enlargements are specified by a centre and positive scale factor

FB10.2h recognise, visualise and construct enlargements of shapes using positive scale factors

FB10.2j distinguish properties that are preserved under particular transformations

Prerequisite knowledge

- Plot points in all four quadrants
- Rotate, reflect and translate shapes on a grid

Useful ICT resources

Introductory powerpoint	B16
Powerpoint worked solution	B16.3
Animation	B16.1, B16.2, B16.3 (x4)
Interactive activity	B16.1 (TI)
Consolidation	B16
Chapter test	B16
Formative on-screen test	B16
Summative on-screen test	B16

RICH TASK COMMENTARY

Students will benefit from using prepared regular polygon shapes for this activity, although they could be asked to construct their own templates. The side lengths of the polygons should be equal, but it is worth tessellating a square or a triangle with their respective enlargements of scale factor 2.

Students should be encouraged to describe the transformations involved in any particular tessellation and could look for reasons as to why some polygons tessellate and some don't.

Further investigation of tessellations could move to work on altering quadrilaterals so that they do tessellate.

- Understand congruence
- Understand similarity of plane figures
- Understand that any two circles and any two squares are mathematically similar, while, in general, two rectangles are not   (FB10.1)

Starter

Imagine a square formed of rods linked together. If the square is distorted by moving the top rod sideways, the square will become a rhombus. The diagonals of the square intersect at 90°. The diagonals of the rhombus also intersect at 90°.

Now imagine a rectangle formed of similar rods. If the rectangle is distorted it will become a parallelogram. The diagonals of the rectangle intersect at different angles depending on the lengths of the sides. Will the diagonals of the parallelogram intersect at the same angle as those of the rectangle? (Yes. This can be shown by drawing a rectangle and several parallelograms with sides of the same length and tracing the angles.)

Resources

Google Images, a sheet of shapes showing reflections and rotations

Teaching notes

There are plenty of congruent shapes that can be found using Google Images. When working with similarity students need to understand what is meant by the word 'corresponding' and examples should be discussed that lead the students to carefully decide which sides correspond. The vocabulary of scale factor is revisited in the example in the text.

One practical approach here is to supply the students with a sheet of shapes some of which are similar and some of which are congruent and ask them to match shapes accordingly. The set of shapes should include reflections and rotations, some students may wish to cut out shapes and compare them directly.

Exercise commentary

Question 1 These questions focus on the basic definitions.

Question 2–3 This question requires students to make their own congruent shapes.

Question 4 This question gives practice looking for similarity by comparing angles.

Question 5 This question also practises plotting points and drawing shapes on coordinate axes.

Question 6 Ratio may need revision here.

Plenary

Provide students with more and different examples of congruence and similarity in geometry. You might want to extend into thinking about 3-D shapes' congruence and similarity using objects in the classroom.

- Transform triangles and other 2D shapes by translation, rotation and reflection and by combinations of these transformations   (FB10.2)

Starter

One of the longest cars in the world is 30.5 m long. If you want to turn it right round in the road in one go, you need the road to be 40 m wide. For every 50 cm less than 40 m you need to do an extra turn, for example a 39 m wide road needs a 2 point turn. How wide is the road for a 7 point turn? (36.5 m) Why will you never need to do a 20 point turn?
(Road would be 30 m wide, car would not fit across the road.)

Resources

Tracing paper, Autograph, squared paper

Teaching notes

This work continues that of chapter 12. Some revision of that work might be necessary before students attempt this section.

Using Autograph may speed things up in this section and enable concentration on the resultant transformations. You may need to revisit the basics of reflection, rotation and translation.

Using drawing or Autograph (without axes if preferred) the students can do a double transformation which as been pre-prepared. If half the group do a double reflection and the other half do a reflection and a rotation then this could provide suitable discussion material before setting the group the exercise.

Emphasise the importance of labelling the shapes and careful measurement.

Students must realise that the description of the overall equivalent single transformation has to be clear and this may involve revision of past work on describing reflections, rotations and translations.

Exercise commentary

Questions 1–5 These questions could be done on Autograph or by drawing, depending on the competence of the group. If drawing, then tracing paper will be a considerable help. Emphasise the use of correct language in describing resultant transformations. The questions themselves are fairly self explanatory.

Question 6 This question applies translations to the context of a crossword puzzle.

Question 7 The Challenge shows applications of transformations in real situations.

Plenary

Students could make designs, then good designs could be printed off to make a classroom display. A glimpse of the extraordinary complexity that is possible could be given by looking at Penrose tiling and/or the tiling at a place like the Alhambra Palace in Granada, Spain.

- Understand that enlargements are specified by a centre and positive scale factor
- Recognise, visualise and construct enlargements of shapes using positive scale factors greater than one   (FB10.2)

Starter

Give pairs of students 10 interlocking cubes. Make a 3-D shape using interlocking cubes without the class seeing. Describe your shape and ask students to make an identical shape.

Compare students' results with the original shape.

Resources

Tracing paper, squared paper interlocking cubes, a few ready-made object–image problems, Autograph would be useful

Teaching notes

Once again Autograph can be used both as a teaching aid and student investigation tool and there are many other excellent demonstration aids on the web.

Recap on similarity and revise that, if objects are mathematically similar, then one object is simply an enlargement of the other. Use an example to show the decision as to whether or not two objects are similar.

Ask students where they meet enlargements in the real world. (Photography, films, zooming on a computer screen, maps etc.) Refer to the example in the book and have a similar one prepared to show to group. Introduce the idea of rays joining the centre of enlargement to the object and image and revise again what is meant by a scale factor of enlargement. Ensure through discussion that students are clear how to locate a centre of enlargement and how to calculate the scale factor of enlargement as described in the textbook. A few ready-made object–image problems can be shown and individual students can volunteer how to find the centre and scale factor. These should be a mixture of problems both without and with coordinate grids. It is a good idea to have an example where the object is inside the image and also to mention that in mathematics, reductions are a subset of enlargements.

Exercise commentary

Questions 1–4 These questions practise enlargements on a coordinate grid.

Questions 5–6 These questions require students to plot coordinates on axes and find scale factors and centres on enlargement.

Question 7 A straightforward drawing is to be done in this question. There is scope for extension here, perhaps considering actual clothing sizes.

Plenary

Question 7 could be extended, or students could try enlarging more complex shapes.

- Understand that enlargements are specified by a centre and positive scale factor
- Recognise, visualise and construct enlargements of shapes using positive scale factors greater than one then positive scale factors less than one (FB10.2)

Starter

The longest dinosaur ever was 48 m long. The smallest was only 60 cm long. What fraction of the longest dinosaur's length is the smallest dinosaur's length? ($\frac{60}{4800} = \frac{1}{80}$)

Resources

Tracing paper, squared paper

Teaching notes

Recap the work on enlargement from the last section. Set the scene for this lesson by using the example in the book or your own example. Project the problem onto the board if possible.

Given their experience of the previous section the students should, with suitable questioning, be able to devise a method for describing any enlargement, using centre and scale factor. Relate all measurements back to the centre of enlargement initially, although eventually some students may discover other equivalent ways of getting the correct distance. You could also provide an enlargement problem where the centre of enlargement is either inside or on the object, and also cover both an enlargement factor greater than one and a fractional enlargement of, for example, $\frac{1}{2}$. Using a suitable example get the students to explain how to calculate missing lengths and a scale factor of enlargement.

Exercise commentary

Question 1 This question is to be done on a coordinate grid. This question allows comparison of positive and negative scale factors.

Question 2 This question is similar to question 7 in section 16.3.

Question 3 This question requires students to plot shapes on axes; some revision of plotting (x, y) coordinates may be necessary.

Question 4 This question covers fractional scale factors.

Questions 5–9 These questions all deal with enlargement in real-life context.

Plenary

Students could investigate how area change relates to length change. Perspective in art could provide a further launch point for investigation. They could also tackle the challenge if it has not already been covered.

Exam-style question commentary

Worked solution	Commentary
1)	1) Ensure that students use lines radiating out from the centre and touching each vertex. The resulting image should have vertices on actual grid points.
2) a) and b) c) Reflection in the y-axis	2) Students often have problems with rotation – encourage the use of tracing paper if helpful. In describing transformations, encourage clear concise language.
3) Translation through vectors (3 −2), (2 3), (−2 2)	3) Encourage students to use translation vectors in their description. QWC can be effective with appropriate use of notation, not just words.

Percentages and proportional change

Objectives covered in this chapter are:

FC4.2a Solve simple percentage problems in real life, including increase and decrease

FC4.3a Solve word problem about proportion, including using informal strategies and the unitary method of solution

Prerequisite knowledge

- Recognise a percentage as a part of 100
- Find equivalent fractions, including reduction to simplest form
- Multiply an integer by a fraction
- Use a calculator for decimal arithmetic

Useful ICT resources

Introductory powerpoint	C17
Starter activity	C17.6
Animation	C17.6 (x2)
Consolidation	C17
Chapter test	C17
Formative on-screen test	C17
Summative on-screen test	C17

RICH TASK COMMENTARY

Percentage increase / decrease problems require some conceptual understanding. Students need to see that 10% of £80 is not the same as 10% of £88.

Students might like to adopt a trial and improvement strategy to find the percentage reduction of 9.1%, and then investigate different starting percentages. Use of a calculator method is vital here and a spreadsheet might prove very useful.

Plotting percentage increase against percentage reduction might be interesting.

(The rule for calculating the percentage decrease is $100x \div (100 + x)$ where x is the percentage increase).

As an extension the students could look at the kinds of offers made in shops in different ways e.g. 3 for 2, BOGOF, 20% extra free, and compare them.

- Know the fraction-to-percentage (or decimal) conversion of familiar simple fractions   (FB3.5)
- Understand the multiplicative nature of percentages as operators   (FB3.6)

Starter

Ask the question: 80% of an amount is £5000.

What is the total amount? Discuss solutions and methods.

Resources

Examples of percentages from the web could be used

Teaching notes

Students have met the idea of percentage already but what they know can be drawn out of them by suitable questioning. Percentages appear in newspapers, on the web and as marks for tests; examples could be presented from the web.

This section is primarily concerned with calculating a percentage of a quantity. The method emphasised in the text is to write the percentage as a fraction and multiply the quantity by that fraction. If using a calculator then a reminder about the use of the fraction button may be helpful. Students can also convert the percentage to a decimal multiplier which is equally valid.

There is a lot of vocabulary in this section which may need explaining such as deposit, tax, commission, discount and personal allowance. This is an excellent area for addressing the functional mathematics dimension of the course.

Most students need careful guidance through the calculation of tax. For example, they need to understand they must subtract the personal allowance first before doing the percentage work.

Exercise commentary

Questions 1–2 these are standard questions set in everyday contexts and some vocabulary may need explaining. For example in question 5 the concept of a pension fund may need clarification.

Question 3 This makes use of the tables for income tax provided earlier and the teacher may need to reiterate some of the key points to enable the calculation.

Question 4 This problem is set in the context of an auction house which may need explanation. The need to split the money up according to the intervals supplied may need emphasising.

Plenary

For homework students could look at the commission structures of Amazon or Ebay.

Alternatively discuss the purpose and meaning of VAT, and how to calculate its correct rate ($17\frac{1}{2}$%)

- Final 10% of the amount
- Halve it (5%)
- Halve it again ($2\frac{1}{2}$%)
- Add them up

- Solve simple percentage problems in real life situations, including increase and decrease (FC4.2)

Starter

Roll two dice. Multiply the first dice by 15 to give a percentage.

Multiply the second dice by 20 to give an amount (ask students to do these calculations). Ask students to work out the percentages of each amount.

Resources

Dice, calculators

Teaching notes

The ideas in this section are key to some of the more advanced work to come. There are two main ways of increasing or decreasing a quantity by a given percentage. The way most students have already used is to work out the required percentage increase or decrease and then add or subtract it from the original quantity. The more powerful method is to use a suitable percentage multiplier. So to increase something by 14% multiply by 1.14. To decrease by 14% multiply by 0.86. This method is very useful when the more difficult percentage work of later sections is attempted, but some students find it hard to understand. The teacher will need to make a judgement about the group or particular student as to which method is best for them.

Whichever way is used, it is worth emphasising the distinction between the percentage found of a quantity and the overall changed quantity itself.

The tasks set in the text provide some good discussion points and can be set to pairs or small groups for consideration.

Exercise commentary

Questions 1–4 These are all basic AO2 questions.

Question 5 The idea of paying for something in instalments may need explaining, with the concept of credit possibly being introduced.

Question 6 This allows students to investigate the effects of various percentage changes.

Question 7 This rich task involves repeated percentage change and can be attempted using either the multiplier method or a repeated step by step approach.

Plenary

The key ideas introduced in question 7 could be further investigated and emphasised as they are essential for understanding reverse percentages later on.

Percentage difference

- Analyse real life problems using mathematical skills
- Apply mathematical skills when solving real life problems   (FC4.1)
- Solve simple percentage problems in real life situations, including increase and decrease.   (FC4.2)

Starter

Ask the students to work on a problem as a pair. Present a scenario of two office workers receiving a similar wage for the same job. One receives a rise of 10% at the end of the year, but the other only receives a rise of 5%. When the second worker discovers this she asks why. The boss agrees it was unfair but to put it right she will receive a 10% rise next year while the other worker will only have 5%. Will each worker now have the same wage? Is this resolution fair? Discuss the findings with the students, sharing the reasoning.

Resources

Some real data on house prices over a period of time could be used, also calculators

Teaching notes

The definition of percentage change should be given, emphasising that it is a measure of comparison with the original quantity. Percentage profit/loss and percentage error are worth considering specifically. The class could be presented with a circle and asked to estimate its area by observation, the percentage error comparing the estimate with the calculated area could be worked out by each student and conclusions drawn about how accurate the group is.

The problem in the text with Stan and Ollie should be given to the class to work on in pairs or small groups. The reasoning of the students can be clarified in a whole class discussion.

The teacher could present some real data on the purchase of houses over a period of time and calculate the percentage profit or loss made.

Exercise commentary

Questions 1–3 This is a mixture of fairly direct increase and decrease problems

Question 4 A slightly more complex problem which may need a little explanation for some.

Plenary

A closer look at percentage error and absolute error could be instigated. The comparison element can be seen very clearly when considering errors. A 0.1 error on a value of 0.5 and a 0.1 error on a value of 100 shows the advantage of percentage error over absolute error.

A mini estimating project could be executed by small groups. The estimation could involve, for example, distances, areas, volumes or duration. This could lead into a substantial data handling project.

The students could investigate the buying and selling of cars or another product in the real world and work out percentage profit and loss.

- Analyse real life problems using mathematical skills
- Apply mathematical skills when solving real life problems   (FC4.1)
- Solve simple percentage problems in real life situations, including increase and decrease. (FC4.2)

Starter

A bank gives customers interest on money left in an account. Is it better to leave this interest in the account or take it out? Ask students to work in pairs, with a whiteboard and allow 2–3 minutes to discuss this before sharing some responses. In order to model the situation say the amount is £500 and the interest rate is 5% p.a. Explore the meaning of p.a. What interest would be received after one year? If the interest is taken out, what is the interest for the next year? What would it be if not taken out?

Resources

Mini whiteboards, calculators

Teaching notes

Ask the students to imagine they have £2000 and that they can invest it at an annual rate of for example 2% p.a. for a number of years. It is worth clarifying the meaning of investment, per annum, interest rate through discussion with the group. Then get them to work out how much interest should be added to the principal amount each year. Make sure students distinguish between the interest earned and the total amount of their investment. It is very important to emphasise that simple interest is calculated only on the original amount invested.

Exercise commentary

Questions 1–2 Distinguish the interest earned from the total amount the investment is worth.

Question 3 Straightforward practice in calculation of the total investment value.

Question 4 That money borrowed is charged for, sometimes excessively as in the example, could be made a class discussion point especially in the light of recent crises in the financial world.

Question 5 This problem requires comparison of two different modes of borrowing money.

Plenary

The ground could be laid for the more important concept of compound interest which arises in the next section.

- Analyse real life problems using mathematical skills
- Apply mathematical skills when solving real life problems (FC4.1)
- Solve simple percentage problems in real life situations, including increase and decrease (FC4.2)

Starter

You have £1000 to invest for up to three years and have two options.

1. An account offering you interest of 10% of £1000 every year.
2. An account offering you interest of 10% of the amount you have at the start of each year and added every year. But you cannot take out any of your money until the end of the three years.

Which is the best option? (1. gives £1300 in total, 2. gives $1100 \rightarrow 1210 \rightarrow £1331$.)

Resources

Sheets of A4 paper, calculators

Teaching notes

Key here is the multiplier approach to percentage increase or decrease by enabling easy handling of repeated changes.

The rich task at the start of this section is the famous problem of folding paper which brings out how extraordinary compound growth can be. Students should try the folding to get a tactile sense to the problem and to come up against the physical barrier of being unable to fold the paper beyond the fifth or sixth fold. They can calculate the thickness stage by stage.

At a suitable moment, intervene and help the group build the simple doubling model and predict the thickness of the folded paper after 20 folds plus, and relate the staggering distances to some real world equivalents.

Then the students can imagine they have some money to invest and work out the compounded growth of their investment under a given fixed interest rate for say five years. A problem involving car depreciation, once again using the multiplier method, should be worked through with the group. Most students find calculating the depreciation multiplier more difficult than the growth multipliers.

Exercise commentary

Question 1 Check students have the correct multiplier and that they distinguish carefully between the interest earned and the value of the total investment. The question leads them step by step to the answer.

Question 2 This question is about depreciation and leads them step by step through the process. Once again they need to be clear on the distinction between the amount lost and the resultant total value of the car.

Question 3 This classic bouncing ball problem can easily be extended for some to considering the total distance covered by the ball after n bounces.

Questions 4–5 These problems are set within the context of population growth and reduction.

Questions 6–7 These questions use more complex percentage increases and the correct multiplier needs to be thought through carefully. You teacher may need to help a lot more with these questions.

Plenary

Students could look at a number of investment schemes and investigate how much profit each offers. This could be built up as a functional maths task to be researched and finished for homework.

More adventurous students might like to investigate the mysterious law of 70 and how it relates to the doubling of an investment.

- Solve word problems about proportion, including using informal strategies and the unitary method of solution   (FC4.3)

Starter

A jeweller can make seven necklaces in two days. How many complete necklaces can he make in: 8 days; 2 weeks; 5 weeks?

Resources

Calculators; OCR AO3 Guide Section 3.10

Teaching notes

Pose the photograph problem to the group and allow them to work out their conclusion in pairs or small groups. This should bring out issues that need to be considered when best value is being calculated.

Pose the best value of shampoo problem from the text to the class and let them come to conclusions backed by calculation in pairs or small groups. Once this problem has been solved fully pose the question as to what price the larger shampoo would need to be placed at in order for its cost to be the same as the smaller size. This leads into the idea of directly proportional quantities. The idea can be further reinforced by looking at an example from physics such as current and voltage where quantities are directly proportional.

The idea of inverse proportionality can be gained from considering pressure and volume of gas in a piston and using the example of building the pyramids. Filling out a table of values can really make clear how trebling one quantity results in the dividing by three of the other quantity.

Exercise commentary

Questions 1–3 These are all basic direct proportion problems.

Question 4 This is a more complex A02 comparison problem and needs careful sorting out. Students must be encouraged to present their final answers in a logical way. The idea of minimum profit may need discussing as well as the meaning of 25%.

Question 5 This question gives a slightly humorous real-life context of how many packets of crisps a child must eat to get their recommended daily calorie intake.

Plenary

The notation for proportionality could be introduced.

Other sorts of proportionality could be investigated and perhaps used to model experimental data in some cross-curricular work with the science department.

Exam-style question commentary

Worked solution	Commentary
1) a) $32\% \times 500 = 0.32 \times 500$ $\quad\quad = 160$ ml b) 12.5% of 140 $\quad\quad = 0.125 \times 140$ $\quad\quad = 17.5$ g	1) Students should have a method of working out percentages of amounts that they understand and are happy with. Many calculators have a percentage key – discourage the blind use of this at least until they are fully confident.
2) $9 \times 25 + 50 = 275$ $\dfrac{275}{20\,000} \times 100\% = 1.375\%$	2) This technique is similar to finding an amount as a fraction of another amount. A common mistake might be to give the answer as £1.38.
3) $\dfrac{285}{100} \approx \dfrac{300}{100} = 3$ $\quad 3 \times 2 = 6$ eggs	3) This problem contains redundant information (the weight of walnuts). Many functional-style problems involve extracting the relevant information. Another valid response is 5 eggs – encourage students to justify their answers.

Area and perimeter

Objectives covered in this chapter are:

FC9.1a find areas of rectangles, recalling the formula, understanding the connection to counting squares

FC9.1b recall and use the formulae for the area of a parallelogram and a triangle

FC9.1c calculate perimeters and areas of shapes made from triangles and rectangles

FC9.1e find circumferences of circles and areas enclosed by circles, recalling relevant formulae

FC9.3b understand that enlargement preserves angle but not length

FC9.3c understand the implications of enlargement for perimeter

FC9.3d understand the implications of enlargement for area

Prerequisite knowledge

- Multiply and divide integers and decimals
- Substitute values into a formula
- Round quantities to a specified accuracy
- Enlarge an object and use scale factors

Useful ICT resources

Introductory powerpoint	C18
Starter activity	C18.4
Powerpoint worked solution	C18.4, C18.5
Animation	C18.1, C18.2(x2), C18.3
Interactive activity	C18.4(AG), C18.2(TI), C18.2(CA)
Consolidation	C18
Chapter test	C18
Formative on-screen test	C18
Summative on-screen test	C18

RICH TASK COMMENTARY

Students might need to start with a smaller example such as 24 m of fencing which they can then represent as rectangles, squares and possibly right-angled triangles. Encourage them to record their results in an ordered table so that they can spot the relationship between the length of side and the area.

In this example the maximum area (3600 m²) occurs when the shape is a square of side length 60 m.

Students could investigate different sized perimeters (p) and might be able to arrive at an optimum side length of $\frac{p}{4}$.

Students could investigate different regular and non-regular shapes, perhaps using a string of fixed length, or a computer program, to see if they could maximise area and may arrive at an intuitive understanding of the final answer of a circle. Why are fields not circular?

Perimeter and area of basic shapes

- Find areas of rectangles, recalling the formula, understanding the connection to counting squares
- Recall and use the formulae for the area of a parallelogram and a triangle
- Calculate perimeters and areas of shapes made from triangles and rectangles (FC9.1)

Starter

How many different rectangles could be made using 24 square units? What is the perimeter of each?

Resources

Counting and estimating squares, tracing paper, an area scale, basic map of the USA, a map of the school area or local grounds might also be useful; OCR AO3 Guide Section 3.1; SMP Problem solving taster pack Task 1

Teaching notes

The students will have met area and perimeter many times before so the idea of estimating using string (perimeter) or superimposing a square grid (area) should be familiar. You want to supply a map of the school grounds or a local area of interest to further practise the counting approach.

The units of perimeter and area and the associated notation should be discussed with some basic examples. Choosing appropriate units could also be mentioned.

Deriving the area of a triangle and parallelogram should be done in discussion. The meaning of base and height of a triangle need to be very clear and using different bases and corresponding heights for a specific triangle could emphasise the key points.

The examples in the text should be tried by all the students.

It may be worth mentioning an obtuse-angled triangle since then the validity of the formula is less obvious. The derivation of the area formula for this type of triangle could be left to the plenary phase of the lesson.

Exercise commentary

Question 1 A simple question requiring accurate use of a ruler.

Question 2 Students may need to revise plotting points on a coordinate grid.

Question 3 A multi-step context question.

Question 4 This question requires counting and estimating squares.

Question 5 This question requires tracing paper and the use of an area scale.

Question 6 This question is AO1 but the last example which involves an obtuse angled triangle may need some support from the teacher.

Question 7 Another context question on area.

Question 8 The rich task requires access to a basic map of the states of the USA.

Plenary

In the rich task a number of reasons could be given for the anomaly in comparing the area of the rectangles to the area given by an encyclopaedia. The curvature of the earth could lead into a discussion about what we mean by area on a sphere and the inevitability of approximation.

The derivation of the area of an obtuse angled triangle could be approached by fitting congruent triangles together to form a parallelogram and using the area of the parallelogram to get the area of the triangle.

As a preparation for the next section the area of a trapezium could be set as a problem.

- Find circumferences of circles and areas enclosed by circles, recalling relevant formulae (FC9.1)

Starter

Students work in small groups to list as many facts about a circle as possible.

Select a few groups to share vocabulary with the class. Try to make sure that the keywords have been covered and include other relevant information, for example π is about 3, or 3.14. You may then wish to show an OHT of parts of a circle.

Resources

Labelled projection of a circle; protractors

Teaching notes

Question the group about the formula for the circumference of a circle and the vocabulary of the parts of a circle, they should have met these before. The first example could be demonstrated to the whole group.

The activity leads to an approximation of the area of a circle, then you can introduce the formula for the area of a circle (if students have not met it before). It is always worth demonstrating a derivation of the formula, by chopping a circle into small sectors that can then be arranged to approximate to a rectangle. This can be done with a paper circle or by using an animated demonstration.

Some simple examples need to be done to ensure that $\pi \times r^2$ is used and not $(\pi r)^2$; a flow chart can help to emphasise this. Students may use 3.14 or their calculator value for π but remind them that even the calculator's value is an approximation.

Exercise commentary

Question 1 This question is about calculating circumference. Students must be clear whether they have been given the radius or the diameter.

Question 2 These circumference questions are set around real-life objects.

Question 3 Some students may need help to relate the question to the circumference of a circle.

Question 4 The rich task is an AO3 question that has cross-curriculum links to science.

Question 5 These questions provide straight forward practice in finding areas.

Questions 6–8 These questions are in context; check that the students state the correct units.

Questions 9–10 These are tougher questions about the area of an annulus. Students may not know about washers or disk brakes, and so need more explanation.

Plenary

This work could easily be extended into some simple sector area work.

- Find areas of rectangles, recalling the formula, understanding the connection to counting squares
- Calculate perimeters and areas of shapes made from triangles and rectangles   (FC9.1)

Starter

Ask students to take measurements and work out the perimeter and area of their desk or table top. They should repeat the task at least twice using different units.

Resources

Measuring tapes; OCR AO3 Guide Section 3.1

Teaching notes

Present an 'L' shape with numerical dimensions to the group. Ask students to find its area and then collect their thoughts on the problem, hopefully they will provide a number of dissections that work.

Then consider the trapezium in the AO2 example in the text as a dissection into a triangle and a rectangle.

Discuss one or two more compound shape examples with students, involving rectangles and triangles. Encourage students to suggest dissections – they should see that there is often more than one way to find the area.

Exercise commentary

Question 1 This question allows practice in dissecting shapes and working out compound areas. Students could compare their methods.

Question 2 A compound area in context. Stress that correct units are important.

Question 3 This question considers various dissections of a compound shape.

Plenary

Some interesting units of area such as acres could be introduced and their history and relationship to metric units considered. There is much history that could be easily accessed about these. Metric land measurements such as hectares could be given as a research topic for homework. A complicated floor map of an interesting-shaped building or car park could be given as an area problem.

- Recall and use the formulae for the area of a parallelogram and a triangle
- Calculate perimeters and areas of shapes made from triangles and rectangles (FC9.1)

Starter

Using mini whiteboards ask students to sketch a parallelogram. Now sketch a different one. Now sketch a more unusual one. Ask students to show their examples, and look at each others'. Draw attention to any features, and correct any errors, emphasising the basic parallelogram properties.
Repeat the activity requesting "normal", different and unusual trapeziums.

Resources

Mini whiteboards

Teaching notes

Using the drawing in the text, relate the area of the parallelogram to that of the equivalent rectangle.

Use the dissection into triangles of a particular trapezium with numerical values, and then work through the derivation of the general formula for the area of a trapezium. The factorisation in the final step may need careful explanation and once again the units of area need to be emphasised.

Practice using the trapezium formula with several examples in different orientations.

Exercise commentary

Question 1-2 These are AO1 questions. Ensure that the students write down sufficient method. Remind them that the area units only need to be put in with the final answer given and that answers should be given to the same accuracy as the values in the question.

Question 3 This is an AO2 question, where the dissection into congruent parallelograms is clear.

Question 4 This rich task is a test of algebraic skill and area work, students may need some hints from the teacher.

Plenary

Picks theorem (requires dotty paper) which is based on comparing dots inside a shape with dots on the perimeter of a shape for a specified area is an excellent investigation which can be attempted by students at a variety of levels. Details are easy to find on the web.

- Find areas of rectangles, recalling the formula
- Recall and use the formulae for the area of a parallelogram and a triangle
- Find circumferences of circles and areas enclosed by circles, recalling relevant formulae   (FC9.1)

Starter

Ask students to draw a circle of at least 4 cm radius as accurately as possible (preferably using compasses). Ask them to measure the circumference using a piece of string, then calculate the value using the correct formula and compare their answers.

Resources

Compasses, string, graph paper

Teaching notes

Begin by getting the group to summarise all the formulae they met for area and perimeter.

It may be worth working through a couple of straight forward applications of the trapezium and circle formulae before moving onto the problems that need rearrangement of the formulae; these make up the core of this section.

Students at this level find algebra difficult and may need a lot of revision of rearrangement skills. Do not assume they can transfer these skills to area work without help and direction.

A reminder about rounding will also be needed.

Exercise commentary

Question 1 This provides some AO1 work to work on the basic idea of substitution and rearrangement. As always students should write down sufficient mathematical argument to justify their answers.

Questions 2–6 Provide a lot of AO2 questions. Working needs to be clear, and units must be given with the final answer. Answers should be given to an appropriate degree of accuracy.

Question 7 This rich task is a variant on the classic farmer's fence problem, and involves drawing and interpreting a graph.

Plenary

The students may like to investigate which shape provides the smallest perimeter for a given area.

A general formula for the area of an annulus may be investigated and some more complex area problems involving parts of circles attempted depending on the confidence and ability of the group.

- Identify the scale factor of an enlargement as the ratio of the lengths of any two corresponding line segments
- Understand that enlargement preserves angle but not length
- Understand the implications of enlargement for area and volume   (FC19.3)

Starter

If you draw a circle inside a square (circumscribe) so that the edges touch, then shade the circle, what fraction of the square is shaded?

You could use sides of length 8, 10 or 60 to establish that the answer is the same for any size or use a general side length of $2x$.

Use an approximation of $\pi = 3$ to establish the answer is approximately $\frac{3}{4}$, or in terms of π that the answer is $\frac{\pi}{4}$.

Resources

Sheets with 3, 4, 5 triangles drawn

Teaching notes

As described in the text, the teacher can provide a sheet with a right-angled triangle with dimensions 3 cm, 4 cm, 5 cm and ask the students to enlarge it by scale factor 2 themselves. The students should measure the angles of the triangles and note that they are the same. They should then measure the perimeter of the enlarged shape and calculate its area and compare these values with the same measures in the original triangle. The whole process could be repeated by enlarging the triangle scale factor 3 and performing the same measurements and calculations. The key facts should become clear, and the conclusions can then be brought together in a discussion and all the key facts summarised.

Exercise commentary

Question 1 This question further reinforces the findings in the class investigation.

Question 2 This requires students to plot their shapes on a coordinate grid.

Question 3 This is a simple application of the idea of scale factor of enlargement in a practical context.

Question 4 This question offers more context calculations.

Question 5 This challenge is set within a practical context.

Plenary

Students could investigate the effect on area of two different stretch factors being used in the x and y directions on a shape.

Exam-style question commentary

Worked solution	Commentary
1) a) trapezium: Area = $\frac{1}{2}$ (5 + 2) × 4 = 14 Triangle (area) = $\frac{1}{2}$ × 12 × 5 = 30 Total area = 14 + 30 = 44 cm² Perimeter = 4 + 12 + 13 + 5 + 2 = 36 cm b) Area = 6 × 8 + 6 × $\frac{8}{2}$ = 72 cm² Perimeter = 6 + 2 + 10 + 14 + 8 = 40 cm	1) Encourage students to split the compound shapes into simpler shapes. Laying out steps clearly should ensure that students maximise their marks.
2) a) i) C and D ii) none b) B and C, also E and F	2) Students will need to be familiar with the area of basic shapes, although at Foundation tier they are given most of these formulae in the exam.
3) Area of large circle = π × 5² = 25π Area of small circle = π × 2² = 4π Shaded area = 25π − 4π = 65.97 cm²	3) This is a multi-step problem requiring subtraction to find a shaded area. Students are less likely at this level to leave their answer in terms of π.

Aim

- To demonstrate how mathematics can be used to plan a holiday
- To show students how the concept of converting units of measure and currency can be applied to real-life situations such as going on holiday

Useful resources

- Holiday starter   Presentation
- Exchange rates   Presentation
- Time zones   Presentation
- Holiday   Worksheet

Teaching notes

Students could work through the example about Louise saving money and then use the first sticky note as a prompt to consider their own fundraising targets.

Use the financial section of a newspaper to discuss currency and conversion rates. Which countries have students visited? Which currencies did they use? What do they know/understand about exchange rates? What do the terms 'strong' and 'weak' currency mean?

Use the *Exchange rates presentation* to help students work through the example on the postcard about exchange rates and then use the sticky note text to prompt their own research into exchange rates and the commission charged by different companies.

Use examples of travel brochures or travel websites to discuss travel options for a trip before students work through the Oxford/Paris example. Discuss the effect of different time-zones on travel plans; the *Time zones presentation* might be helpful.

Use the next sticky note to prompt students to research travel options from their home to a chosen destination using websites, brochures or newspapers.

Did students notice a difference in the units of measure used for distances/temperature/etc when they visited a different country on holiday?

Students could work through the material in the blue panel. They could then use the text in the sticky note as a prompt to carry out more calculations using the values for that day's maximum and minimum temperatures.

Extension

Students could look at other units of measure and conversion rates. For example, miles/kilometres, grams/ounces, centimetres/inches, etc.

Students could prepare a fact sheet for travellers about a chosen destination.

Students could use question 3 on the worksheet to plot a graph of the equation that links temperature in °C and temperature in °F which they could use to convert between temperatures.

Simplification

Students could use the global time zones map from the *Time zones presentation* and make a chart to show what children around the world would be doing (for example, sleeping, having breakfast) when it is lunchtime in the UK.

Algebraic manipulation

Objectives covered in this chapter are:

FC6.1a understand that the transformation of algebraic expressions obeys and generalises the rules of general arithmetic

FC6.1b manipulate algebraic expressions by collecting like terms, by multiplying a single term over a bracket, and by taking out common factors

FC6.2a use systematic trial and improvement to find approximate solutions of equations where there is no simple analytical method of solving them

Prerequisite knowledge

- Collect like terms
- Expand brackets
- Factorise expressions
- Substitute values into a non-linear expression

Useful ICT resources

Introductory powerpoint	C19
Starter activity	C19.1 (x2)
Animation	C19.2
Consolidation	C19
Chapter test	C19
Formative on-screen test	C19
Summative on-screen test	C19

RICH TASK COMMENTARY

This is a nice opportunity for using algebra in context.

There is a need to simplify, and substitute when the algebra is used to explain the trick.

Students will probably try lots of different numbers before they are convinced.

Try altering the question to Add 10. Can they predict the answer?

A little bit of algebra makes sense of why the answer is always half of what you add.

Can the students invent their own magic trick and use algebra to show why it works?

- Distinguish in meaning between the words 'equation', 'formula' and 'expression' (FC5.2)
- Understand that the transformation of algebraic expressions obeys and generalises the rules of general arithmetic
- Manipulate algebraic expressions by collecting like terms, by multiplying a single term over a bracket, and by taking out common factors (FC6.1)

Starter

A warm up mental quiz reviewing directed number multiplication.

Resources

None required

Teaching notes

Students will have encountered this area before in section 7, and much of this section is a revision and progression from that work.

Present to the group a couple of examples, without brackets, which involve collecting together like terms and simplifying. Emphasise that the sign to the left of the term stays with that term.

Using the example in the text illustrate the difference between an identity and an equation. At this level an identity is simply a different way of writing an expression. When multiplying out or expanding the brackets think lines can be used to ensure everything inside the bracket is multiplied by what is outside. Pay special attention to the directed number rules.

The opposite process of factorising relies on picking out common factors from the expression given. The highest common factors should be taken to ensure complete factorisation and a number of key examples are given in the text. Students should be encouraged to multiply out the brackets in their mind's eye as a check on the factorisation.

Exercise commentary

Question 1 This requires interpretation of a diagram and the simplest expression to be given.

Question 2 These involve collecting like terms. Students who find this work challenging are well advised to rearrange the expression with the like terms collected together, keeping the sign to the left of each term with the term, before finding the resultant term.

Question 3 This uses an identity approach to simplifying an expression which is a progression from earlier work in this area. Basically they should follow the same routine as in question 2 then equate the relevant coefficients to a and to b.

Question 4 These cover all the permutations of expanding and simplifying two bracket expressions. The key is to be careful with the directed number arithmetic and to set out work systematically.

Question 5 This is a factorisation exercise, some questions require full factorisation. Students should be encouraged to check their answers by multiplying out the brackets.

Question 6 This question reminds students that there are many ways an expression can be factorised.

Plenary

Students could try expanding brackets with three or four terms, for example, $3(x + 2y - 4z)$.

- Use systematic trial and improvement to find approximate solutions of equations where there is no simple analytical method of solving them (FC6.2)

Starter

I have a large 5 litre jug and I want to fill it as much as possible using 2 other jugs. The small one holds 300 ml, the other holds 1.5 litres. I can use these two smaller jugs as many times as I like but I must use all the liquid in them. How can this be done?

[One option is 3 = 1.5 = 4.5 litres plus 1 × 300 = 300 ml. Total = 4.8 litres. Other possibilities are 2 medium and 6 small (4.8 litres) or 1 medium and 11 small (4.8 litres) or 0 medium and 16 small (4.8 litres).]

Resources

A spreadsheet, graphical calculator, Autograph could be useful for Question 5

Teaching notes

Present a number of examples of equations that students have met and solved over the course. These might include linear, quadratics and simple cubic equations. Present to the group an equation which they cannot solve using manipulative or formula methods and ask them what could be done. The idea of trial and error may arise in discussion, or you can prompt the idea and let them try it. Once everyone has had a go at the process and gained solutions of various kinds and accuracy, collect together the findings and then suggest a more systematic approach of interval bisection. That is, if the solution is between 3 and 4 then try 3.5 to further the process. A lot of the students will have been more intuitive in their choice of values, which should be valued, but for purposes of showing a systematic method this bisection approach helps them to really justify what they are doing.

It is important they write what they are doing down. Their partner should be able to follow their route to the answer easily. They need to work to at least 1 d.p. more than is required in the question.

Exercise commentary

Question 1 The method can also be used to find exact solutions and in fact can be used with any equation which has a solution.

Question 2 The table needs to be drawn and the method shown. If some realise that they can calculate the cube root directly using their calculator it is worth explaining that it is the method which is significant here and such a method which will transfer to much more complex equations.

Question 3 This should be written down fully and students need to justify that their answer is indeed the best to 1 d.p. Some may wish to rewrite the equation equal to zero which is equally valid.

Question 4 These are trial and improvement questions which again must be set out as in the lesson and text. Some may observe that part **f** can be rearranged and factorised giving one obvious solution of zero and leaving a quadratic to be solved for two solutions.

Question 5 A spreadsheet can speed things up if set up correctly. Also the use of a graphical calculator or Autograph could enable students to see how many solutions there and get good starting values to locate them more accurately.

Plenary

The rich task concerning Mr Gupta's central heating could now be attempted or revisited.

- Use systematic trial and improvement to find
  approximate solutions of equations where there
  is no simple analytical method of solving them   (FC6.2)

Starter

Ask students to give answers on whiteboards. Ask for the
squares of some numbers. Now ask for a couple of cubes and
some square roots.

Now ask for an estimate of the square root of 90. Make sure no
student uses a calculator at this point. Encourage better
estimates, praising responses of 'about 9' or equivalent. Write
up some of the suggested values.

Resources

Mini whiteboards, a spreadsheet or graphical calculator is useful
for question 7

Teaching notes

This section extends the challenges met in the last section.
There are often several ways of setting up these problems.
With the example in the text the students can compare
directly the two algebraic expressions. Zero is also an
obvious solution and the equation can be reduced to a
quadratic for which there are two distinct solutions. It is
worth working through this problem carefully with the
group to illustrate that there may be more than one solution
to find. As before the students should ensure that the
solution they find to one decimal place is actually the
best one.

Exercise commentary

Questions 1–5 These all require the
students to build their own algebraic
equation which they then need to
solve by trial and improvement,
though some of the solutions may be
clear as in question 4 which has a
trivial solution of zero as well as two
other less obvious ones.

Question 6 The hints given will lead
to a solution of each equation but
students can be encouraged to
investigate for other possible
solutions. They may find access to a
graphical calculator or a spreadsheet
helpful here.

Question 7 This challenge requires
the multiplication of three brackets
together but it is not necessary for
the brackets to be expanded. A
spreadsheet or table of values
application on a graphical calculator
will be helpful.

Plenary

Students could research the web to find
how computers are used to find very
accurate values of numbers such as π.

Summary

Exam-style question commentary

Worked solution	Commentary
1) a) $x(4x + 7) = 4x^2 + 7x$ b) $2(3x - 3) + 3(x + 5)$ $= 6x - 6 + 3x + 15$ $= 9x + 9$ or $9(x + 1)$	1) 10 Students may need reminding how to expand brackets, particularly when negatives are involved. Gauge students' confidence in multiplying terms such as x by $4x$. In b), students may not factorise at the end.
2) $x = 2$, $x^3 - x = 6$, too low $x = 3$, $x^3 - x = 24$, too high $x = 2.5$, $x^3 - x = 13.125$, too low $x = 2.7$, $x^3 - x = 16.983$, too low $x = 2.8$, $x^3 - x = 19.152$, too high $x = 2.75$, $x^3 - x = 18.0469$, too high To 1 d.p. the solution is $x = 2.7$	2) Encourage students to show their working systematically and clearly, perhaps in a table. It is important that the trial and improvement process is clearly displayed in order to satisfy QWC.
3) $x + x^3 = 465$ $7 + 7^3 = 350$ $8 + 8^3 = 520$ $7.6 + 7.6^3 = 446.6$ $7.7 + 7.7^3 = 464.233$ 7.7 points were scored	3) This problem is typical of the new style of questioning, whereby students are left to find a strategy. They may need a hint to use trial and improvement.

Objectives covered in this chapter are:

FC9.2a explore the geometry of cuboids (including cubes) and objects made from cuboids

FC9.2b use 2D representations of 3D objects; analyse 3D objects through 2D projections (including plan and elevation) and cross-sections

FC9.2c draw nets of 3D objects

FC9.2d solve problems involving the surface area of prisms

FC9.2e construct nets of cubes, regular tetrahedra, square-based pyramids and other 3D shapes from given information.

Prerequisite knowledge

- Recognise standard 2D and 3D shapes
- Find the area of a rectangle, a triangle and a circle

Useful ICT resources

Introductory powerpoint	C20
Starter activity	C20.1, C20.2, C20.3, C20.4
Powerpoint worked solution	C20.1, C20.4
Interactive activity	C20.4(AG)
Consolidation	C20
Chapter test	C20
Formative on-screen test	C20
Summative on-screen test	C20

RICH TASK COMMENTARY

Students should get lots of practice in drawing 3D views and plans and elevations.

Trying to uniquely define a 3D shape using only the front and side view is possible for some simple 3D shapes.

This is the 3D shape from which the front and side view were given.

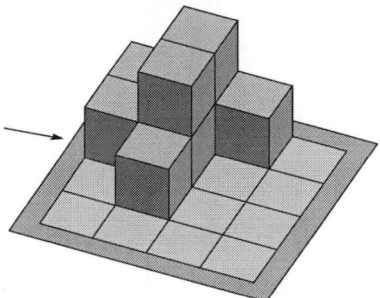

Could students find a 3D shape using less than 10 cubes, which can by uniquely defined by just the front and side view? How can they check?

Can you find a 3D solid using less than 10 cubes, which is not uniquely defined by its front, side and plan view?

- Explore the geometry of cuboids (including cubes) and objects made from cuboids
- Use 2D representations of 3D objects   (FC9.2)

Starter

Ask students to work in pairs. Ask them to sketch, on squared paper, as many shapes as possible made up of 6 linked squares, in 2 minutes (hexominoes—there are 35 different shapes). Students can compare their results with another pair.
Now ask them to sort the shapes carefully and identify those that could be a net of a cube.

Resources

Some solid shapes (cuboids, pyramids etc.), Cabri, isometric paper, mini whiteboards, web resources

Teaching notes

Show the group some actual solid objects. Define for them the meaning of vertex and vertices, faces and edges. Ask students to describe how many faces, edges and vertices each shape has. The text asks them to think about why the cuboid is such a common man-made shape so be prepared to provide some suggestions if they cannot think of any.

The next area of focus is using isometric paper to draw 3D objects; students may have done this in other areas of the curriculum. The key point is to get the paper the correct way up; once this is done then they can experiment drawing some simple shapes. The idea of a cross-section is very important and a lot of examples can be projected from the web or using Cabri 3D. Present a couple of objects, either on screen or using 3D models, and ask students to sketch each cross-section on their mini whiteboards.

From the idea of cross-section introduce the idea of a plane of symmetry.

Exercise commentary

Question 1 Ensure students have the paper in the correct orientation and have a supply of paper so they can experiment with their own drawings.

Question 2 This question involves the use of visualisation skills. Some students may also consider the other possible conic sections.

Question 3 This question is more difficult since the students need to perform a mental transformation of the object and draw the result. Encourage them to make rough sketch before drawing the accurate diagram. The actual drawing attempt often helps to get to the answer even if the initial effort is incorrect. Some students may need extra support.

Question 4 For the rich task you may wish to have a cube ready to demonstrate what is meant by the question. Encourage students to look at cubes of different sizes, but as always get them to consider smaller cases first so they can predict what may happen for a large cube such as a $20 \times 20 \times 20$.

Plenary

The rich task could be extended here if necessary. The investigation is presented in 'Virtual textbook'.

For those with good 3D skills introduce the idea of an axis of rotational symmetry. How many axes of symmetry does a cube have?

- Analyse 3D objects through 2D projections
  (including plan and elevation) and cross-sections (FC9.2)

Starter

Ask students to visualise putting 3 multilink cubes together. Ask each student to describe the shape they see to a neighbour. Are they seeing the same shape? How many different shapes are possible? Now model the possible shapes with 3 cubes.

Allocate multilink cubes to each pair of students and ask them to produce all possible shapes with 4 cubes (8 possible shapes).

Resources

Multilink cubes, mini whiteboards

Teaching notes

Present a side elevation and a plan view of a simple object such as a cylinder. Ask students to suggest what the object is that you are looking at. Repeat with a more difficult object, which perhaps might require more information for a unique answer. Use these examples along with the example in the text to introduce the vocabulary of this topic area. Get them to draw a plan and elevation of an object on their mini whiteboards. The emphasis at present is a correct basic sketch not an accurate scale drawing.

Working in pairs, and perhaps using mini whiteboards, students can quiz each other on shapes for which they have drawn plans and elevations. Be prepared to arbitrate any heated discussions that might arise. They meet this task again in Question 6 in the exercise.

Exercise commentary

Question 1 This question provides basic AO1 practice.

Question 2 For this question it can help to do a rough free hand sketch first, and then a more accurate diagram.

Question 3 This question involves visualisation.

Question 4 Is more challenging and could be done in pairs.

Question 5 Again this question may provoke lively discussion.

Question 6 This is a return to the activity from the teaching notes; after practice they should be more accurate and adventurous.

Question 7 This discussion is an extension of the question posed in question 4. It may be useful to have a couple of objects to illustrate possible solutions.

Plenary

There may be some cross-curricula links available here with design technology. Students could try doing plans and elevations for their school or a local building. Encourage them to look at some architectural drawings on the web to put the subject in a practical context. This work could form part of a more general functional mathematics task of producing accurate plans for a building or the design of a new toy.

Nets

- Draw nets of 3D objects
- Construct nets of cubes, regular tetrahedra, square-based pyramids and other 3D shapes from given information   (FC9.2)

Starter

Give students 2 minutes to write as many facts about triangles as possible. Ask each student to share a list with a neighbour and add facts if appropriate.

Which student pair has the most? Prompt further by asking if students can remember the special names, or have they remembered about symmetry, and so on.

Compile a list from those offered by the pairs.

Resources

Cabri 3D, a large ready-made net to fold up to make a well known 3D object, mini whiteboards

Teaching notes

Illustrate a net by folding up your ready-prepared net. Ask students to sketch a net for a cuboid on a mini whiteboard. If you can find one that works and one that doesn't, then use these to illustrate the idea further.

This should also bring out the fact that a solid object may have a number of nets. It will probably arise in discussion that extra tabs will have to added if the net is to be stuck together.

Exercise commentary

Question 1 This question is practice in visualisation.

Question 2 The reasoning given here should be a clearly expressed one. Students might wish to try out their explanation for clarity on their partners.

Question 3 This question is quite challenging so be prepared to provide hints on its solution.

Question 4 This introduces notation by labelling the faces. It is a good exercise in visualisation; students who cannot see it may need to look at a pre-prepared net.

Question 5 A revision of what an equilateral triangle is may be required.

Question 6 This rich task could be a group task for which the results are drawn together and the different nets being displayed.

Plenary

There are some quite complex nets available on the web; students may wish to use some to make objects for class room displays. The problem of the shortest distance between two points on the surface of a cube can be considered using nets.

- Work out the surface area of simple shapes using the area formulae for triangles and rectangles (FC9.1)
- Draw nets of 3D objects
- Solve problems involving the surface area of prisms (FC9.2)

Starter

Ask the question: If a cuboid has a surface area of 52 m^2, a base of 12 m^2 and a front face of 6 m^2, what is the area of one of the side faces? (8 m^2)

Students should sketch a cuboid to help visualise the faces. You can extend this starter to ask what the dimensions of the cuboid must be. (Only solution is 2 by 3 by 4)

Resources

Solid objects

Teaching notes

If possible, have some solid objects to show the group to emphasise surface area. Ask students to calculate the surface area and volume of a cuboid, either one whose dimensions are given or an actual cuboid which has to have its dimensions measured.

The surface area of a cuboid or other polygonal prism is best investigated by drawing the net of each shape as in the example given. The surface area of a cylinder could also be shown by cutting along a side of a cylinder and unfolding into a rectangle, either practically, or as a visualisation exercise.

Exercise commentary

Question 1 This question gives simple practice; students must remember a cuboid has 6 faces.

Question 2 This question uses a net to help find the surface area of a cuboid.

Question 3 This question has a variety of context problems.

Question 4 This mini functional maths task needs careful setting out.

Question 5 The key to this question is drawing a correct net. Some revision of percentages may be needed.

Plenary

Students could find the dimensions of three different boxes with a volume of 24 cm^3 and find which has the smallest surface area.

- Work out the surface area of simple shapes using the area formulae for triangles and rectangles (FC9.1)
- Draw nets of 3D objects
- Solve problems involving the surface area of prisms (FC9.2)

Starter

Ask students to list all the units of area and volume that they know, both imperial and metric.

Resources

None needed, but it may help students to construct a cylinder from paper

Teaching notes

This continues the work of C20.4. The formulae for circumference and area of a circle should be revised and then the area of the circular ends and the curved surface of a cylinder discussed. It may help students to construct a cylinder from paper to illustrate the fact that the curved face is actually a rectangle. The net of the cylinder relates to the work of C20.3. Students should work through the example and they should note that the final answer is not rounded until the calculation is complete.

Exercise commentary

Question 1 This question gives simple practice; here the students are finding only the curved surface area.

Question 2 This question is similar to question 1 but set in context.

Question 3 This question requires total surface area.

Question 4 In this question students should compare their answers to the two parts.

Question 5 This two-part shape needs more thought.

Question 6 For this question some revision of percentages may be needed.

Question 7 This question needs a clear method and reasoning.

Question 8 This rich task poses a real-life packaging problem.

Plenary

Students could extend the rich task to other shapes of packaging. It is also interesting to work out the percentage of wasted space in a box of 24 cans of baked beans (packed $4 \times 3 \times 2$).

Summary

Exam-style question commentary

Worked solution	Commentary
1)	1) You may need to remind some students that their net should have six faces (rectangles). Students will have varying degrees of confidence in moving between 2D and 3D representations; encourage them to visualise a box unfolding.
2) Area of triangle = $\frac{1}{2} \times 3 \times 4 = 6$ cm^2 $6 \times 2 = 12$ cm^2 Area of rectangles = $3 \times 6 + 4 \times 6 + 5 \times 6$ $= 18 + 24 + 30 = 72$ cm^2 Surface area = $72 + 12 = 84$ cm^2	2) This is a multi-step problem that can be broken down into working out the area of simple shapes. Encourage students to show their working clearly (QWC). Some may need reminding of the units.
3) The smallest surface area is when the 5×4 faces are joined because this face has the largest area that is not joined. Surface area = 112 cm^2	3) An important part of this question is the justification – some students may struggle with this. Encourage them to consider the different arrangements and the differences between them – what makes their surface areas different?

Graphs

Objectives covered in this chapter are:

FC5.3b understand that one coordinate identifies a point on a number line, two coordinates identify a point in a plane and three coordinates identify a point in space, using the terms '1D', '2D' and '3D'.

FC7.1a discuss and interpret graphs modelling real situations

FC7.2a generate points and plot graphs of simple quadratic functions

FC7.2b find approximate solutions of a quadratic equation from the graph of the corresponding quadratic function

Prerequisite knowledge

- Create a table of values
- Substitute values into an equation including a squared term
- Plot points in all four quadrants

Useful ICT resources

Introductory powerpoint	C21
Powerpoint worked solution	C21.1
Animation	C21.1 (x2)
Interactive activity	C21.1 (AG)
Consolidation	C21
Chapter test	C21
Formative on-screen test	C21
Summative on-screen test	C21

RICH TASK COMMENTARY

Students often do not understand what graphs are all about. This activity provides an opportunity for them to develop their understanding.

Encourage students to think of their own context such as: 'A boy goes for a bike ride – he travels fairly quickly along the first part of the journey, then he has a rest. He goes slowly up a hill and comes quickly down again as he heads for home. Unfortunately he has a crash and eventually an ambulance comes and takes him to hospital'.

The next level is to ask the students how long, how far, how fast and then how can they show this on their graphs so that they now have to have scales on their axes.

As an extension a student could be given another student's work and asked to write the story and compare it with the author's intention.

Starter

Display a journey graph with the scale and axes labels hidden other than Time and Distance. Say that this is a graph of a journey. Ask the students to work in pairs to find a story of a journey which would fit the graph. Allow 3–4 minutes for this before selecting two or three pairs of students to tell their story to the whole group.

Resources

A journey graph with the scale and axes labels hidden other than Time and Distance (to show the whole class)

Teaching notes

Distance-time graphs may have already been encountered in physics so there is the possibility of some cross-curricula work here. It is worth quickly revising the relationship between distance, time and speed and looking at the formula triangle

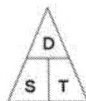

used to express the relations between these three quantities. It is particularly important that students grasp that the average speed over a journey is the total distance travelled divided by the total time taken, and not the mean of several mean speeds for parts of the journey.

Present the diagram from the text and get the students working in pairs to describe what is going on in words. The fact that the gradient of a distance-time graph gives the speed may need reinforcing. The meaning of a negative gradient will arise and discussions about velocity can be developed as far as you feel the group is capable, but students should appreciate that a change of sign implies a change of direction.

Plenary

Continuing the idea in question 14 local train or bus timetables could be used to provide data for a distance-time graph. There are some excellent distance-time graphs on, for example the recent world record 100 m run by Usain Bolt, which illustrate the shape of the race. There is potential here for some functional maths work.

- Discuss and interpret graphs modelling real situations (FC7.2)

Exercise commentary

Questions 1–2 These are basic questions on interpreting a distance-time graph in words.

Question 3 This is about fitting the correct graph to a simply-described situation and brings out the meaning of positive and negative gradients. Some explanation of the notation for units of speed may be needed.

Question 4 In this question students have to match the graph to the transport category. It clearly emphasises that the steepness of the line says much about how fast an object is travelling. More practice is provided in calculating speed.

Questions 5–6 These AO2 questions require the calculation of an overall average speed. Students must be careful not to think that the mean of the speeds for different parts of the journey will give the overall average speed. The emphasis is on the total distance travelled divided by the total time taken.

Question 7 This question requires some drawing and the meaning of mph may need clarifying.

Question 8 This is a dual graph describing the journeys of two people. It needs to be clear in the student's mind that the vertical axis represents the distance from a specified point. The differences in the sign of the gradients of the lines indicates they are travelling in opposite directions. Once again the method for overall average speed may need clarifying.

Questions 9–12 These are more unusual situations which may catch some students out. In question **10** it may not be immediately clear that depth of oil is in fact a distance travelled.

Question 13 This question requires the student to interpret a coach timetable as well as draw a graph and calculate speeds.

Question 14 This could be the basis of a homework task or be based on data already collected as part of a homework task.

Interpreting graphs

- Discuss and interpret graphs modelling real situations (FC7.2)

Starter

Display a spider diagram and write a speed in the centre: 40 km/h. Add a leg to the diagram and enter '80 km in 2 hours'. Ask students to write an equivalent statement on whiteboards. Choose some students to add theirs to the diagram. Repeat the activity for a different speed.

Resources

Mini whiteboards; OCR AO3 Guide Section 3.7

Teaching notes

The web and the newspapers are full of graphs that need interpreting or checking. Graphs are pictures which should enhance a person's understanding of a situation, not mislead.

The rich task on resting heart rate can be presented carefully to the group and students can work in pairs or small groups to interpret what they see. They should ask themselves what story does the graph tell? There is clearly a possibility of linking up with PE or Biology with this topic. Some explanation of the squiggle on the vertical axis may be needed and emphasised as a useful technique to make a graph fit the page more effectively.

The Royal Mail graph provides an excellent example of a discontinuous step-graph which students may not have encountered before. The difference between a shaded and an unshaded dot will need explaining. The questions asked should be attempted by the students and then checked at a suitable moment.

Exercise commentary

Questions 1–3 These are closely structured questions which lead students through the discussion of graphs.

Question 4 The idea of efficiency may need clarifying. Part **b** is one for discussion and at some stage it would be interesting and useful to bring together the students' responses.

Questions 5–6 More basic interpretation questions.

Questions 7 and 9 This involves fitting a graph to a situation.

Question 8 This graph requires some explanation and is a chance to practice QWC.

Question 10 The use of the squiggle appears again. Careful explanation is required to develop the quality of the students' communication as well as reinforce their mathematical understanding.

Question 11 Careful thought is required in this AO3 question.

Question 12 Students may research data for this question for homework if they have access to the web. It is a question that could be developed by some into a functional maths task.

Plenary

Students could extend question 12 into a functional maths project or develop a similar task.

Some students may want to find graphs in other more unusual areas or the infamous 'hockey stick graph' at the centre of some climate-change debates.

- Generate points and plot graphs of simple quadratic
  functions   (FC7.2)

Starter

Ask students to give the square of various values, starting with
integers up to 20, and then including fractions and simple
decimals up to 2 d.p. (eg the square of 0.12, which will involve
knowledge of times tables and place value).

Resources

2 mm graph paper, Autograph, graphics calculators

(e.g. TI-nSpire)

Teaching notes

Introduce the parabola, through real-life contexts eg path
of a projectile, or the shape of a curved mirror. Say that it
can be described by an equation in much the same way as a
linear graph, but it includes an x^2 term.

Using Autograph, show the shape of the basic quadratic
function $y = x^2$ and guide students through the steps
involved in recreating this, either on graph paper from a
table of values, or using graphical software in pairs or
individually.

It is well worth spending time to show students how to
draw an appropriate set of axes, and how to draw a smooth
curve by hand.

The example in the student book shows how a parabolic
graph can be used to provide an approximate solution to
quadratic equations (introduce this term carefully as
students will not be familiar with it).

Students will need time to devote to the exercise, which
could potentially involve drawing a lot of graphs by hand.
Access to Autograph or the TI-nSpire would be a great
help, once students have mastered the skill of drawing
graphs by hand.

Exercise commentary

Throughout this exercise, 2 mm
graph paper will provide sufficient
accuracy and clarity.

Question 1 This provides practice in
drawing simple quadratic graphs,
with a restricted domain and a
suggested set of axes. Students will
need to take care of completing the
rows, particularly with negative
values of x. Students may also need
help in interpreting how the graphs
are transformed.

Questions 2 and 3 These provide
further basic practice in drawing a
parabola from a table of values. The
flow diagrams in question 2 help in
fixing the correct order of operations.

Questions 4–6 These illustrate the
use of parabolic curves in context,
and require students to interpret.

Questions 7–10 These involve
drawing harder parabolas, and using
them to find approximate solutions to
equations.

Questions 11-12 These ICT
Challenges require students to
replicate the work they have done by
hand, using graphing software.

Plenary

Using Autograph, tackle the rich task
as a whole-class activity. Encourage
students to describe the shape and
symmetry properties of each curve as
it is displayed.

There is scope here for students to
explore simple transformations of graphs
in pairs or small groups, if an ICT-based
lesson can be devoted to this.

Points in three dimensions

C21.4

- Understand that three coordinates identify a point in space, using the term '3D'   (FC5.3)

Starter

Sketch the plan and elevations of a variety of shapes on the board, and ask students to identify the solid shape. They can either call out the name, or preferably sketch it on mini-whiteboards. You can use some of the plans and elevations on page 293 in the student book for inspiration.

Resources

Mini-whiteboards for starter activity, 3D geometry software such as Cabri 3D may also be useful

Teaching notes

Ask students to imagine how they could describe the location of a point on an infinite straight line (1D) – you may get responses like 'say how far along it is'. Remind them that it's infinite, and elicit the need for an origin. Move onto a plane (2D), again eliciting the need for an origin (you can discuss positive and negative coordinates within quadrants). Then extend to describing the location of a point in space (3D), and introduce the z axis.

Access to 3D graphing software would be an advantage in consolidating the idea of three coordinates, as it is difficult to draw points and axes on a 2D board.

Discuss the example of coordinates of points on a church.

Exercise commentary

Question 1 This gives a fairly straight-forward grid of buildings, continuing the theme of the example. Ensure students get the coordinates the right way around – with some students, it's hard enough with x and y coordinates in 2D.

Questions 2 and 3 These show contours on a coastline, continuing the theme of the rich task.

Question 4 This involves researching 6-figure grid references. Although this gives a different type of real-life coordinate, it is 2D rather than 3D, but worth including here.

Question 5 For those who find it easy to visualise and solve problems in 3D, they will relish the challenge of playing a few games of 3D noughts and crosses with a partner!

Plenary

Address the rich task through discussion – perhaps by showing two maps of Europe, one political and one physical, then asking what the main differences between the two are. Ask how you could locate a point – which map would give you the most useful information as to where it was positioned?

154

Exam-style question commentary

Worked solution	Commentary
1) a) missing value 0 b) 	1) a) Students should be careful to follow the correct order of operations. b) Ensure that the y-axis is scaled appropriately, and the points are joined with a smooth symmetrical curve.
2) a) speedy, cheaper by £1.60 b) just under 6 miles (approx 5.8 miles)	2) Some students may be put off by the awkward scale used – ask them to consider what one small square represents on each axis.
3) a) b) 53 m c) Yes, Speed of 44 gives skid mark of 83 83 close to 80 & driver unlikely to deliberately over-estimate speed	3) Ensure that the axes are scaled appropriately – the y-axis will need to stretch beyond 100. Part c) provides a good example of functional mathematics – ensure that students realise they are meant to use their graph. Ensure clear justification for full QWC marks.

Aim

- To introduce students to the mathematics behind radio transmission;
- To demonstrate how mathematics can be applied to organise and run a radio station and to plan radio programmes

Useful resources

- Radio starter   Presentation
- Radio waves   Presentation
- Radio   Worksheet

Teaching notes

Demonstrate a wave using a 'Mexican wave' with the students. Describe how energy is passed along the wave. You could use a rope and a spring to show the difference between longitudinal and transverse waves.

Use the sine wave diagram on the Case study to show what a sine wave looks like before the students convert the given values in Hz, kHz, MHz and GHz.

Explain how the amplitude and frequency of a wave affect its characteristics. This should be covered in very general terms, and students can check that they understand the concept by discussing the three waveforms shown in the Case study. They could also practise sketching their own wave diagrams and comparing them.

Ensure that students understand how the frequency of a radio station is linked to its name using the text at the bottom of the page and the sticky note hint.

Make sure that students understand the equation linking wave speed, frequency and wavelength before they answer the first set of questions on the second page. Some may need help with this work.

Discuss the hour wheel diagram (pointing out that it is simply a pie chart) and how it can be used to plan the timing of a radio programme and then allow the students to answer the related questions.

Encourage students to consider real-life radio stations and radio shows.

Extension

Students could attempt to create a time-plan for their own radio show. They should understand how to represent units of time on the wheel diagram.

Students could carry out further research into different types of waves and their frequencies and wavelengths (for example, radio waves, x-rays, etc.)

Simplification

Students could use the internet, or a TV listings magazine, to make a table of popular radio stations listed according to their frequencies

Everyday arithmetic and bounds

Objectives covered in this chapter are:

FC4.1a analyse real life problems using mathematical skills

FC4.1b apply mathematical skills when solving real life problems

FC4.1c communicate findings from solutions to real life problems

FC4.1d interpret solutions to real life problems

FC4.4a explore and solve problems in real life contexts that use common measures (including time, money, mass, length, area and volume)

FC4.4b explore and solve problems in real life contexts that use common compound measures such as speed and density

FC4.4c use checking procedures, including inverse operations; work to stated levels of accuracy.

Prerequisite knowledge

- Substitute a value into a formula
- Give answers to a specified degree of accuracy

Useful ICT resources

Introductory powerpoint	C22
Starter activity	C22.2
Powerpoint worked solution	C22.2, C22.3, C22.5
Consolidation	C22
Chapter test	C22
Formative on-screen test	C22
Summative on-screen test	C22

RICH TASK COMMENTARY

Students will need to be clear about what they are trying to do and this calls for some trial and improvement:

A	B	2AB	100A + B
10	10	200	1010
15	15	450	1515
etc			

They may be able to get closer as they think about the size of the number made by multiplying (and doubling) two 2-digit numbers and what happens when you write them as a 4-digit number i.e. how many thousands you are aiming at.

A bit of reasoning gives

$$2AB = 100A + B$$
$$\text{and } B = 100A \div (2A - 1)$$

Substituting for $A = 10$ and $A = 99$ (because it is a 2-digit number), narrows down to a limited set of possible integer values for B (51 or 52).

The final answer is $B = 52$ and $A = 13$.

What about investigating for when $100A + B = 3AB$ ($A = 17$ and $B = 34$) etc?

• Explore and solve problems in real life contexts that use common measures (including time, money, mass, length, area and volume) (FC4.4)

Starter

Ask students to prepare for recording rapidly on whiteboards. The first task is to count on in 0.3s as fast as possible, writing each value, starting from 2.3s. Allow one minute for this task, and see who gets the furthest. The whiteboard will act as a check. Students may also check their results with a neighbour. Now try counting on in 0.7s, starting from 3.4. Finally, count back in 0.4s, starting from 5.9.

Resources

Local train timetables or similar, mini whiteboards; SMP problem solving taster pack Tasks 2 and 4

Teaching notes

This section builds on topics encountered before and is firmly in the functional mathematics area of the curriculum.

Begin by getting the students to look at the postal charges table in pairs and ask them to answer the given questions and perhaps others created by the teacher. Collect together their responses and check they have dealt with the table correctly.

Distribute some train timetables (preferably from local stations) to the group working in pairs and ask them to work out a few journey plans. The students can present their answers to the rest of the group before working on the exercise.

Exercise commentary

Question 1 Students may not all be familiar with Fahrenheit measure so this may need comment.

Question 2 The relation between kilometres and miles naturally arises out of this problem. Some students may get caught out by the anticlockwise orientation of the scale.

Question 3 The students may need reminding about the conversion process between miles and km.

Question 4 This timetable reading question uses the 24 hour clock.

Part c requires some interpretation of the structure of the table.

Plenary

If the students have access to the web then they could try working out a more complex cross-country journey which involves different regional railway lines; for example, Tunbridge Wells to Bristol.

- Substitute positive and negative numbers into expressions such as $3x^2 + 4$ and $2x^3$ and evaluate the outcome   (FC2.4)
- Explore and solve problems in real life contexts that use common measures (including time, money, mass, length, area and volume)   (FC4.4)

Starter

Say to the students that you are going to make them all think of the number 3.

They should use whiteboards and start with any number they wish and perform the following steps:

Add 2; then multiply by 5; subtract 4; add the first number thought of; half this result; now take away 3 lots of the first number.

Resources

Mini whiteboards

Teaching notes

The rich task provides a good starting point for this section. It is worth checking students' initial answers since some are likely to miss enclosing the denominator in brackets in the 'child dose' formula.

Present the two formulae suggested in the text to illustrate examples of formulae used in an everyday context. Though students have met substitution into formulae before, it is worth reminding them that the formula should be written down and the substitution shown before giving the final rounded answer, with units if appropriate.

The example in the text concerning the resistors either requires brackets around the denominator or an equivalent method.

Exercise commentary

Question 1 The substitution should be shown. Brackets and the use of the fraction button provide one route to the answer; alternatively the students may wish to view the formula as multiplying by 5 and then dividing by 9.

Question 2 This medical formula requires some unit conversion and therefore revision of changing between imperial and metric units may be required.

Question 3 The numerator needs to be enclosed in brackets before division by 25 or calculated first and then use divided by 25 as a separate step.

Question 4 This question uses mg and it may be informative for the students to discuss how much substance this represents.

Plenary

Students could research other common scientific formulae on the internet and experiment with rearranging them to find different information.

- Solve word problems about proportion, including using informal strategies and the unitary method of solution   (FC4.3)
- Explore and solve problems in real life contexts that use common measures (including time, money, mass, length, area and volume)   (FC4.4)

Starter

Ask students to respond on whiteboards. Display a table of values showing £ and €.

£	5	10	15	–	50	90
€	–	14	–	28	–	–

Highlight one of the empty cells and ask for the values (€28; £5; £15; £50; £90; solutions: £20; €7; €21; €70; €126). Explore the strategies used by some of the students. What is the exchange rate for this set of data? (£1=€1.40) Explore what this means in terms of scale factors.

Resources

Mini whiteboards; SMP problem solving taster pack Tasks 2 and 4

Teaching notes

This section draws on earlier ones and uses previously encountered knowledge in everyday situations. It lies very firmly in the functional mathematics strand of the course. Using the example in the text or a similar problem will motivate this lesson. It is worth revising the powerful unitary method for dealing with conversion problems in currency.

The advice presented in the text should be stressed; a lot of this work is about sifting the information required by reading the question carefully.

Plenary

Students could investigate petrol prices in local garages and convert the cost to £ per gallon. They might like to compare petrol prices internationally.

The time zone context could be extended by use of the web and form the basis of a short functional mathematics project or group presentation.

- Explore and solve problems in real life contexts that use common compound measures such as speed and density   (FC4.4)

Starter

Ask some questions based around travelling at 45 miles per hour.

For example, how long would it take to travel 180 miles? What distance would be covered in 5½ hours?

Ask which is faster: 45 miles/hour or 45 km/hr.

Resources

A world map would be useful

Teaching notes

The problem centred on Togo is a good entry point here and introduces students to the idea of population density. Access to the web could quickly extend this problem either now or later in the lesson.

Many of these compound measures may have already been encountered in physics and there is the possibility of some cross-curricula work here. It is worth quickly revising with the group the relationship between distance, time and speed and revising the formula triangle

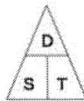

used in physics to express the relations between these three quantities. There is a triangle approach available with density which is introduced here via the rich task about the two boxes.

Exercise commentary

Questions 1–4 These provide examples with speed. Students may need reminding to convert the minutes into hours, either as fractions of one hour or as decimals.

Question 5 This is an AO2 density problem.

Question 6 This revisits the idea of population density. Students will need to think carefully about the degree of accuracy they can meaningfully use in this question. It may be of interest to locate Armenia on a world map.

Question 7 Some may need reminding about how many ml there are in a litre. Get them to think of the problem visually. Each second a 2ml drop falls out of the tap so after 10 seconds how much water will have dropped out?

Plenary

The population density of cities around the world makes for interesting reading. Students could use the web, or a geography textbook, to investigate which cities have the highest density and compare densities of cities or countries.

- Recognise that measurements given to the nearest whole unit may be inaccurate by up to one half in either direction   (FC3.1)

Starter

A review quiz on rounding numbers to one or two decimal places or one or two s.f. Students could suggest their own questions to solve in small groups.

Resources

A dynamic number line would be useful

Teaching notes

Begin with a review quiz on rounding numbers to one or two decimal places or one or two significant figures.

Present a number like 9.2 which has been rounded to one d.p. and obtain from students a variety of numbers that the original number could have been. This should build up a picture of the interval of possible values. On the whole students have little trouble getting the lower possible bound but the upper bound is more contentious. The idea to get across is that we get as close as we like to the upper bound without actually achieving it and for practical purposes, in the above case, we can use 9.25 even though this would officially round up to 9.3.

The problem about motorway junctions can then be given to the group to develop this notion of lower and upper bounds.

Exercise commentary

Questions 1–2 These provide a broad range of rounded numbers to consider.

Question 3 This AO2 problem is set within the context of a sports day.

Question 4 A quick review of how to find the percentage of a given quantity may be required.

Plenary

The possible errors in measurement could lead students to wonder about what world records in, for example, the 100 m sprint actually mean. Does 9.58 seconds mean exactly that time or a range of times? This could be extended to a general consideration of various world records.

Exam-style question commentary

Worked solution	Commentary
1) 3 mins 59.35 s (smallest) 3 mins 59.45 s (largest)	1) Students often find bounds of measurement rather a difficult topic. You could encourage the use of a number line marked in tenths (59.3, 59.4, 59.5…)

2) a) 2 h 40 min = 160 min
 	
   160 miles ÷ 160 min = 1 mile per min = 60 mph
   b) $4\frac{1}{2}$ litres ≈ 1 gallon
   18 ÷ 4.5 = 4 gallons
   160 ÷ 4 = 40 mpg
	2) a) Students may have problems calculating with time involving mixed units. Encourage converting to either hours or minutes, but ensure the final answer is in miles per hour.
	
	   b) Students will need to know basic imperial-metric conversions, including litres to a gallon.

3) £4.50 → 2 kg
        → 25 washes
 	
   450 ÷ 25 = 18p per wash
   New box size is 17p per wash
   17 × 30 = £5.10
   $\frac{30}{25} = \frac{6}{5} = 1.2$
 	
   1.2 × 2 kg = 2.4 kg
	3) There is a lot of information contained in this AO2-type problem. Students will need to use proportional reasoning.
	Encourage scaling up or down using multiplication or division (not addition or subtraction).

Area and volume

Objectives covered in this chapter are:

FC9.1f   find volumes of cuboids, recalling the formula and understanding the connection to counting cubes

FC9.1g   calculate volumes of right prisms and of shapes made from cubes and cuboids

FC9.2d   solve problems involving the surface area and volume of prisms

FC9.3d   understand the implications of enlargement for area and volume

Prerequisite knowledge

- Find the area of a rectangle, triangle and circle
- Substitute values into a formula
- Give answers to a required degree of accuracy

Useful ICT resources

Introductory powerpoint	C23
Powerpoint worked solution	C23.1
Animation	C23.1 (x3), C23.2, C23.3 (x3), C23.4, C23.5
Consolidation	C23
Chapter test	C23
Formative on-screen test	C23
Summative on-screen test	C23

RICH TASK COMMENTARY

This is an opportunity to investigate the properties of different triangles as you should get equilateral, isosceles and right-angled triangles.

Students will need to describe their triangles and measure the angles fairly accurately.

Each of the angles in every triangle is a multiple of 15; when one side is the diameter of the circle you get a right angle, if you start a circle at two fixed points and move the third point you get the same angle – so you can discover circle theorems!

An extension could be to look at the angle made at the centre of the circle...

Volume of cuboids

- Find volumes of cuboids, recalling the formula and understanding the connection to counting cubes   (FC9.1)

Starter

Draw up a chart for the whole group with columns headed Length, Area, Capacity/Volume. Explain that you will give each student one minute to think of as many units as they can under these headings. They may want to jot thoughts down on mini whiteboards. Now select as many individuals as possible to record a unit in the columns. Encourage unusual ones, and accept imperial measures as well as metric. Where any errors occur, allow other students to make corrections.

Resources

Mini whiteboards

Teaching notes

This is a topic students will have encountered a number of times already and so is best started by quizzing them on what they know. Ask for the volume of a given cuboid but leave off any units. Ask them to explain what they mean by their answer so that the idea of filling the box with a standardised cube of side 1 cm or 1 m is revised for all. Emphasise the importance of writing down the correct cubic unit and ensure they are familiar with the vocabulary of length, height, width, depth and dimension.

The word capacity and its meaning needs to be highlighted and the relationship between cm^3 and litres revisited with a couple of examples of conversion, covering both directions of calculation.

Exercise commentary

Question 1 This question emphasises what is meant by volume.

Question 2 This requires information to be used from a table.

Question 3 The key phrase here is that the object has a square base.

Questions 4–5 These questions link units of volume and capacity.

Question 6 This is a multi-stage calculation which involves finding a percentage.

Questions 7–8 These questions find a missing length from a given volume.

Question 9 This is an AO2 problem. You could encourage students to sketch the situation.

Questions 10–11 The rich tasks require clear working and explanations.

Plenary

Given a piece of card 10 cm by 8 cm what size square should be cut from each corner to make a net of an open box with the maximum volume?

- Calculate volumes of right prisms and of shapes made from cubes and cuboids   (FC9.1)

Starter

Ask students, in pairs, to look at two sheets of A4 paper. Do students all agree that they have the same area?

By joining either the widths or the lengths together two different cylinders can be formed. Ask students to try this and decide which of the two cylinders has the larger volume. Share their results, and ask how they might be tested.

From student responses, revise how to find the volume of any prism. What shape is the cross-section? Estimating π as about 3, ask students to establish rough values for the volumes and hence which is larger.

There is potential to examine methods of estimation here, if appropriate for the students' needs.

Resources

Sheets of A4 paper, prism and non-prism solid models

Teaching notes

You should ideally have a number of solid models to show the group, some of which are prisms and some non-prisms. By asking questions like 'What is special about this set of objects?' students should notice that some objects have a constant cross-section.

To arrive at the volume of a prism begin with a cuboid and invite the students to consider its volume, which can be seen as area of cross-section multiplied by length. Then by comparing with a cuboid the volume of a triangular prism should emerge. A trapezoid can be split into two triangular prisms and once again the area of the cross-section times the length gives the volume. This discussion plus the explanation in the text should lead to the general formula for any prism.

All working needs to be clearly laid out and the units given at final stage. Once again answers should not be rounded until the final answer in order to avoid rounding errors.

With more complex composite cross-sections it can help students to draw the cross-section.

Exercise commentary

Question 1 The cross-sectional area is already calculated in these problems.

Question 2 This problem is simple but requires interpretation without the aid of a diagram.

Question 3 This problem could lead to some practical work on finding the volume of unusual objects.

Question 4 Drawing the cross-section first can help with these composite area problems.

Question 5 Once again drawing the flat cross-section can help with this AO2 problem.

Question 6 This AO3 question requires good visualisation skills and some careful drawing.

Question 7 Students should recognise that these apparently complex shapes obey the same rules.

Plenary

Challenge the students to investigate the volume of non-prismatic shapes such as spheres or cones.

- Calculate volumes of right prisms
- Use π in exact calculations   (FC9.1)

Starter

At the front of a block of flats, the first floor has 16 windows and the number of windows halves each time you go up one floor. All floors have windows. There are equal numbers of windows on each of the four sides of the building. How many floors are there and how many windows altogether?
(5 floors; $16 + 8 + 4 + 2 + 1 = 31$; $31 \times 4 = 124$.)

Resources

A solid cylinder, some cylindrical bottles

Teaching notes

The lesson can be started by a recap quiz on the volume of a prism. A cylinder can then be presented to the class and it should be clear to students that the object is a prism with a circular cross-section. Fully justifying the volume formula is difficult at this level but it should be fairly intuitive. The general formula should be derived as a subset of the general formula for the volume of a prism.

The group may need reminding about pipes and solid cylinders and the annular cross-section in the second text example may need explaining.
As before emphasise that units are important in the final answer and remind students about litres and millilitres.

Exercise commentary

Question 1 As the question warns, students need to be wary of confusing diameter and radius.

Question 2 The word capacity may need revising again; and also how to round to the nearest 10 ml.

Question 3 This is annular cross-section (as in the second example in the text) which can be calculated exactly.

Question 4 This is an AO2 problem which needs working to back up the answer. Students should ensure their working convinces their neighbour.

Question 5 The context of this question may need explaining since some will be unfamiliar with engine capacity.

Questions 6–7 These questions require students to work back from volume to find a length. Some revision of cube roots and calculator functions may be needed.

Plenary

The story of Archimedes and his principle could be investigated as a cross-curricula exercise. The problem of finding the volume of irregular shapes could then become a functional maths task.

- Identify a scale factor and understand the implications of enlargement for area and volume (FC9.2)

Starter

Ask students to find the dimensions of a cylindrical can that holds 1 litre of liquid.

Resources

None, but different sized cubes would be useful, also multilink cubes

Teaching notes

The class can be set the task of enlarging a 2 × 2 × 2 cube by scale factor 2. Make it very clear that it is just the lengths that are being enlarged by this factor. Students should calculate the new volume and surface area of the enlarged object. A diagram on the whiteboard may help make things clearer. They can then try the same thing with a linear scale factor of enlargement of three. At a suitable moment bring together and refine the findings then the key facts can be summarised.

Exercise commentary

Question 1 This question reinforces the findings of the class investigation, this time using a cuboid.

Question 2 This problem provides basic drill in the application of scale factors. Some students may need reminding about how to convert cm^3 into litres.

Question 3 This is a reverse problem requiring cube rooting and then squaring to get the length scale factors and area factor.

Question 4 This challenge practises scale factors in context.

Question 5 This challenge may require a quick review of the meaning of the ratio 1 : 15.

Plenary

The large size of the volume factor compared with a length factor, if it is greater than one, can surprise students. The conversion of area and volume units often catches students out and this could be looked at again, for example, how many mm^3 are needed to make one m^3?

Exam-style question commentary

Worked solution	Commentary

1) a) area of cross-section = $\frac{1}{2}$ × 6 × 8 = 24 cm²
 	
 Volume = 24 × 13 = 312 cm²
 	
 b) area of circle = π × 2²
             = 12.57 cm²
 volume = 12.57 × 9
          = 113.10 cm³ (2 dp)
	1) Encourage students to show their working clearly, giving an answer for the cross-sectional area and then multiplying by the length. In b) students will need to take care about rounding.

2) 150 ÷ 6 = 25 cm² (area of each face) Length of side =$\sqrt{25}$ = 5 cm Volume = 5³ = 125 cm³	2) This AO3-type question requires three steps: work out the area of each face, then the length of each side, then the volume. Encourage correct use of units.

3) a) area = 4² × 100
          = 1600 cm²
 	
 b) space needed = 800 ÷ 4³
                = 12.5 cm³
	3) This AO2-type question requires the knowledge of the effect of scale factor on area and volume. If students are unsure whether to multiply or divide, ask them if their answer is sensible in the context.

Study of chance

Objectives covered in this chapter are:

FC10.1a use the vocabulary of probability to interpret results involving uncertainty and prediction

FC10.1b understand and use the probability scale

FC10.1c understand and use estimates or measures of probability from theoretical models (including equally-likely outcomes), or from relative frequency

FC10.1d list all outcomes for single events, and for two successive events, in a systematic way

FC10.1e identify different mutually exclusive outcomes

FC10.1f know that the sum of the probabilities of all the possible mutually exclusive outcomes is 1

FC10.1g understand that if they repeat an experiment, they may (and usually will) get different outcomes, and that increasing sample size generally leads to better estimates of probability

FC10.1h compare experimental data to theoretical probabilities

Prerequisite knowledge

- Convert between fractions, decimals and percentages
- Add and subtract fractions
- Multiply a fraction by an integer
- Simplify a fraction

Useful ICT resources

Introductory powerpoint	C24
Starter activity	C24.4
Powerpoint worked solution	C24.3 (x2), C24.6
Animation	C24.6
Interactive activity	C24.2 (TI), C24.5 (TI)
Consolidation	C24
Chapter test	C24
Formative on-screen test	C24
Summative on-screen test	C24

RICH TASK COMMENTARY

Students should enjoy playing the game! They need to record the choices made by the two participants and how many times each player wins. Students should convert the relative frequency into a decimal/percentage. The game is fair and mathematically the probability of winning each time is $\frac{1}{3}$.

Students could make a two way table to list all the 9 possible outcomes and demonstrate that from one person's point of view the chance of them winning is $\frac{3}{9}$.

Students could investigate other games to see if they are fair, such as the Monty Hall puzzle: There are three boxes. One box has a real car inside, the others have model cars inside. A contestant picks a box but does not open the box. The host opens one of the other boxes and reveals a model car. The host offers a switch. Would you take it?

- Use the vocabulary of probability to interpret results involving uncertainty and prediction
- Understand and use the probability scale (FC10.1)

Starter

The students should work in pairs to place these quantities into five groups, each group totalling 1: $\frac{1}{3}$, $\frac{2}{3}$, 0.5, 20%, 0.3, 30%, $\frac{3}{5}$, 0.1, 0.6, $\frac{2}{5}$, 0.125, 25% $\frac{5}{8}$.

The quantities show a mix of fractions, decimals and percentages.

Check the results and discuss with the students whether other groups which make 1 are possible.

Resources

Blank probability scale

Teaching notes

The students can either draw their own likelihood scale or the teacher can provide a photocopied version. Through discussion the students can allocate the events on the scale. Some of the statements should provide disagreement and this could provoke a discussion about the need to be able to quantify probability in some way, by collecting data or making assumptions for the situation.

Present the probability scale ranging from 0 to 1 and review the key facts about probability highlighted in the text. When expressing probabilities in fraction, decimal or percentage form it is worth emphasising that they should not use ratio to describe a probability.

The basic notation for probability needs to be defined and shown.

Exercise commentary

Question 1 Students need to refer back to the likelihood scale and discuss the best place to allocate the described events. Once again disagreements can point to the need for data collection to verify intuitions.

Question 2 They can draw their own scale or the teacher may wish to speed things up with a photocopied version.

Question 3 This provides a reinforcement of the notation described earlier.

Question 4 The structure of a pack of playing cards may need to be explained.

Plenary

Prepare the ground for quantifying probability in the next section either by collecting data or by using the symmetry of the situation as we do with dice or coins.

- Understand and use estimates or measures of probability from theoretical models (including equally likely outcomes)
- List all outcomes for single events, and for two successive events, in a systematic way (FC10.1)

Starter

Display a table of events with given probabilities.
Ask students to write responses to questions such as:
What is the probability of *not* getting ... ?
What is the probability of getting either ... or ... ?
What is the total probability? and so on.

Resources

Mini whiteboards

Teaching notes

The notation for probability can be revisited using the dice situation by focusing on $P(6) = \frac{1}{6}$. Establish clearly and simply the distinction between outcomes and events, then move swiftly on!

The next archetypal situation to look at is the spin of a coin. The probability of gaining a head will be forthcoming, though once again it may be worth mentioning that this could be tested experimentally as well. If the possibility of landing on its side is brought up then this will highlight that we are simplifying what really occurs in order to make our model more manageable, and that it is sensible in a simple model of a simple situation to ignore improbable events.

The marble example should be set to the group since it brings out a number of important ideas and practise in the use of the notation. The probability of an event not happening is worth reinforcing with a number of similar examples.

Exercise commentary

Questions 1–2 The answers to these standard AO1 problems are best given as fractions.

Question 3 This simple question should be written out clearly to cement understanding of complement probabilities.

Question 4 These question requires more thought about how the number of marbles relates to the theoretical probability.

Question 5 This AO3 problem needs the student to clearly lay out their answer in proper notation and to explain their thoughts.

Plenary

The probability of getting a head or throwing a six based on experimental data could be researched on the web and the slight differences from the theoretical probability noted. Other sorts of dice or spinner could be considered.

- Identify different mutually exclusive outcomes
- Know that the sum of the probabilities of all the possible mutually exclusive outcomes is 1   (FC10.1)

Starter

Ask students to consider the outcome of a situation such as a topical sporting event, for example, a football game. What outcomes are possible? (win, lose, draw) Would an individual be correct in saying, therefore, that the probability of a particular team winning is $\frac{1}{3}$?

Is a home win or an away win more likely? What difference does it make to an estimate of the probability of winning if a person has prior knowledge of team performance?

Resources

Spinners and dice may be useful as props

Teaching notes

Define what mutually exclusive outcomes are and provide clear simple examples. Ask students to produce some examples of their own of outcomes which are mutually exclusive and some examples which are not mutually exclusive; these can be discussed in pairs and then brought together in a class summary.

The sum of two dice scores generates a possibility space that provides a fertile ground for the different types of event and can also bring out the summation rule for mutually exclusive outcomes. The use of the word 'or' needs to be highlighted and the notation introduced in the previous section reinforced.

The example provided in the text can then be attempted by the students to reinforce the addition rule idea. It is worth emphasising once again that if they get an answer greater than 1 then they should to go back and check their working.

Exercise commentary

Question 1 Encourage the pupils to write down their answers properly using the notation introduced earlier. Fractions are the obvious mode of expression here.

Question 2 This question is in terms of decimals.

Question 3 The phrase 'equally likely' may need revising in this question.

Question 4 This is an AO3 question which demands careful thought on the part of the student. The events need to be described accurately in correct notation. In part **c** the explanation should clearly indicate elements in common between the defined events. You might be advised to have a variety of responses to hand to help students if they struggle.

Plenary

The students could collect data from their class or environment and create their own questions similar to question 3 and test them on their peers.

Starter

Write down sums and products of fractions, for example:

$\frac{2}{3} + \frac{1}{4}$

$\frac{2}{5} + \frac{3}{8}$

$\frac{4}{9} \times \frac{3}{10}$

$\frac{7}{12} \times \frac{6}{11}$

Resources

Spinners and biased dice

Teaching notes

Using an unbiased five-sided spinner as in the text, get the students individually or in pairs to predict how many times each number will appear if they spin the spinner 100 times. This will either revise or introduce the method for calculating expected numbers. Let them complete the experiment and record the results for comparison and discussion. Discuss the results as a group and consider how to improve the experiment. This should lead to the key idea of more data giving a more accurate result.

If available the group could investigate experimentally the behaviour of a loaded die, once again noting how increasing the number of trials improves the accuracy of the calculated probability. The lack of symmetry prevents the use of theoretical probabilities based on equally likely outcomes.

Exercise commentary

Questions 1–2 These provide practice in the calculation of expected number. Students could consider what range of values they would consider acceptable in each situation before questioning the probability given.

Question 3 This estimate of probability is easy to calculate. Students may be asked to consider how to improve the estimate.

Questions 4–5 Answers to these questions should be expressed clearly in the notation encountered earlier.

Question 6 Introduces the word survey and enables a discussion about samples and surveys at a very simple level. Once again the students could reflect on how to improve the survey but should realise that surveying greater numbers needs more time and resources.

Plenary

The complexities of taking a sample could be further investigated and the use of surveys to mislead in advertising may interest some students.

- Understand and use estimates probability from relative frequency
- Understand that if they repeat an experiment, they may (and usually will) get different outcomes, and that increasing sample size generally leads to better estimates of probability   (FC10.1)

Starter

The seedings of the winners of the men's singles at Wimbledon for the past 20 years were 1, 1, 4, 1, U, 1, 1, 1, 1, 5, 2, 1, 1, 12, 6, 3, 3, 3, 11, 4. U stands for unseeded.

What seeded player is most likely to win based on the past records? (Number one seed.)

Is the chance that the number one seeded player wins greater than 0.5? (No, only nine times out of last 20 years.)

Resources

Spinners and biased dice

Teaching notes

Go through Laura's experiment paying special attention to how the table for relative frequency is constructed. This will necessitate a definition of relative frequency which is a concept students will have met before. Ask them individually, or in pairs, to repeat the experiment and record their results in a similar table and to write down their conclusions. Discussion with the class might suggest that some coins are slightly biased; these could be spun further to get more accurate data. The students should observe that the relative frequency approaches the theoretical probability as the number of trials increases.

A similar experiment using a six-sided die could be attempted and similar conclusions drawn.

Exercise commentary

Question 1 The students need to be encouraged to write their reasoning down clearly to justify what might seem to them an obvious conclusion.

Questions 2–3 The meaning of frequency may need re-emphasising to some. Once again clear justification for answers must be provided.

Question 4 This is a table like the one they would have filled out during the initial part of the lesson. They may need a reminder about how to get started. Part **b** requires clear justification for their conclusion.

Question 5 This question is based on raw data which needs to be summarised by using a tally method before. As before, conclusions must be made with clear reference to the data.

Plenary

If not encountered already students could investigate the behaviour of loaded dice. There are a number of coin and dice simulations on the web which can be used to investigate bias.

- List all outcomes for two successive events, in a systematic way (FC10.1)

Starter

Ask students to find products of fractions, for example:

$\frac{1}{2} \times \frac{5}{12}$, $\frac{1}{3} \times \frac{6}{7}$, $\frac{2}{5} \times \frac{3}{4}$

Encourage students to simplify their answer.

Resources

None required, but the SMP Problem solving taster pack Task 3 is directly relevant

Teaching notes

The money tree example in the text can provide an activity to start this lesson. The vocabulary needs to be defined a little more rigorously at this stage and the phrase 'sample space diagram' or 'possibility space' carefully explained. Once the table has been completed for this situation a number of suitable questions could be posed to the group to illustrate its use. Correct notation should be used to write down answers.

Discuss why a table is often better than listing outcomes for two events (you ensure that all outcomes are accounted for).

Exercise commentary

Questions 1–2 Students may need a little help to get started with this so be prepared to show to the group how to set up the sample space diagram. These tables should be drawn neatly with a ruler.

Question 3 Students should be made aware that they can abbreviate the names to ease the drawing of their diagram but that a key should be given. Part **c** requires a clear explanation to be given.

Question 4 This is a classic problem with two dice but involves multiplying the uppermost numbers, not summing which they have met before; make sure the students read the question correctly.

Question 5 Similar to question 4 but with spinners.

Plenary

Students could investigate the number of outcomes there are when tossing two, three, four .....coins and come up with a general rule. A similar investigation in other situations might lead to an appreciation of the multiplier principle. More able students might investigate the concepts of permutations and combinations.

Exam-style question commentary

Worked solution	Commentary
1) For example: a) b) c) 	1) There is no unique solution, and students should use their own initiative to arrive at a possible answer. They should appreciate that a probability of 1 equates to a certainty.
2) a) $\frac{11}{44} = \frac{1}{4}$ b) $\frac{22}{44} = \frac{1}{2}$	2) This is a fairly straight-forward question where students can arrive at the correct answer in a single step. Possible pitfalls include giving an answer to a) of 11, or $44 \div 11 = 4$
3) $\frac{15}{36} = \frac{5}{12}$	3) Many students will immediately give an answer of $\frac{1}{2}$. They may need prompting that the scores can be the same, though it's not simply half and half. Students will not often readily draw a sample space diagram, so you may need to encourage them along.

Aim

- To show the importance of mathematics and taking accurate measurements as a basis to create weather predictions
- To introduce how mathematics is used to formulate a weather forecast

Useful resources

- Weather starter   Presentation
- Weather maps   Presentation
- Weather forecasts   Presentation
- Weather   Worksheet

Teaching notes

Start with a discussion about the variables included in a weather report, for example, temperature, wind speed and direction, etc.

Use the examples in the case study to ensure that students are comfortable with taking readings from thermometers.

Show students the temperature map. Let students discuss the map and what it shows before they answer the related questions. You could use the *Weather maps presentation* to illustrate this.

Use the Internet to research if there have been any changes to these records since 2000.

You could introduce the second section of the case study by first showing students a weather map from a newspaper. Look particularly at the symbols for wind speed and direction. Students could use the Internet to research the 'Beaufort Scale'.

Ensure that students understand how to interpret symbols to show wind speed and direction before they answer the wind-related questions on the case study.

Discuss the inaccuracy involved in weather reporting and the unpredictable behaviour of nature. The *Weather forecast presentation* could help with this.

Let students discuss the graph showing the temperatures in Exeter. Encourage them to use statistical vocabulary to suggest how a weather forecaster could interpret this graph into a weather forecast.

Extension

Students could use the Met office website (http://www.metoffice.gov.uk) to gather and interpret other national, local or international weather data. They could then present their findings using a range of tables, charts and diagrams.

Students could research chaos and the 'butterfly effect' to see how this places an intrinsic limit on the accuracy of long term weather predictions and what this might mean for global warming predictions.

Simplification

Students could use a protractor to draw their own compass, marking it with degrees (0°, 10°, 20° etc.) and compass points. This ties in with work on bearings, which could be revisited at this point.

Student book answers

A1 Integers and decimals

Check in

1 −8, −5, −3, −1, 2, 4

2 a 7 **b** −10 **c** −12 **d** −3

3 1, 2, 3, 4, 6, 8, 12, 16, 24, 48

Ex A1.1

A1.1 Rich task

Correct, incorrect, correct

1 a one thousand three hundred and seven

b twenty nine thousand and six

c three hundred thousand

d six hundred and five thousand and thirty

2 a 8043 **b** 70 000 000 **c** 200 051 **d** 2010

3 a 8000 **b** 40 **c** 70

4 a largest − 95, smallest − 59

   i largest − smallest = 36 **ii** 9

   iii It is always 9

b largest: 821, smallest: 128

   i largest − smallest = 693 **ii** Always get 495

   iii Students will find the number is always divisible by 99. This can be proven algebraically:

Using a place value table:

100s	10s	1s
x	y	z

$(100x + 10y + z) − (100z + 10y + x) = 99x − 99z$
$= 99 (x − z)$

Students may find something similar using numbers rather than algebra.

Ex A1.2

1 a 1 **b** −2 **c** −4 **d** 1

  e −12 **f** −15 **g** −9 **h** −10

  i 7 **j** 15 **k** −19 **l** −12

  m −8 **n** −5 **o** 5 **p** 8

2 a −12 **b** −35 **c** −32 **d** −27 **e** 20

  f 36 **g** 20 **h** 21 **i** −9 **j** −3

  k −2 **l** −3 **m** 3 **n** 4 **o** 8

  p 9 **q** 77 **r** 12 **s** −5

3 a 16, 23, 7; 23, 22, 1 **b** 8°C

4 a 36, −24 **b** 4 × 3 + 6 × −2 = 0

  c eg. Answer 4, all correct; Answer 9, 6 correct.

Ex A1.3

A1.3 Rich task

Yes, they would both be 180° because 350° F= 176.7°C is 180° to the nearest 10, and 360°F = 182.2°C is also 180° to the nearest 10.

1 a 630 m **b** 220 m **c** 200 m **d** 200 m

2 a 7700 g **b** 5500 g **c** 3100 g **d** 2600 g

3 a 40 730, 40 700 **b** 310, 300

  c 590, 600 **d** 150 900, 150 900

4 302 km 254 km

5 a 19.37 **b** 19.4 **c** 0.00752 **d** 0.008

  e 153.262 **f** 153.26 **g** 34.16 **h** 4.90

6 a 76 000 **b** 76 300 **c** 23 400 **d** 58 000

  e 46 000 **f** 23.40 **g** 23.4 **h** 7.184

7 a 165 m to 175 m **b** 50, 51, 52, 53, 54 kg

Ex A1.4

1 a 61 **b** 23.83 **c** 1.5625 **d** 0.35

  e 1.33 **f** 156.25 **g** 500 **h** 7.5

2 a 1.736 307 692 1.7 **b** −1.693 877 551 −1.69

  c −0.191 345 436 −0.19 **d** 12.68 283 582 12.7

  e 3.839 270 764 3.84 **f** 2.370 021 097 2.4

3 a 0.25 **b** 0.i̇ **c** 0.4 **d** 0.2̇7̇ **e** 5

  f 6.25 **g** 2 **h** 4 **i** 2.5

4 a 1296 **b** 78125 **c** 100000

  d 262144 **e** 410.0625 **f** 0.004096

5 This is an investigative task and students' answers will vary, it's an opportunity to practice QWC skills so students should be encouraged to write clear instructions both in terms of language used and mathematical notation used.

Exam practice

1 a 2.71828 **b** 2.72

2 a 1.716961498 **b** 2

3 Missing numbers are bottom row −1 middle row −6, 2

A2 Summary statistics

Check in

1 a 44, 47, 48, 55, 56, 59, 61, 65

  b 0.5, 0.8, 1.5, 1.7, 2.1, 2.5

  c 13.1, 13.2, 21.3, 23.1, 31.2, 32.1

2 a 81 **b** 179 **c** 105 **d** 205 **e** 441
f 108 **g** 135 **h** 177 **i** 219 **j** 41

Ex A2.1

1 a i 1 **ii** 3 **b i** 5 **ii** 10
d No. 18 cells, only 16 poems
3 a 11 **b** % of Welsh with AB for example

Ex A2.2

1 a i cont. **ii** disc **b i** cont. **ii** disc
c i disc **ii** cont **d i** disc **ii** cont
2 a secondary **b** a survey, primary

Ex A2.3

1 a 75 **b** 63 **c** 60.1 **d** 63
2 a 71 **b** bimodal **c** 40.4 **d** 37
3 a £26 **b** bimodal **c** £84.20 **d** £87.00
4 a i £72 000 **ii** £27 000 **iii** £46 900 **iv** £34 000
b lowest price
5 Rich task

This is an investigative task and students can experiment with different spreads of data and their averages. They should be encouraged to consider whether different averages are representative by choosing data with a large spread, a small spread. It's also an opportunity to practice QWC.

Ex A2.4

1 a

```
4 | 5 8                7 | 4 means 74%
5 | 1 1 2 4 9 9
6 | 1 2 3 6 9
7 | 0 1 4 5 7 8
8 | 1 2 9
9 | 3
```

b i 48% **ii** 66%

2 a

```
2 | 6 8 9              5 | 8 means 58 mins
3 | 0 3 7 8 9
4 | 0 1 3 3 4 7 9
5 | 2 5 8 9
6 | 0 1 3 6 7 9
7 | 1 3 5 7
8 | 0 4
```

b i 58 mins **ii** 52 mins

3 a

```
0 | 3 5 6 7 8 9
1 | 0 1 2 2 5 6 7 8 9
2 | 0 1 2 4 6 7 7 9 9
3 | 1 2 3 4 5 7
4 | 0 1
```

1 | 7 means 17 mins

b i 38 mins **ii** 20.5 mins

4 a

```
3 | 2 6 7 9
4 | 2 5 7 8 9
5 | 1 2 4 6 6 6 7 8 9
6 | 0 1 3 6
7 | 0
```

4 | 5 means 45 kg

b i 38 kg **ii** 54 kg

5 a

```
14 | 6 7 9
15 | 0 0 2 2 3 4 5 5 7 8 9
16 | 0 2 3 5 7 8
17 | 1 2 2
```

16 | 0 means 160 cm

b i 26 cm **ii** 157 cm

6 a

```
 8 | 8 9
 9 | 1 2 4 8
10 | 1 3 4 5 6 7 8 8 9
11 | 0 2 4 6 6 7 7 8 9
12 | 1 5 6 7 9
13 | 1 3
```

11 | 2 means IQ score of 112

b i 45 **ii** 110

7 a

```
0 | 3 6 8 9 9
1 | 0 1 2 5 6 7 8 9
2 | 1 1 2 3 3 5 7
3 | 0 2 3
```

2 | 3 means 23 mins

b i 30 mins **ii** 18 mins

A2.5 Rich task

Mike is correct. There is a smaller range in the girls' data. Students may observe that the boys' data is grouped around the higher values on the diagram showing that they tend to spend more time on the internet. This is an opportunity for students to practice QWC in their explanation.

Ex A2.5

1 Boys' range is 4.0 secs, girls' is 4.2 secs so girls' is larger. Median for boys is 5.3 and for girls is 6.3, so on average girls have longer reaction times.

2 a Puzzle P   Puzzle Z

```
            9 8 8 6 | 0 | 8 9
9 8 7 7 4 3 2 1 0 | 1 | 1 2 4 5 6 7 7 8 9
          9 7 4 2 | 2 | 1 3 4 5 8 9
              7 1 | 3 | 2 3
```

1 | 3 | 2 means puzzle P 31, puzzle Z 32 minute

b **i** P 31, Z 25 **ii** P 2 modes, Z 17

iii P 17.5, Z 19.5 **iv** P 17, Z 18

c not much difference, but range for Z is larger and Z is more difficult because takes more time on average.

3 a class X   Class Y

```
               9 | 8  | 7
           9 8 6 | 9  | 3 7 9
     9 8 6 5 5 4 3 | 10 | 2 3 4 6 7 7 9
 8 8 7 7 6 5 5 2 0 0 | 11 | 3 4 4 4 6 8 8 8 9 9
     9 6 4 3 3 2 1 | 12 | 1 1 4 6 6 8 9
           4 1 0 | 13 | 0 1 2
```

3 | 10 | 2 means 103 for X, 102 for Y

b X and Y have same range, 45, median for Y is 116 and for X is 115 so Y have slightly higher IQ.

A2.6 Rich task

If students try calculating summary statistics they may find that the mean and median are very similar. They could use this to support Thao's argument that the recall of both groups is the same.

To argue that 15 yr olds can recall more objects than 11 yr olds, students might argue that the data for 15 yr olds is spread over higher values than the data for 11yr olds. Also the mean is higher and the total number of objects recalled is higher.

Ex A2.6

1 a i 6 **ii** 6 **iii** 5.8 **iv** 4

  b i 5 **ii** 5 **iii** 5 **iv** 4

2 a and **b** Mean greater for boys (16.2, 16.1)
Mode greater for boys (18, 15) Median 16 for both; no evidence girls have better recall.

Ex A2.7

1 a $10 < B \le 20$ **b** £24.20 **c** uses all data

  d 11, 45; 12, 46; 13, 47; 14, 48; 15, 49; 16, 50

2 a £88.00 **b** $0 < M \le 40$

  c Min value $\le$ £40; Max value = £250;
Yes, Range 200 − 40 = 160

3 Modal value and median same for both groups;
Mean = 11.5 km for teachers, 14.1 km for office workers; conclusion supported.

A2.8 Rich task

This should be a class/student discussion and answers may vary.

Ex A2.8

1 a eg. Assumes show is liked

  b eg. boxes don't cover all answers, assumes people listen, "per day" not specified.

2 Rich task

Students' answers will vary. Attention should be paid to whether they are using open or closed questions, how they are constructing the answer choice boxes, whether their questions are biased or unbiased and so on.

Exam practice

1 a Charlie **b** Charlie leaves, Ellen joins

2 a 4.13 mins **b** $4 \le m < 5$

3

	Mean	Median	Range
Girls	64.7	62	46
Boys	64	66	44

Not a great deal of difference – boys did slightly better

A3 Constructions

Check in

1 a 45° **b** 135°

2 Check construction

3 a 65.5 mm **b** 6.55 cm

Ex A3.1

1 168.2 units

2 a 23 cm **b** 38 cm **c** 46 cm

  d 162 kg **e** 177 kg **f** 189 kg

  g 640 g **h** 780 g **i** 850 g

  j 10.4°C **k** 11.9°C **l** 12.6°C

  m 3.26 l **n** 3.38 l **o** 3.42 l

  p $7\frac{1}{4}$ oz **q** $8\frac{3}{4}$ oz **r** $9\frac{1}{2}$ oz

3 a 07 : 10, 19 : 10 **b** 09.35, 21.35

4 17 : 37

5 a 1.25 kg **b** 2.65 m **c** 63.5°C

  d 36.5 t **e** 39.5 t **f** 135 volts

  g 155 volts **h** 0.605 l **i** 0.685 l

A3.2 Discussion

This is a group or class discussion and students answers may vary, encourage them to think about different contexts in which we use measures.

Ex A3.2

1 a i 6 m **ii** 8 m **iii** 14 m

  b i 18 feet **ii** 24 feet **iii** 42 feet

2 a i 8 m **ii** 6 m **iii** 8 m **iv** 20 m

  b i 20 feet **ii** 15 feet **iii** 20 feet **iv** 50 feet

3 3 km

4 1.189 m by 0.841 m

5 a i 60 cm **ii** 24 km **iii** 2.5 kg

    iv 27 L **v** 2 L

b i 3 feet   **ii** 25 miles   **iii** 18 lbs

   iv 36 pints   **v** 4 pints

6 196 lbs and 169 lbs, 27 lbs lost

7 Research

This is an opportunity to practice QWC and look at different systems of measurement.

Ex A3.3

1 AB = 11 km   YZ = 12.1 km

2 $a = 70°$ $x = 5.0$ cm $y = 5.5$ cm

   $b = 81°$ $c = 61°$ $z = 4.5$ cm

3 AB = 6.6 km   BC = 7.3 km

4 7.3 m, 62°

5 2 km

A3.4 Rich task

The answer is 36 m, students should be encouraged to practice accurate scale drawing but may also spot the shortcut that it's the side length of the equilateral triangle multiplied by three. Both approaches are equally valid but it should be emphasised that this is an opportunity to develop the ability to draw accurate constructions to scales.

Ex A3.4

1 b W   41°   56°   83°

    X   119°   32°   29°

    Y   37°   53°   90°

    Z   44°   68°   68°

   c Y is right-angled

    Z is isosceles

2 39°

3 1.2 m

4 d triangular based pyramid (tetrahedron)

5 c parallelogram   **d** 29°   29° they are the same

6 Students' own answers, paying attention to QWC.

7 Challenge

Students should be encouraged to think about how within a 9 cm equilateral triangle, there are 9 smaller triangles, each of side length 3 cm. They can use this fact to construct a central hexagon of 6 equilateral triangles with a further 6 attached to the outside edges of the hexagon. Once this has been drawn, the construction lines inside the triangle can be erased to show two overlapping equilateral triangles constructing the Star of David.

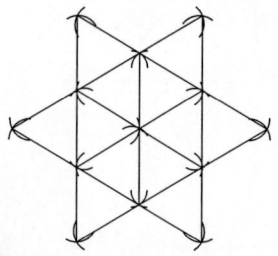

Ex A3.5

1 b

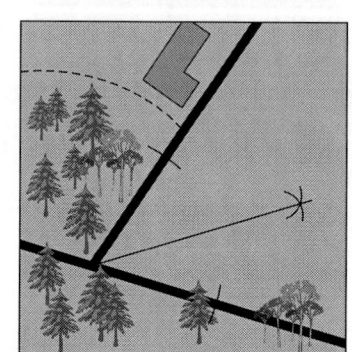

3 b

4 a

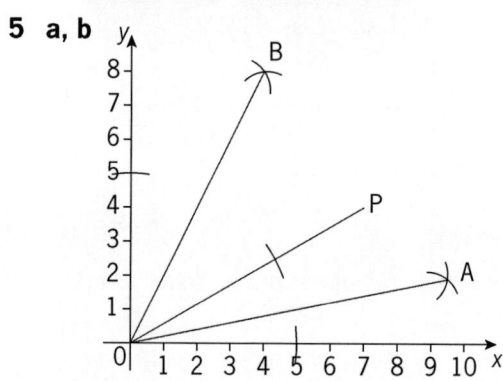

   b

5 a, b

   c 45° This is half of the angle between the x and y axes

6 5.7 m

A3.6 Rich task

Construct a perpendicular bisector of the line PQ.

Ex A3.6

1 a

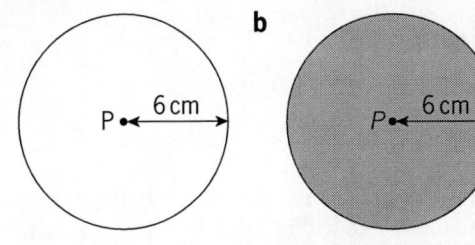

the circle

b

the area inside the circle

c

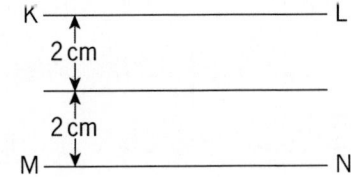

the line bisecting
the angle AOB

d

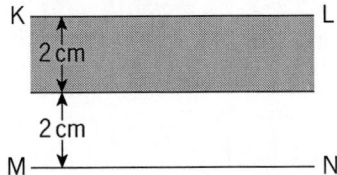

the area between the
line OA and the bisector

e

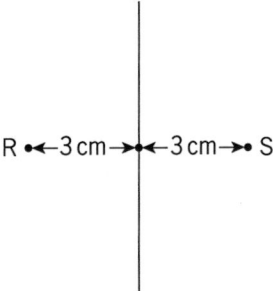

the line parallel to KL and MN and midway
between them

f

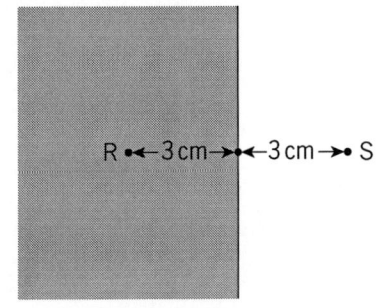

the area between the line KL and the mid-line

g

R •←3 cm→•←3 cm→• S

the perpendicular bisector of the line RS

h

R •←3 cm→•←3 cm→• S

the area on the side of the perpendicular bisector
that contains R

2

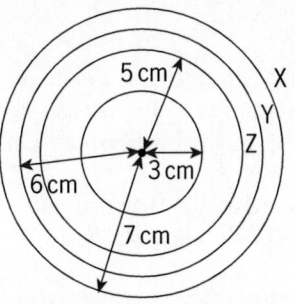

3

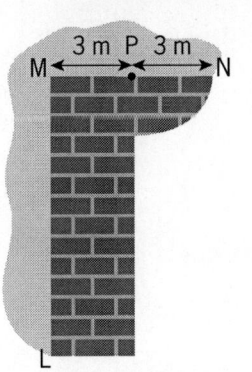

4

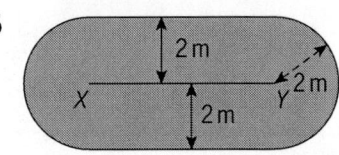

5

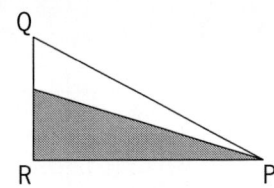

6 a

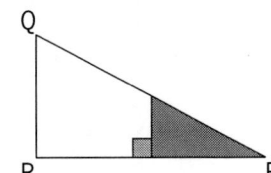

b

7

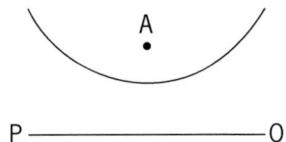

8 Challenge

This is an investigative activity, students are encouraged to think about real life examples of loci. They can use the internet to find animations which will help them to visualise loci more easily.

A hypocycloid is a curve generated by the trace of a fixed point on a small circle that moves around a larger circle.

Exam practice

1 3.4 cm, 42°, 88°

2 44 lbs

Case study 1

  a Results given to 0.01 s

  b Reaction times given to 0.001 s

  a Range = 0.76 s

  b Median = 9.93 s

  c Mean = 9.92 s

  a Men: Thompson 0.019 above limit

  b Women: Ferguson-McKenzie 0.03 above limit

Range for reaction times:

  a Men = 0.046 s

  b Women = 0.043 s

Men altered times:

Name	Nationality	Time (s)	Reaction (s)	Time with 0.1 s reaction
Bailey	ANT	9.93	0.129	9.90
Bolt	JAM	9.58	0.146	9.53
Burns	TRI	10.00	0.165	9.94
Chambers	GBR	10.00	0.123	9.98
Gay	USA	9.71	0.144	9.67
Patton	USA	10.34	0.149	10.29
Powell	JAM	9.84	0.134	9.81
Thompson	TRI	9.93	0.119	9.91

Name	Nationality	Time (s)	Reaction (s)	Time with 0.1 s reaction
Fraser	JAM	10.73	0.146	10.68
Stewart	JAM	10.75	0.170	10.68
Jeter	USA	10.90	0.160	10.84
Campbell-Brown	JAM	10.95	0.135	10.92
Williams	USA	11.01	0.158	10.95
Ferguson-McKenzie	BAH	11.05	0.130	11.02
Sturrup	BAH	11.05	0.137	11.01
Bailey	JAM	11.16	0.173	11.09

A4 Factors, multiples and ratio

Check in

1 240 miles   **2** 15 miles

A4.1 Activity

Students play the game and try to answers the questions as a result. They may need some specific guidance on some aspects.

Ex A4.1

1 a 3, 4   **b** 5, 25   **c** 3, 21, 24, 30
  d 21, 28   **e** 4, 25   **f** 3, 5, 17, 23

2 a 1, 3, 5, 15   **b** 1, 2, 3, 4, 6, 12   **c** 1, 2, 11, 22
  d 1, 5, 25   **e** 1, 2, 4, 5, 8, 10, 20, 40

3 55

4 42, 48

5 31, 37

6 a i 1, 2, 11, 22   **ii** 1, 2, 3, 6, 11, 22, 33, 66
  b 22 is factor of 66

7 a 1, 3   **b** 1, 2, 3, 6   **c** 1, 7   **d** 1, 2, 3, 6

8 a 4, 8, 12   **b** 2, 4, 6, 8, 10, 12
  c 4 is multiple of 2

9 a eg 12, 24 **b** eg 30, 60   **c** eg 21, 42   **d** eg 18, 36

10 a eg 24   **b** eg 1, 4, 16

A4.2 Activity

Students investigate prime factors by playing a game.

Ex A4.2

1 a $2^4 \times 3$ **b** 3^3 **c** 2×3^3 **d** $2^3 \times 3 \times 5$
  e $2^3 \times 3^2$ **f** $2 \times 3 \times 7^2$ **g** 7×53

2 a 504, 4 **b** 3960, 3   **c** 3384, 2
  d 196, 7 **e** 390, 5

3 a 12   **b** 48

4 The 3 factors are 1, prime number and the number itself

A4.4 Rich task

The ratio tends to 1:1.61803 – the golden ratio.

Ex A4.3

1 a 1:3 **b** 2:3 **c** 2:3 **d** 5:8   **e** 3:7

2 a 1:2.5 **b** 1:1.8 **c** 1:3.8 **d** 3.3:1   **e** 2.5:1

3 a £4.95 **b** £24.30 **c** £25.08 **d** £23.45

4 Students play a game to investigate ratios. Their answer will vary. It's an opportunity to practice QWC where they have to comment and explain.

A4.4 Rich task

Fred is 2, Marvin is 6.

Fred will be 8, Marvin will be 12.

Ex A4.4

1 a £8 : £40 **b** £56 : £8 **c** £24 : £84

d £56 : £40 **e** £60 : £120 : £240 **f** £75 : £150 : £200

2 £45.30

3 £8.40

4 93.75

5 137.5

6 680 g

7 a 6 : 5 **b** 7 : 6 **c** 6 and 3 years old

Exam practice

1 a i 24 **ii** 25 **iii** 23 **b** $2^2 \times 7$

2 45

3 a $\frac{3}{5}$ **b** 5 : 3

A5 Sequences

Check in

1 a 3 **b** 6 **c** 5 **d** 6

2 a 3 **b** 4 **c** 5 **d** 4

3 a 4, 8, 12, 16, 20, 24 **b** 3, 6, 9, 12, 15, 18

c 5, 10, 15, 20, 25, 30 **d** 6, 12, 18, 24, 30, 36

A5.1 Rich task

Students will find answers by investigating using numbers which correspond to 2^n where n is the number of hours that have elapsed.

They can then use the internet to investigate how different types of bacteria grows.

Ex A5.1

1 a 80, 75, 70, 65, 60, 55, 50 **b** 16

2 a 5, 9, 13, 17 **b** 21, 25, 29 Add 4 each time **c** 81

3 a

No. of columns	1	2	3	4	5
No. of tiles used	2	5	8	11	14

b 59. Number of tiles = Treble the number of columns and subtract 1

4 a 18, 20, 22. 48 **b** 20, 23, 26. 62

A5.2 Rich task

Aya needs 7 rods for the first section, 4 rods for the next section. This is a total of 11 rods. The term-to-term rule is start with 7 and add 4 each time.

Ex A5.2

1 a

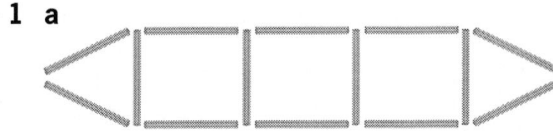

5, 8, 11, 14

b Start with 5 and add 3 each time. 17, 20, 23

2 a 3, 8, 18, 38, 78 **b** 1, 6, 21, 66, 201

c $\frac{1}{4}$, $1\frac{1}{2}$, 4, 9, 19 **d** 20, 17, 14, 11, 8

e 600, 280, 120, 40, 0 **f** 4, 4, 4, 4, 4

3 a 2, 44, 128, 296 **b** 50, 140, 320, 680

c −30, −20, 0, 40

4

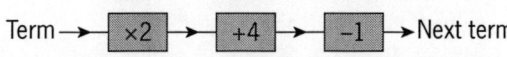

5 a Start with 8 and add 3 each time. 20, 23, 26

b Start with 30 and subtract 3 each time. 18, 15, 12

c Start with 1, then double and add 1 each time. 31, 63, 127

d Start with 3, then double and subtract 1 each time. 33, 65, 129

e Start with 1, then treble and add 1 each time. 121, 364, 1093

f Start with 10, then subtract 3 each time. −2, −5, −8

g Start with 200, then halve each time. 12.5, 6.25, 3.125

h Start with $\frac{1}{2}$, then double and add 2 each time. 38, 78, 158

i Start with −7 and add 3 each time. 5, 8, 11

6 5, 11, 23, 47, 95

A5.3 Rich task

Students look at Hayley's method for finding a position to term rule. The values in the table for the 4th position are 12 and 11.

Hayley is correct in saying the 100th position will use 299 tiles.

Ex A5.3

1 a 4

b

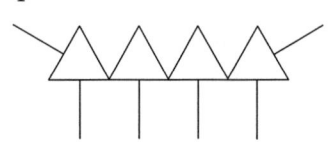

c Start with 6 and add 4 each time

d

Position	1	2	3	4	5
4 × table	4	8	12	16	20
Term	6	10	14	18	22

Multiply position by 4 and add 2

e 202

2 a ii Multiply the position by 4 and subtract 1.

iii 23, 27, 399

b ii Multiply the position by 3 and add 1.

iii 19, 22, 301

c **ii** Multiply the position by 2 and subtract 1.

  iii 11, 13, 199

d **ii** Multiply the position by 4 and add 1.

  iii 25, 29, 401

e **ii** Multiply the position by 5 and subtract 2.

  iii 28, 33, 498

f **ii** Multiply the position by 6 and add 1.

  iii 37, 43, 601

g **ii** Multiply the position by $\frac{1}{2}$ and add 3.

  iii $6, 6\frac{1}{2}, 53$

h **ii** Multiply the position by −2 and add 8.

  iii −4, −6, −192

3 **a** 19, 37, 301   **b** $5, 9\frac{1}{2}, 77$

4 **a** 00139   **b** 00243

5 Multiply the position by 3 and add 12, 102 mm

6 Because it turns 6 revolutions every minute.

Multiply the position by 6 and add 325, 685

A5.4 Rich task

$3n + 1$

Ex A5.4

1 **a** 4

b

Position	1	2	3	4	5	.....	n
4 × table	4	8	12	16	20		4n
Term	3	7	11	15	19		4n−1

c $4n - 1$ **d** 23, 199

2 **a** $2n + 1, 201$ **b** $3n + 1, 301$

c $4n, 400$ **d** $4n + 1, 401$

3 **a** Multiply the position by 2 and add 5.

  $T(n) = 2n + 5, 17, 85$

b Multiply the position by 3 and subtract 1.

  $T(n) = 3n - 1, 17, 119$

c Multiply the position by 1 and add 4.

  $T(n) = n + 4, 10, 44$

d Multiply the position by 5 and subtract 2.

  $T(n) = 5n - 2, 28, 198$

e Multiply the position by 6 and add 1.

  $T(n) = 6n + 1, 37, 241$

f Multiply the position by 5 and add 1.

  $T(n) = 5n + 1, 31, 201$

g Multiply the position by 4 and subtract 5.

  $T(n) = 4n - 5, 19, 155$

h Multiply the position by 7 and add 3.

  $T(n) = 7n + 3, 45, 283$

i Multiply the position by 3 and subtract 7.

  $T(n) = 3n - 7, 11, 113$

j Multiply the position by −2 and add 10.

  $T(n) = -2n + 10, -2, -70$

4 **a** 21 31 501   **b** 32 62 1002

  c 15 23 399   **d** 29 45 797

5 4 6 8 10 12. 19

Ex A5.5

1 **a** **i** 10 12 14 16 18

  ii 6 4 2 0 −2

  iii The first sequence is increasing, the second sequence is decreasing.

b **i** 11 13 15 17 19

  ii 7 5 3 1 −1

  iii The first sequence is increasing, the second sequence is decreasing.

c $T(n) = 2n + 5$ **d** 0 2 4 6 8

  It starts with zero and increases by 2 metres each time.

2 **a** 1 4 9 16 25 36   **b** $T(n) = n^2$

  c **i** 81   **ii** 144   **iii** 400   **d** 8

3 **a** 1 3 6 10

b $T(1) = 1$

  $T(2) = 1 + 2 = 3$

  $T(3) = 1 + 2 + 3 = 6$

  $T(4) = 1 + 2 + 3 + 4 = 10$

  $T(5) = 1 + 2 + 3 + 4 + 5 = 15$

c $T(1) = \frac{1}{2} \times 1 \times (1 + 1) = 1$

  $T(2) = \frac{1}{2} \times 2 \times (2 + 1) = 3$

  $T(3) = \frac{1}{2} \times 3 \times (3 + 1) = 6$

  $T(4) = \frac{1}{2} \times 4 \times (4 + 1) = 10$

  $T(5) = \frac{1}{2} \times 5 \times (5 + 1) = 15$

d $T(6) = \frac{1}{2} \times 6 \times (6 + 1) = 21$

  $T(6) = 1 + 2 + 3 + 4 + 5 + 6 = 21$

4 **a** **i** 1   **b** 3   **c** 6

  5 people = 10 handshakes, 6 people = 15 handshakes.
  It is the same sequence of triangle numbers.
  4950 handshakes for 100 people.

5 Using the second method, Sue would get

10p + 20p + 40p + 80p + 160p + 320p + 640p = £12.70 per week.

Sue should opt for this method.

Exam practice

1 a 16, 19 **b** double previous term **c** 2, 5, 10

2 a i 21 **ii** 61 **b** 4n – 3

3 10 more minutes

A6 Representing and interpreting data

Check In

1 a 4, 5.5, 6.5, 7, 8 **b** 2.3, 2.4, 3.2, 3.4, 4.2, 4.3

c 7.5, 7.9, 8.3, 8.6, 9.1

2 a 6, 6, 7, 8, 8, 9, 9, 9, 9, 9

b 100, 100, 101, 102, 102, 104, 104, 104, 104, 104

A6.1 Activity

China won the most gold medals.
The USA won the most silver and bronze medals.
The USA won the most medals overall.

Rich task

Students might consider using total number of medals won or some kind of points system. Encourage students to discuss answers.

Ex A6.1

1 Bar chart

2 a Bar chart

b Higher proportion of girls recalled the Rabbit first recall similar otherwise.

3 eg. most popular; total number sold; preferences by gender

4 a i car **ii** microwave

Ex A6.2

1 Histogram

2 a Histograms **b** $15 \leq t < 20$ $20 \leq t < 25$

c $15 \leq t < 20$ $15 \leq t < 20$

d eg. boys quicker – modal class

3 eg range is same, modal class on patio is $12 < m \leq 16$, but greenhouse is $4 < m \leq 8$ so weights larger on patio.

A6.3 Activity

Elastic band.

Ex A6.3

1 Pie chart

2 a pie chart **b i** England **ii** 54%

3 a 6.5 million tonnes **b** 21.6°

A6.4 Rich task

Students answers may vary but ought to include the fact that the largest segment of the girls' pie chart is a higher earning one.

Ex A6.4

1 a baths, showers, hand-washing

b 4100 megalitres

2 a leisure, recreation, holidays **b** rail

c no connection between the sets of data.

3 pie charts

Ex A6.5

1 a polygon **b i** $20 < t \leq 30$ $30 < t \leq 40$

ii 50 mins, 50 mins

c office workers take longer

2 a polygon **b i** $40 < m \leq 60, 40 < m \leq 60$,

ii 100 miles, 80 miles

c eg smaller range in Jan because no short journeys

3 a polygons

b eg modal class D $0 < t \leq 5$, P $5 < t \leq 10$; range same for both, median in class $10 < t \leq 15$ for both; Powerblast better buy because of shape of distribution and modal class.

4 eg 2002–2003 may have range 67, and median in class 50–60, so could be $52\frac{1}{2}$

5 eg higher proportion of 40 – 60 year olds, the highest spending group, on weekdays, so more money spent per person on weekday.

Exam practice

1 a i 9 **ii** –6 **b i** 7 **ii** –3

c i –10 **ii** 10

2 a 15 **b** £0–£10

c Because we do not know the exact amount spent

3 a polygon

b the modal class for both months is 5–10 mins. The range is larger for August than July.

Case study: Sandwich shop

Day	Number of Customers	
	Week 1	Week 2
Monday	50	54
Tuesday	68	60
Wednesday	47	53
Thursday	58	57
Friday	52	56
Saturday	76	70
TOTAL	351	350

a Busiest day: first Saturday

b Range = 76 – 47 = 29

Variety	Mon	Tues	Weds	Thurs	Fri	Sat	Total	Average
Ham	14	16	13	14	17	18	92	15
Cheese	9	11	12	10	8	12	62	10
Hummus	6	5	7	4	6	8	36	6
Tuna	7	6	6	8	6	9	42	7
Chicken	18	22	15	21	19	23	118	20
Total	54	60	53	57	56	70	350	58

Product	Stock (packs)	Portions per pack	Portions left	Stock needed	Amount to order
Bread	6	20	120	18	12
Ham	2.5	10	25	10	8
Cheese	3	10	30	7	4
Hummus	2	14	28	3	1
Tuna	1.5	8	12	6	5
Chicken	1	10	10	12	11

Estimate of stock left on Wednesday morning:

Bread 4
Ham −5 (will have none left)
Cheese 10
Hummus 16
Tuna −2 (will have none left)
Chicken −30 (will have none left)

A7 Formulae and equations

Check in

1 16 cm

2 a x **b** m **c** $3n$ **d** $2p$

A7.1 Activity

You subtract 7 from both sides.

The solution is $x = 2$

Activity 2

You substitute 2 for A and 1 for C.

$P = ((21 \times 2) + (8 \times 1))/2 = 50/2 = 25$

Ex A7.1

1 a formula   **b** equation   **c** expression

2 a 14   **b** 2   **c** 14

3 a formula   **b** equation   **c** expression

4 a formula   **b** expression   **c** equation

5 a i 16   **ii** 5

 b i 2   **ii** 5

 c i $5x + 3$ **ii** $5x - 1$

Ex A7.2

1 $4x + 5y$

2 a $6x + 8y$ **b** $8x + 8x^2$ **c** $4x + 3y$

 d $x^2 + 8$ **e** $8m + 2n$ **f** $6p + 2q + 7$

g $6a - 2b + 9$ **h** $9x^2 + 8x + 7$

3 a $6x + 10$ **b** $10x + 20$ **c** $18y - 12$

 d $8z - 12$ **e** $15 + 20a$ **f** $10 - 6c$

 g $2a + 10b$ **h** $8x - 12y$ **i** $18a - 6b + 3c$

 j $12 + 6x^2$ **k** $15y^2 + 10y$ **l** $4 + 8x + 12x^2$

4 a $23x + 12$ **b** $18x + 10$ **c** $9p + 4$

 d $18q + 8$ **e** $13m + 3$ **f** $19n$

5 a $2(3x + 4)$ **b** $3(3x + 2)$ **c** $4(2x + 3)$

 d $5(x + 2)$ **e** $3(x + 3)$ **f** $6(x - 3)$

 g $4(3y + 2)$ **h** $5(3a - 2)$ **i** $2(2z - 1)$

 j $2(4c + 3d)$ **k** $5(2x + 3y)$ **l** $3(3s - 2t)$

6 a $5(2x + 3)$ **b** $4(2y + 3)$ **c** $16(z + 1)$

 d $4(2p + q)$ **e** $3(3a + 2b)$ **f** $2(4s + t)$

 g $8(1 + m)$ **h** $6(3c - 1)$ **i** $7(2 + z)$

7 3 ways using whole numbers. If fractions are used there are an infinite number of ways.

8 Length could be $(12x + 24)$, $(6x + 12)$, $(4x + 8)$, $(3x + 6)$, $(2x + 4)$, or $(x + 2)$ with corresponding widths 1, 2, 3, 4, 6, and 12

9 $4x + 3y$.

 The different lengths are:

$3x + 3y$	$2x + 3y$	$x + 3y$	$3y$
$4x + 2y$	$3x + 2y$	$2x + 2y$	$x + 2y$ $2y$
$4x + y$	$3x + y$	$2x + y$	$x + y$ y
$4x$	$3x$	$2x$	x

A7.3 Activity

$I^2 = 25$
$10 \times 25 = 250$
$E = 250$

Ex A7.3

1 a £22   **b** £31

2 a £636   **b** £1237.75

3 a X   41.5 mpg
    Y   38.8 mpg
    Z   39.9 mpg

 b Z likely to be more accurate as it uses a longer distance and therefore is likely to be based on more varied driving conditions. Yes, the journeys are consecutive so you could use the total mileage and the total fuel used to get a more accurate result.

4 a 42   **b** 30   **c** 19.6   **d** 9.4

5 a 18   **b** 11   **c** 8.4   **d** −2

6 a 48   **b** 10   **c** 37.5

7 25.5

A7.4 Rich task

$P = 12 + 16 + 10 + 2x + 4$
This simplifies to $P = 2x + 42$
If $P = 50$, $x = 4$

Ex A7.4

1 a 2   **b** 1.5   **c** 4
   d 5.5   **e** 4   **f** 10

2 a 2   **b** 6   **c** 5   **d** 4
   e 10   **f** 7   **g** 4   **h** 4

3 a 5   **b** 4   **c** 32   **d** 4.56

4 $x = 20$, $q = 56$, $a = 5\frac{2}{3}$

A7.5 Rich task

Students explore the area of the shape. They will find that if $x = 5$ then the four squares will meet in the middle.

Ex A7.5

1 a $n = x + 1$

   b 5   Yes, if you like strong tea

2 a Area $= 20 + 2x$ cm²   **b** Area $= 8 + 6x$ cm²
   c Area $= 10 + 7x$ cm²   **d** Area $= 24 + 5x$ cm²

3 a 45910   **b** $45670 + 50x$

4 a 8 hours   **b** $5 + x$ hours

5 $100 \times$ integer + my age

A7.6 Rich task

$3x + 8 = 50$

$x = 14$, $14 < 15$, therefore the Smith's luggage is allowed on the plane.

Ex A7.6

1 a 5   **b** 13   **c** 5   **d** 20
   e 1   **f** 5   **g** 6   **h** 8
   i −3   **j** 15   **k** 3   **l** 4

2 a 4   **b** $\frac{1}{2}$

3 a 2   **b** 5   **c** 1   **d** 3
   e 9   **f** $1\frac{1}{2}$ **g** $1\frac{1}{4}$ **h** 0
   i 4   **j** $\frac{1}{2}$ **k** $\frac{1}{2}$ **l** $16\frac{1}{2}$

4 7

5 a 9   **b** 7

6 12 years old

7 $x = 13$
   $y = 12$

A7.7 Rich task

A brick weighs a kilo.

Ex A7.7

1 a 2   **b** 1   **c** 4   **d** 3   **e** 1
   f 3   **g** 2   **h** 4   **i** 4   **j** 6
   k $\frac{1}{2}$ **l** $1\frac{1}{4}$

2 a 2   **b** 1   **c** 0   **d** 3   **e** 2
   f 3   **g** 1   **h** 0   **i** 10   **j** 4

3 a 5   **b** $3\frac{1}{2}$ **c** $1\frac{1}{2}$ **d** $2\frac{1}{3}$ **e** 3
   f 6   **g** 9   **h** 3   **i** 2   **j** $1\frac{1}{4}$
   k $3\frac{1}{2}$ **l** $1\frac{1}{4}$ **m** $2\frac{1}{2}$ **n** $2\frac{2}{3}$ **o** $6\frac{1}{2}$
   p 2   **q** 1   **r** 5

4 $3(x - 4) = 24$
   $x = 12$

5 $30x + 40 = 220$
   £6 an hour

6 $2(x - 12) - 10 = 16$
   $x = 25$
   £13

7 B $2x + 6$
   C $x + 8$
   $2x + 6 + x + 8 = x + 100$
   $x = 43$

A7.8 Activity 1

$11 - 4x = 2$

$9 = 4x$

$\frac{9}{4} = x$

$= 2\frac{1}{4}$

Activity 2

$2(4x + 3) - 3(x - 5) = 36$

$8x + 6 - 3x + 15 = 36$

$5x + 21 = 36$

$5x = 15$

$x = 3$

Activity 3

$8 = \frac{x}{3}$

$x = 24$

Activity 4

$3 = \frac{12}{x}$

$3x = 12$

$x = 4$

Ex A7.8

1 a 20   **b** 15   **c** 16   **d** 30
   e 7   **f** 3   **g** 5   **h** 5
   i 4   **j** 6   **k** 4   **l** 2

2 a 3   **b** 4   **c** 6   **d** $1\frac{1}{2}$
   e $\frac{1}{2}$ **f** $1\frac{1}{4}$ **g** 3   **h** $3\frac{1}{3}$
   i 3   **j** 4   **k** $3\frac{1}{2}$ **l** $2\frac{1}{4}$
   m −2   **n** −2   **o** −1   **p** −3
   q $-1\frac{1}{2}$ **r** −7   **s** $-1\frac{1}{4}$ **t** $-1\frac{1}{3}$

3 a 2 **b** 1 **c** 3 **d** 5 **e** 1
  f 2 **g** 4 **h** 2 **i** −2 **j** −3
4 a 3 **b** −1 **c** 5 **d** −2
  e $1\frac{1}{2}$ **f** −3 **g** $\frac{1}{2}$ **h** $1\frac{1}{4}$
  i $\frac{1}{4}$ **j** 0 **k** $1\frac{1}{2}$ **l** $-1\frac{1}{4}$
5 £40
6 16 years old

Ex A7.9

1 a (2, 3) **b** (3, −2) **c** (−3, 2)
  d (−4, −3) **e** (−3, −5) **f** Post Office
  g Rail bridge over road **h** Crossroads **i** School
2 a Yes **b** Yes
  c i (2, 4) **ii** (5, 7) **d** S(3, 2.5) T(6.5, 3)
3 a (10, 10) **b** (4, 9)
4 (30, 25) (30, 25) It is a parallelogram
5 a (14, 14) **b** (16, 9) A quarter of the total length

Exam practice

1 a $3a + 4b$ **b i** $5(x − 3)$ **ii** $x(x + 4)$ **c** $4\frac{3}{5}$
2 $b = \frac{4}{5}(e − 32)$
3 a No
  since $3 + 2 \neq 3$
  b $2n − 3$

A8 Bearings and Pythagoras

Check in

1 a 180° **b** 180° **c** 360°
2 a 50° **b** 70°

Ex A8.1

1 a i 035° **ii** 130° **iii** 207°
  iv 225° **v** 035° **vi** 0°
  b i 067° **ii** 247° **c** 15 km
  d i 57 km **ii** 69 km **iii** 33 km **iv** 73 km
2 a 180° **b** 045° **c** 225°
3 a 33 m **b** 14 m
4 a 24 km **b** 51 km
5 a 49 km **b** 70 km
6 a Drogheda to Douglas: bearing 066°, distance 140 km
  Douglas to Heysham: bearing 097°, distance 110 km
  b 260°
7 95 m
8 150°, 240° 330°, just over 1 hour
9 a 500 km **b** 2500 km **c** 3200 km

A8.2 Rich task

Number of tiles inside

Pattern	A small square	The other small square	The large square
A	2	2	4
B	8	8	16
C	4	4	8
D	16	16	32

Students should notice that the total number of tiles in the small squares is the same as the number of tiles in the large square

Activity

Students should find that X and Y should fit together inside square Z.

They should conclude from this that the area of X plus the area of Y equals the area of Z. This ought to lead them into thinking about Pythagoras' theorem

Ex A8.2

1 a $p = 5$ cm **b** $q = 13$ cm **c** $c = 10$ cm
  d $r = 6.4$ cm **e** $s = 7.8$ cm **f** $t = 7.3$ cm
2 6.8 m
3 5.57 m
4 6.5 miles
5 2.28 km
6 Jim's error is in his first line as $x^2 = 3^2 + 5^2$
  Jan's error is in her last line as $x = \sqrt{34} = 5.83$ cm

Ex A8.3

1 a $w = 9.2$ cm **b** $x = 8.7$ cm
  c $y = 9.4$ cm **d** $z = 9$ cm
2 a $p = 12$ cm **b** $q = 6$ cm
  c $r = 4.9$ cm **d** $s = 7$ cm
3 3.04 m
4 1.4 km
5 21 m

Exam practice

1 9.49 cm
2 a 110 km, 100° **b** 170 km, 71° **c** 95 km, 246°
3 31

B9 Fractions, decimals and percentages

Check in

1 0.1, $\frac{1}{4}$, $\frac{1}{2}$ = 0.5, 23% = $\frac{23}{100}$
2 a 0.375 **b** 0.8$\dot{3}$

Ex B9.1

1 a $\frac{2}{3}$ b $\frac{1}{3}$ c $\frac{3}{8}$ d $\frac{3}{5}$ e $\frac{2}{3}$ f $\frac{5}{7}$

2 a $\frac{1}{4}$ b $\frac{1}{3}$ c $\frac{3}{5}$

3 a $\frac{3}{8}$ b $\frac{2}{3}$ c $\frac{2}{5}$

4 $\frac{9}{30} = \frac{3}{10}$

5 $\frac{30}{40}, \frac{6}{8}, \frac{9}{12}$

6 a $\frac{1}{9}$ $\frac{1}{4}$ $\frac{1}{3}$ $\frac{1}{2}$ b $\frac{2}{7}$ $\frac{4}{7}$ $\frac{5}{7}$

  c $\frac{3}{8}$ $\frac{1}{2}$ $\frac{5}{6}$ d $\frac{2}{3}$ $\frac{3}{4}$ $\frac{5}{6}$

7 $\frac{21}{40}$

Ex B9.2

1 a 25% b 60%

2 0.5 50%, $\frac{1}{4}$ 25%, $\frac{3}{4}$ 0.75, $\frac{1}{10}$ 0.1, 0.2 20%, $\frac{7}{10}$ 70%, $\frac{23}{100}$ 0.23, 0.6 60%

3 a $\frac{1}{4}$ 40% 0.7 b 40% 0.45 $\frac{4}{5}$

  c 0.09 15% $\frac{2}{5}$ d 7% $\frac{11}{20}$ 0.6

4 0.625 62.5%

5 $\frac{2}{5}$

6 15%

7 a 45% b 80%

8 32%

9 60%

Ex B9.3

1 a 0.205 0.3 0.43 0.61 b 0.205 0.701 0.84 0.9

  c 0.405 0.41 0.415 0.45 d 0.809 0.89 0.908 0.98

  e 0.2 0.205 0.25 0.5 0.52

2 a 9.3 b 10.44 c 9.49 d 9.25

  e 4.2 f 22.89 g 141.65 h 15.14

3 a 4.3 b 11.2 c 27.7 d 3.2

  e 1.5 f 3.4 g 2.45 h 4.74

4 a 0.06 b 0.48 c 1.15 d 0.48

  e 0.6 f 0.72 g 0.126 h 0.345

5 a 3 b 52 c 200 d 72.8

  e 32 f 272.5 g 100 h 49

6 a 0.2, 0.25 b $2 \div 0.2 = 10$

7 c 19.38

B9.4 Activity

Students play game, outcomes will vary.

Ex B9.4

1 a 53 b 21 c 8 d 22.5

  e 4.2 f 50 g 5 h 3.2

2 a 18 b 800 c 10.8 d 25.5

  e 8.4 f 50 g 20 h 3

3 a 67.2 b 45 c 66 d 10.4

  e 1.26 f 98 g 60 h 28.8

4 25% of 60

5 50% of 30

6 25

7 a 400 b 350

B9.5 Activity

a six squares b 4 squares c 2 squares

Ex B9.5

1 a £22.50 b £21 c £10 d £16

2 a $\frac{4}{5}$ b $\frac{1}{2}$

3 a $\frac{1}{2}$ b $\frac{11}{16}$ c $\frac{27}{70}$ d $\frac{59}{60}$

4 a $\frac{1}{4}$ b $\frac{16}{27}$ c $\frac{1}{10}$ d $\frac{5}{12}$

Ex B9.6

1 a $\frac{1}{6}$ b $\frac{3}{35}$ c $\frac{24}{35}$ d $\frac{1}{6}$

2 a $\frac{1}{10}$ b $\frac{1}{4}$ c $\frac{3}{20}$ d $\frac{3}{20}$

  e $\frac{2}{5}$ f $\frac{8}{9}$ g $\frac{15}{16}$ h $\frac{3}{4}$

3 a i $\frac{1}{10}, \frac{3}{8}$ ii $\frac{1}{2}, \frac{2}{5}, \frac{1}{10}$

  b i $\frac{1}{5}, \frac{2}{7}$ ii $\frac{1}{2}, \frac{1}{5}, \frac{3}{10}$

Ex B9.7

1 a $1\frac{3}{5}$ b $7\frac{1}{2}$ c $7\frac{1}{2}$ d $\frac{3}{4}$

  e $9\frac{1}{6}$ f $2\frac{2}{3}$ g $12\frac{1}{2}$ h $\frac{6}{7}$

2 6 cans

3 a 5 b 6 c 13

4 a $3\frac{31}{40}$ b $11\frac{3}{4}$ c $8\frac{1}{12}$ d $5\frac{2}{5}$

  e $2\frac{5}{26}$ f $1\frac{13}{20}$ g $-\frac{5}{12}$ h $-\frac{11}{12}$

B9.8 Rich task

Students may notice that all of these fractions convert to recurring decimals.

Ex B9.8

1 a $0.\dot{1}$ $0.\dot{2}$ $0.\dot{3}$ $0.\dot{4}$ $0.\dot{5}$ $0.\dot{6}$ $0.\dot{7}$ $0.\dot{8}$

  b All digits the same as numerator

2 3.14, π

3 a i 0.1$\dot{6}$ **ii** 0.8$\dot{3}$

 b i 0.167 **ii** 0.833

4 a i 4 **ii** 3.996 **iii** 3.6

 b i 0.333 **ii** 0.3

Exam practice

1 a 13 **b** £80

2 $\frac{7}{30}$

3 a i $\frac{1}{8}$ **ii** $\frac{5}{8}$

 b i 0.125 **ii** 0.625

Business

Original table:

	January (£)	February (£)	March (£)
Quantity of standard	22	28	25
TOTAL INCOME	56.10	71.40	63.75
Materials used	6.60	8.40	7.50
Wages	22.00	28.00	25.00
Craft fair fees	10.00	10.00	10.00
Advertising	5.00	5.00	5.00
TOTAL EXPENDITURE	43.60	51.40	47.50
NET CASH SURPLUS/ DEFICIT	12.50	20.00	16.25
CASH BALANCE BROUGHT FORWARD	–	12.50	32.50
CASH BALANCE TO CARRY FORWARD	12.50	32.50	48.75

Fee fairs £15:

	January (£)	February (£)	March (£)
Quantity of standard	22	28	25
TOTAL INCOME	56.10	71.40	63.75
Materials used	6.60	8.40	7.50
Wages	22.00	28.00	25.00
Craft fair fees	15.00	15.00	15.00
Advertising	5.00	5.00	5.00
TOTAL EXPENDITURE	48.60	56.40	52.50
NET CASH SURPLUS/ DEFICIT	7.50	15.00	11.25
CASH BALANCE BROUGHT FORWARD	–	7.50	22.50
CASH BALANCE TO CARRY FORWARD	7.50	22.50	33.75

Materials £0.40:

	January (£)	February (£)	March (£)
Quantity of standard	22	28	25
TOTAL INCOME	56.10	71.40	63.75
Materials used	8.80	11.20	10.00
Wages	22.00	28.00	25.00
Craft fair fees	10.00	10.00	10.00
Advertising	5.00	5.00	5.00
TOTAL EXPENDITURE	45.80	54.20	50.00
NET CASH SURPLUS/ DEFICIT	10.30	17.20	13.75
CASH BALANCE BROUGHT FORWARD	–	10.30	27.50
CASH BALANCE TO CARRY FORWARD	10.30	27.50	41.25

Selling price £2.75:

	January (£)	February (£)	March (£)
Quantity of standard	22	28	25
TOTAL INCOME	60.50	77.00	68.75
Materials used	6.60	8.40	7.50
Wages	22.00	28.00	25.00
Craft fair fees	10.00	10.00	10.00
Advertising	5.00	5.00	5.00
TOTAL EXPENDITURE	43.60	51.40	47.50
NET CASH SURPLUS/ DEFICIT	16.90	25.60	21.25
CASH BALANCE BROUGHT FORWARD	–	16.90	42.50
CASH BALANCE TO CARRY FORWARD	16.90	42.50	63.75

Data for breakeven charts

Original:

Number of cards	Fixed cost	Total cost	Revenue
0	15	15.00	0.00
5	15	21.50	12.75
10	15	28.00	25.50
15	15	34.50	38.25
20	15	41.00	51.00
25	15	47.50	63.75
30	15	54.00	76.50

Fair fees £15:

Number of cards	Fixed cost	Total cost	Revenue
0	20	20.00	0.00
5	20	26.50	12.75
10	20	33.00	25.50
15	20	39.50	38.25
20	20	46.00	51.00
25	20	52.50	63.75
30	20	59.00	76.50

Materials £0.40:

Number of cards	Fixed cost	Total cost	Revenue
0	15	15.00	0.00
5	15	22.00	12.75
10	15	29.00	25.50
15	15	36.00	38.25
20	15	43.00	51.00
25	15	50.00	63.75
30	15	57.00	76.50

Selling price £2.75:

Number of cards	Fixed cost	Total cost	Revenue
0	15	15.00	0.00
5	15	21.50	13.75
10	15	28.00	27.50
15	15	34.50	41.25
20	15	41.00	55.00
25	15	47.50	68.75
30	15	54.00	82.50

B10 Circles, angles and lines

Check in

1 a Diameter **b** Circumference **c** Radius
2 $360°$

Ex B10.1

1 a semicircle **b** quadrant
2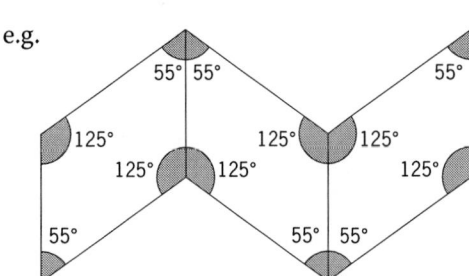
   AX = BX. Symmetry about the line joining X to the centre of the circle.

3
   $90°$, yes

4 Cone, yes
5 a i 2   ii 4   iii 7   iv 11
6 They are all prehistoric constructions based on circles and connected with the movement of the sun. Stonehenge is another famous example.

Ex B10.2

1 a acute $20°$ **b** right-angle $90°$
   c acute $60°$ **d** obtuse $140°$
   e Straight line $180°$ **f** reflex $220°$
2 p right-angle $90°$ **q** acute $70°$
   r right-angle $90°$ **s** obtuse $110°$

---

   t acute $20°$ **u** reflex $210°$
   v acute $20°$ **w** obtuse $110°$
3 a obtuse $180°$ **b** right-angle $90°$
   c reflex $270°$ **d** obtuse $135°$
4 a $x = 70°$ **b** $y = 160°$ **c** $z = 130°$
   d $u = 180°$ **e** $v = 80°$ **f** $w = 100°$
5 $120°$
6 4 angles $72°$ $144°$ $216°$ $288°$

Ex B10.3

1 a $50°$ **b** $100°$ **c** $55°$
   d $110°$ **e** $70°$ **f** $70°$
   g $30°$ **h** $150°$ **i** $150°$
2 p $45°$ **q** $25°$ **r** $125°$ **s** $55°$
   t $60°$ **u** $40°$ **v** $70°$ **w** $60°$
   x $120°$ **y** $80°$
3 p $50°$ **q** $130°$ **r** $90°$
   s $130°$ **t** $200°$ **u** $220°$

Ex B10.4

2 a $a = 50°$ $b = c = 130°$ **b** $d = 120°$ $e = f = 60°$
   c $h = 70°$ $g = i = 110°$ **d** $l = 65°$ $j = k = 115°$
3 $a = 120°$ $b = c = 60°$ $d = e = f = 110°$
   $g = h = 70°$ $i = 120°$ $j = 50°$ $k = 130°$
4 $a = 120°$ $b = 140°$ $c = 60°$ $d = 130°$
   $e = 50°$ $f = 125°$ $g = 55°$
   $h = j = 120°$ $i = 60°$ $k = l = 70°$
   $m = n = 50°$ $p = q = 65°$ $r = s = 115°$
5 $p = 135°$
   $q = 45°$
6 $x = 145°$
   $y = z = 35°$
7 $p = q = t = 125°$
   $r = s = u = 55°$
8 e.g.

9 $y = 180° - x$

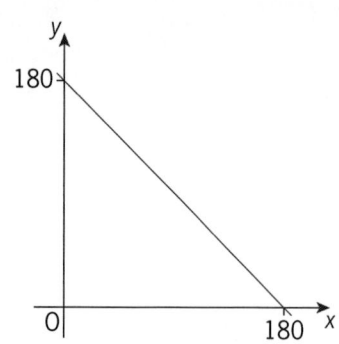

Closed when
$x = 0$ or 180
$y = 180$ or 0

Ex B10.5

1 $a = 35°$

2 $m = 20°$ $n = 20°$ $p = 70°$ $q = 70°$

3 $e = 20°$ $f = 80°$ $g = 20°$

4 $x = 50°$

5 $v = 60°$

6 $x = y = 38°$

7 $u = 30°$ $v = 60°$ $w = 60°$

8 $a = 60°$ $b = 30°$

9 $c = 90°$

10 $43\frac{1}{3}°$

11 $24°$ $48°$ $96°$ $192°$

Ex B10.6

1

Regular polygon	Number of sides	Each interior angle	Each exterior angle	Sum of all interior angles
Triangle	3	60°	120°	180°
Quadrilateral	4	90°	90°	360°
Pentagon	5	108°	72°	540°
Hexagon	6	120°	60°	720°
Octagon	8	135°	45°	1080°
Decagon	10	144°	36°	1440°

2 a $a = 120°$ $b = 60°$ $c = 60°$

   b $x = 140°$ $y = 110°$ $z = 40°$

   c $s = 30°$ $t = 120°$ $u = 150°$

3 a $103°$, $103°$, $103°$, $132°$, $93°$, $186°$

   b $102°$, $102°$, $112°$, $112°$, $112°$

4 $40°$, $40°$, $40°$, $30°$, $30°$

Exam practice

1 No, because $66° + 71° + 53° \neq 180°$

2 $x = 24°$
   $y = 48°$

3 $102°$

B11 Straight lines and inequalities

Check in

1 a 6   **b** 11   **c** 9   **d** 6

2 a $3x + 3$ **b** $2x - 2$ **c** $8x + 12$ **d** $12x - 6$

3 a 4   **b** 6

4 a $4(x + 2)$ **b** $3(y + 6)$ **c** $3(y - 3)$

B11.1 Activity

Students should see the equivalence between the formula and flow diagram.

By substituting zero into the formula, they find the temperature at which water freezes in Fahrenheit. By substituting 100°C into the formula, they find that water boils at 212°F.

Ex B11.1

1

No. of seconds, x	5	10	15	20	25	30
No. of miles away, y	1	2	3	4	5	6

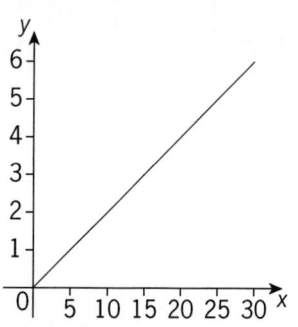

2

No. of hours, x	1	2	3	4	5
Cost, $£C$	6	8	10	12	14

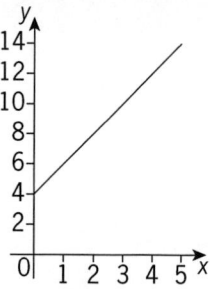

   a 3.5 hrs

   b 8.5 hrs

3

x, miles	50	100	200	300
C, £	21	22	24	26

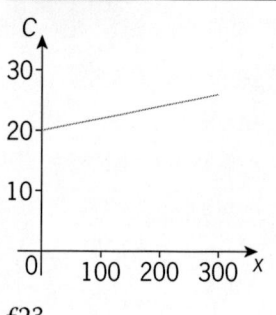

£23

4 For example:

a, age in years	0	4	8	12	16
h, no. of hours sleep required	17	15	13	11	9

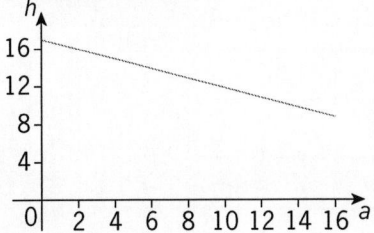

5 For example:

h, height in cms	160	170	180	190	200
m, mass in kg	54	63	72	81	90

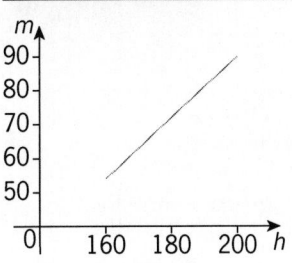

B11.2 Activity

If $x = 60$, $y = 120$

The values are correct because they all add up to $180°$

x cannot have values greater than 180, because $x + y = 180$.
This would be the equivalent of the windscreen wiper going off the windscreen!

Ex B11.2

1 a

Length of sides, *x*	5	6	7	8	9	10
Length of edging, *y*	20	24	28	32	36	40

b

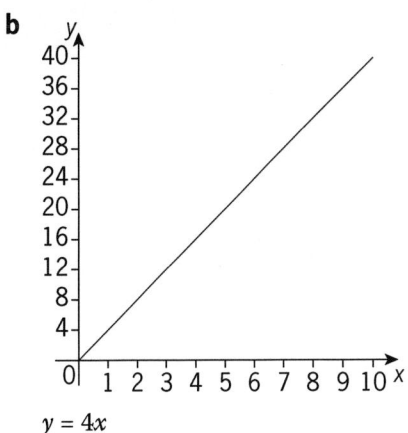

$y = 4x$

c 100 m

2 a

Amount used, *x* litres	0	10	20	30	40
Amount left in tank, *y* litres	40	30	20	10	0

b

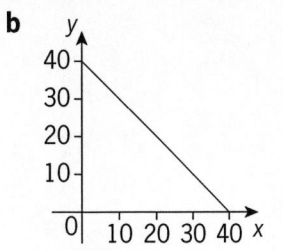

$y = 40 - x$

c 5, 420 miles

3 a

Length of journey, *x* km	1	2	3	4	5
Cost, £*y*	5	8	11	14	17

b

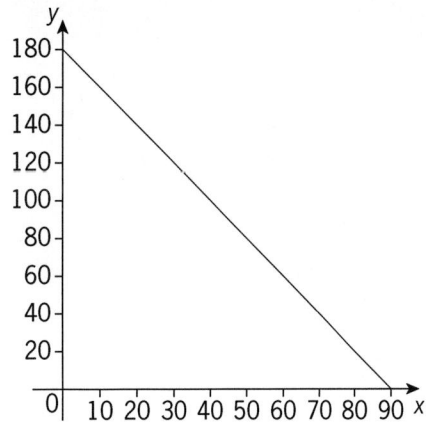

$y = 3x + 2$

c 23, No

4 For example:

x, in degrees	10	20	30	40	50	60	70	80
y, in degrees	160	140	120	100	80	60	40	20

$y = 180 - 2x$

5 a 360°

b 180°

c 6°

For example:

x, minutes	10	20	30	40	50	60
y, degrees	60	120	180	240	300	360

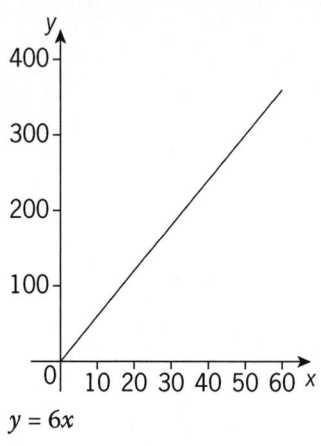

$y = 6x$

B11.3 Rich task

A leaves at 2pm, B leaves at 1pm. A takes 2 hours, B takes 4 hours. A sets off last and gets there first. A travels faster. They cross at 3pm, 50 miles away from HQ.

Ex B11.3

1 a 20°C **b** 50°C **c** 40°C

d 8 mins **e** 5°C

2 a 750 L **b** 250 L **c** 8 weeks

d 16 weeks **e** After 12 weeks

3 a i $70 **ii** £25

b No, because the exchange rates are different. She will get less than £40 back.

4 50 miles

a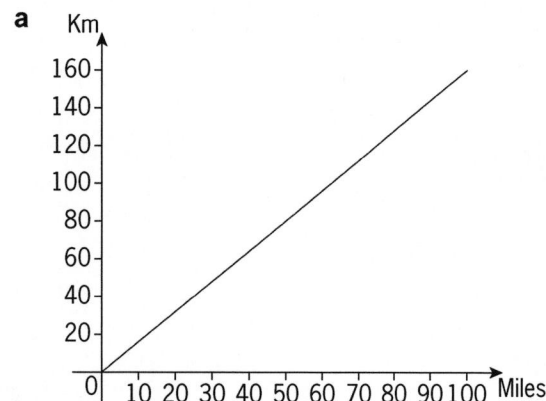

b 48 km, 128 km

B11.4 Rich task

Constructed as an inequality; $4x + 3 > 2x + 11$ so $2x > 8$, so $x > 4$

Ex B11.4

1 a equation **b** identity

c inequality **d** inequality

2 a $x < 7$ **b** $x > 7$ **c** $x \geq 7$ **d** $x \leq 7$

3 a $x > 2$ **b** $x \geq 0$ **c** $x \geq 1$

d $x < 1$ **e** $x < -2$ **f** $x \geq -1$

g $x < 0$ **h** $1 \leq x \leq 2$ **i** $-1 \leq x \leq 2$

4 a ⊶ –4 –3 –2 –1 0 1 2 3 4

b ●– –4 –3 –2 –1 0 1 2 3 4

c ◄————● –4 –3 –2 –1 0 1 2 3 4

d ◄—○ –4 –3 –2 –1 0 1 2 3 4

e ●— –4 –3 –2 –1 0 1 2 3 4

f —●— –4 –3 –2 –1 0 1 2 3 4

g ○——○ –4 –3 –2 –1 0 1 2 3 4

h ●——● –4 –3 –2 –1 0 1 2 3 4

5 a $x > 3$ ○—→ 0 1 2 3 4 5 6

b $x < 2$ ◄——○ –2 –1 0 1 2 3 4

c $x \geq 4$ ●—→ 0 1 2 3 4 5 6

d $x \leq 3$ ◄——● –1 0 1 2 3 4 5

e $x > 5$ ○—→ 0 1 2 3 4 5 6 7 8

f $x < 5$ ◄——○ 0 1 2 3 4 5 6 7

g $x > 5$ ○—→ 0 1 2 3 4 5 6 7 8

h $x < -2$ ◄——○ –4 –3 –2 –1 0 1 2

i $x < 3$ ◄——○ –1 0 1 2 3 4 5 6

j $x \geq 4$ ●—→ 0 1 2 3 4 5 6 7 8

k $x < 5$ ◄——○ –1 0 1 2 3 4 5 6 7

l $x \leq 1$ ◄——● –2 –1 0 1 2 3

m $x < 2$ ◄——○ –2 –1 0 1 2 3 4

n $x \geq 3$ ●—→ 0 1 2 3 4 5 6

o $x \leq -1$ ◄——● –3 –2 –1 0 1 2 3

p $x > -2$ ○—→ –4 –3 –2 –1 0 1 2 3

6 a $3 < x < 5$ ○——○ 0 1 2 3 4 5 6 7

b $3 \leq x \leq 5$ ●——● 0 1 2 3 4 5 6 7

c $5 < x < 7$ ○——○ 2 3 4 5 6 7 8 9

7 a 6, 7, 8 **b** 5, 6, 7, 8, 9 **c** −1, 0, 1

8 a 7, 9 **b** 1, 3, 5 **c** −3, −1, 1

Exam practice

1 a $x \geq 7.5$

b i ●—→ 5 6 7 8 9 **ii** 8, 9

2 a graph horizontal for call times between 0 and 1 minute

b $C = 10 + 30m$ (only valid when $m \geq 1$)

3 a at least 16 times

B12 Transformations

Check in

1 a 180° **b** 270° **c** 90° **d** 180°

2 a Clockwise **b** Anti-clockwise

Ex B12.1

1 a

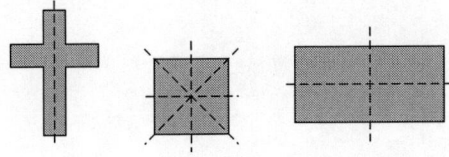

b

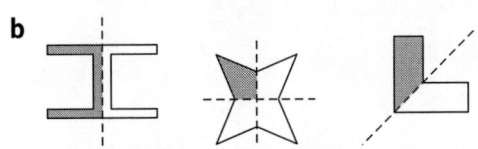

2 a 4 **b** 2 **c** 1 **d** 3

3 1 line: A C D E M T U V W Y K B

0 line: L Q F G J N P R S Z

2 lines: H I X

2 or infinite lines: O

dependent on the shape of font

4

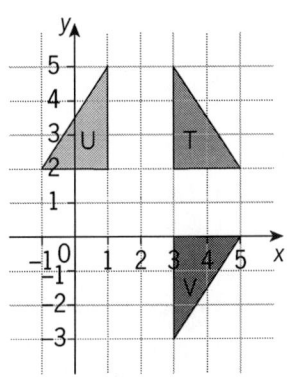

Ex B12.2

1

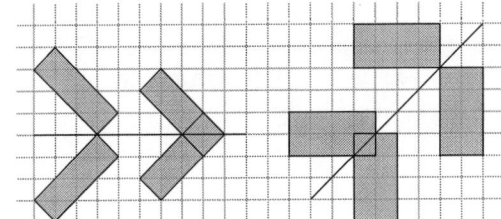

2 a

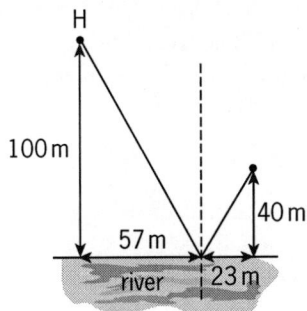

3

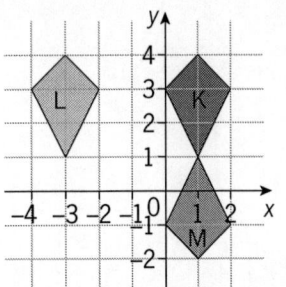

4

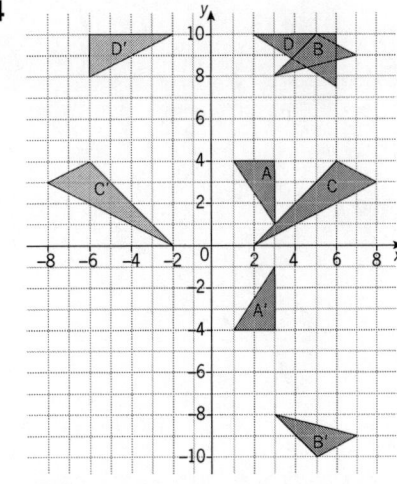

Ex B12.3

1 a 180° **b** 90° anticlockwise

2

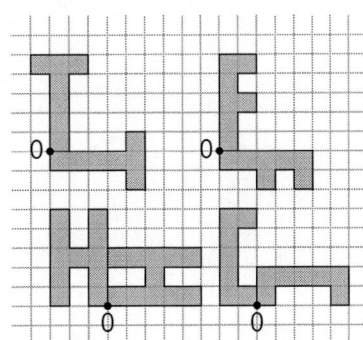

3

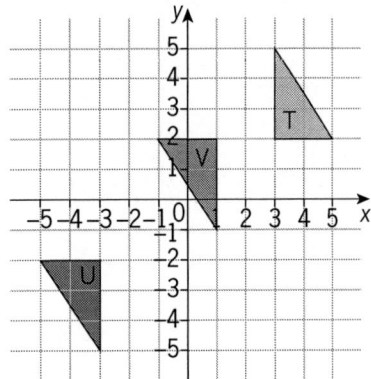

4

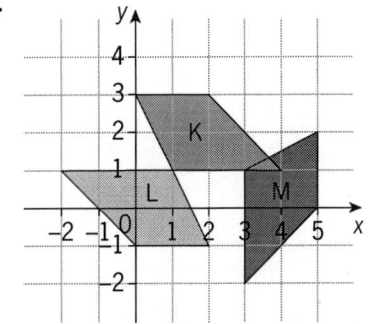

Ex B12.4

1 a $(4, 5), (7, 3), (8, 2), (5, 9), (6, -2), (6, -1)$

b $\begin{pmatrix} 4 \\ 2 \end{pmatrix}, \begin{pmatrix} 2 \\ -2 \end{pmatrix}, \begin{pmatrix} 4 \\ 0 \end{pmatrix}, \begin{pmatrix} -7 \\ -4 \end{pmatrix}, \begin{pmatrix} -2 \\ 2 \end{pmatrix}, \begin{pmatrix} -4 \\ 0 \end{pmatrix}$

2 a $\begin{pmatrix} 3 \\ 2 \end{pmatrix}$ **b** $\begin{pmatrix} 5 \\ 1 \end{pmatrix}$ **c** $\begin{pmatrix} 2 \\ -1 \end{pmatrix}$ **d** $\begin{pmatrix} -3 \\ -2 \end{pmatrix}$

3 a

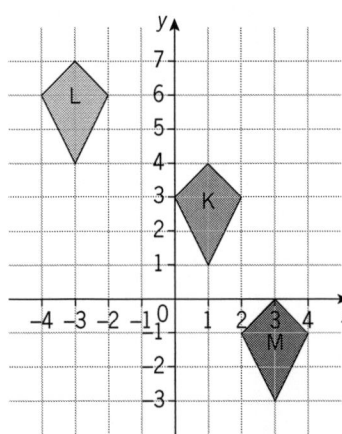

4 $\begin{pmatrix} 2 \\ 1 \end{pmatrix}, \begin{pmatrix} 2 \\ -1 \end{pmatrix}, \begin{pmatrix} -2 \\ 1 \end{pmatrix}, \begin{pmatrix} -2 \\ -1 \end{pmatrix}, \begin{pmatrix} 1 \\ 2 \end{pmatrix}, \begin{pmatrix} 1 \\ -2 \end{pmatrix}, \begin{pmatrix} -1 \\ 2 \end{pmatrix}, \begin{pmatrix} -1 \\ -2 \end{pmatrix}$

Exam practice

1 a i no line symmetry

　　ii rotational symmetry of order 1

　b i no line symmetry

　　ii rotational symmetry of order 5

2 a $(0, 1) (3, 2) (2, 3)$ R **b** $(1, 0) (2, 3) (3, 2)$ S

3 a S is $(1, -2) (1, 0) (2, 1) (4, 1)$

　b T is $(0, 0) (0, 2) (1, 3) (3, 3)$

Case study: Art

1 a 30 **b** 4.44 m

　c length = 40 hands; height = 29.6 hands

2 a i 2 trapeziums, 1 parallelogram, 2 rectangles

　　ii 3 trapeziums, 1 parallelogram, 1 rectangle

　b i $(-2, 0), (0, 5), (1, 5), (1, 0), (0.4, 0), (0.4, 2),$
　　　$(-0.6, 2), (-0.6, 0)$

　　ii $(2, -1), (1.6, 1), (1.6, 6), (3, 6), (3.6, 5), (2.4, 5),$
　　　$(2.4, 1), (3.6, 1), (3.8, 2), (3.4, 2), (3, 3), (4.4, 3),$
　　　$(3.6, -1)$

3 a 2 **b** scale factor 4

　c i 120 cm² **ii** 480 cm²

B13 Bivariate data and time series

Check in

1

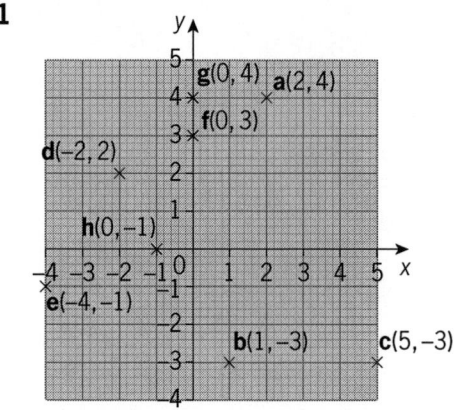

2 a 10 **b** 25 **c** 20 **d** 12.5 **e** 27.5

B13.1 Rich task

Yes, where you live does affect your lung capacity. From the graph you can see that those living at a higher altitude tend to have better lung capacity.
Students answers will vary regarding other possible data to collect.

Ex B13.1

1 graph

2 graph

3 more alcohol associated with longer reaction times
More time on games associated with shorter reaction times. Longer reaction times at 3.0 am for all subjects

Ex B13.2

1 Positive; people from higher altitudes have larger lung capacity.

2 Positive; good at both subjects
Positive; tall people have long arms

3 b positive

　c all except one subject take longer with left hand than right.

4 b no correlation. Number of deaths not related to magnitude. Density of population and type of buildings very important.

Ex B13.3

1 a £108 **b** £97

2 a 4.9 litres

　b i beyond data range

　　ii relationship only established for men

3 a graph

　b If results for black bear and horse are ignored, correlation very weak so estimates are inaccurate

Ex B13.4

1 Highest in June and December, which are holiday months.

2 2005 higher than 2004, but same monthly pattern. Cost per unit may have increased. Highest in Jan-March then Oct-Dec, the coldest months.

3 Highest in warmer months of August, July and June. Also peak in December, a holiday period.

4 Earns most in May-August, maybe school holidays. Earnings increased each year, maybe better rates as older.

5 Highest in April-June, Lowest in Oct-Dec. 2005 less than 2004, maybe economising.

Exam practice

1 No consistent pattern. Average temperature ranged from 13.6°C to 16.7°C

2 More marriages in summer months.

3 Question not valid as data is artificially paired

B14 More straight-line graphs

Check in

1 1, 3, 5, 7, 9

B14.1 Activity

When $x = 2$, $y = 8$. When $x = 3$, $y = 10$.

The coordinates are (0, 4), (1, 6), (2, 8), (3, 10)

Ex B14.1

1

x	0	1	2	3
y	1	3	5	7

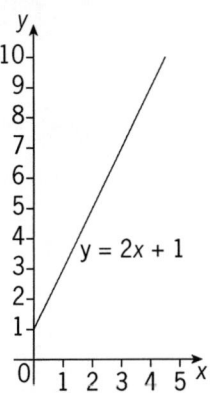

$y = 2x + 1$

2 a

x	0	1	2	3	4
y	3	4	5	6	7

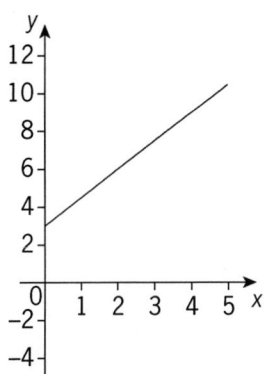

b

x	0	1	2	3	4
y	-3	-2	-1	0	1

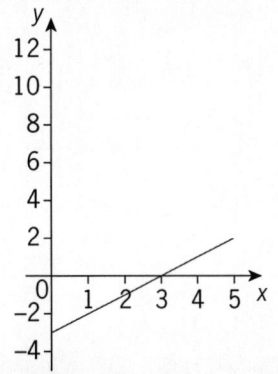

c

x	0	1	2	3	4
y	1	3	5	7	9

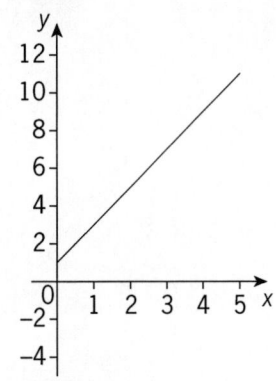

d

x	0	1	2	3	4
y	-2	0	2	4	6

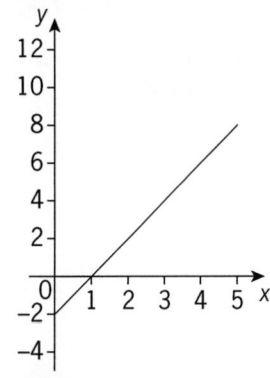

e

x	0	1	2	3	4
y	12	11	10	9	8

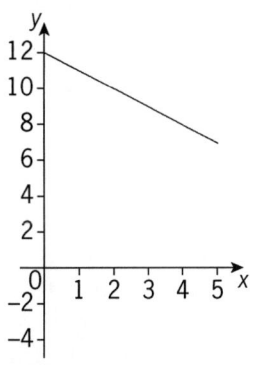

f

x	0	1	2	3	4
y	3	2	1	0	-1

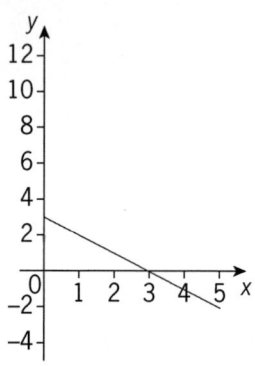

3 a Yes   **b** Yes   **c** No

  d Yes   **e** Yes   **f** No

4 a ROAD NORTH

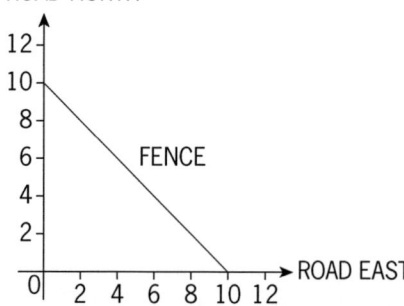

  b 50

5 a

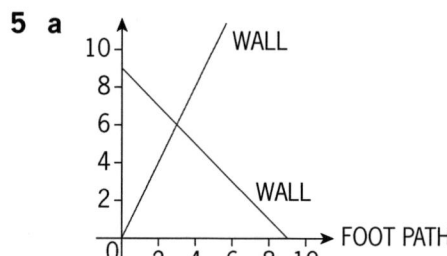

  b 27

6

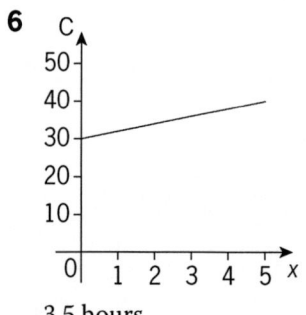

3.5 hours

7 (20, 52)

B14.2 Rich task

The ratio is often said to be "rise over run". Run is the *horizontal distance* and rise is the *vertical distance* travelled. Cyclists and cars can typically cope with a gradient of no more than 1:10.

The steepest roads are in Rosedale Abbey, N Yorks which is 1:3 and Ffordd Penllech, Harlech, Wales (officially described as not suitable for motor vehicles) which is 1:2.91 at its steepest point.

Ex B14.2

1 P   3   Q   2   R   1   S   −2

    T   0.5   U   −1   V   0

2 a 2   **b** 3   **c** 0.5

  d 0   **e** −1   **f** −2

3 a 5   **b** 4   **c** 1   **d** $\frac{1}{2}$

  e −6   **f** −3   **g** −8   **h** −8

  i −4   **j** −1   **k** $-\frac{1}{2}$ **l** 3

4 $y = 2x + 1$ and $y = 2x - 1$

    $y = 4 - x$ and $y = -x + 5$

    $y = \frac{1}{2}x + 3$ and $y = 1 + \frac{1}{2}x$

    $y = -2x + 7$ and $y = 6 - 2x$

Rich Task

The graphs of $y = mx + 3$ all pass through (0, 3)

The graphs of $y = 2x + c$ are all parallel lines

B14.3 Rich task

There are 19 combinations of seedlings (where he buys both apple and pair seedlings at the same time) he can buy ranging from $x = 1$, $y = 38$ to $x = 19$, $y = 2$

The graph of $10x + 5y = 200$ will intersect the y axis at (0, 40) and the x axis at (20, 0).

Ex B14.3

1 a   (4, 0)   (0, 6)

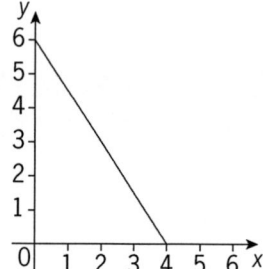

  b   (5, 0)   (0, 2)

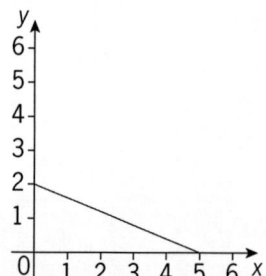

  c   (5, 0)   (0, 3)

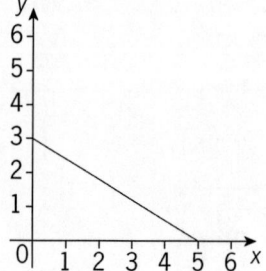

d (3, 0) (0, 4)

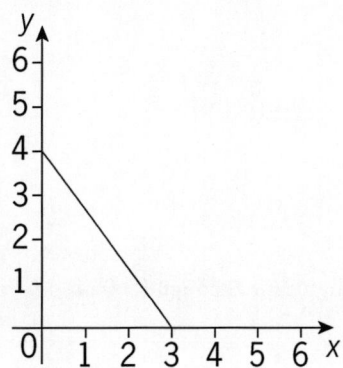

e (4.5, 0) (0, 3)

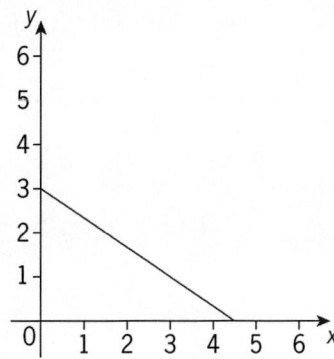

f (6, 0)   (0, 2)

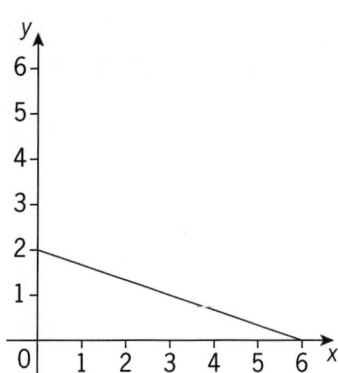

2 a (4, 0)   (0, −2)

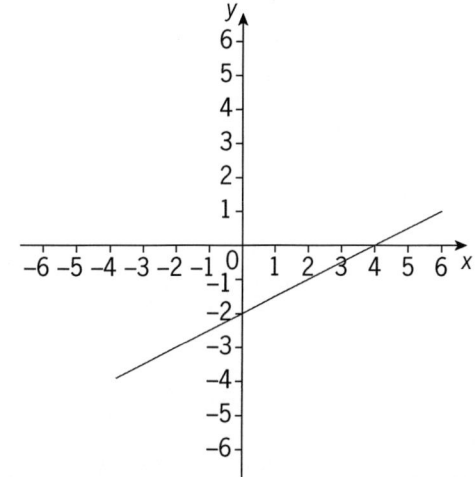

b (5, 0)   (0, −6)

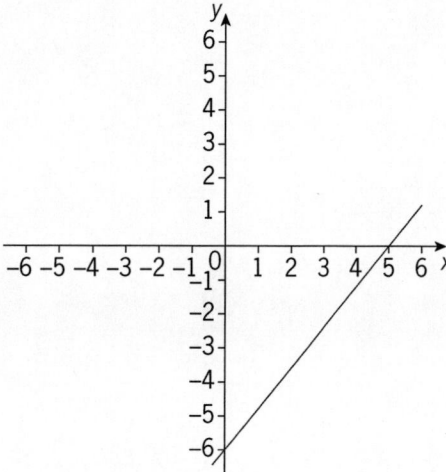

c (−4, 0)   (0, −3)

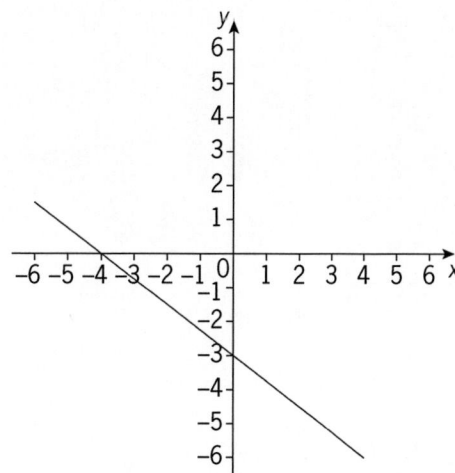

3 a gradient = −2

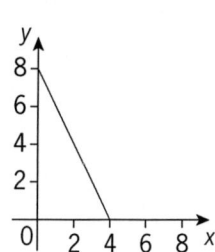

b gradient = −3

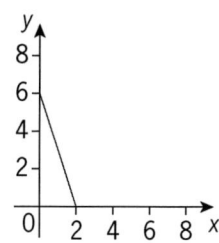

c gradient = $-\frac{1}{2}$

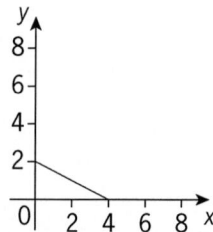

4 a gradient = −2

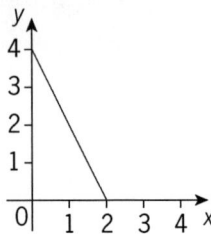

b gradient = −3

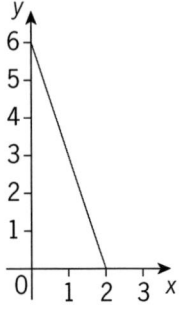

c gradient = 3

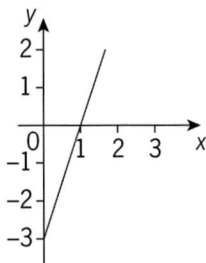

d gradient = −3

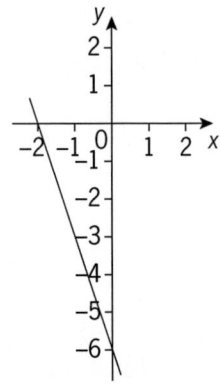

e gradient = $-\frac{1}{2}$

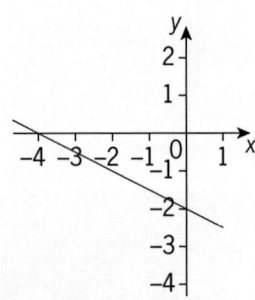

f gradient = 2

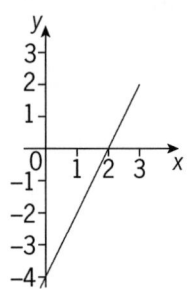

5 Graph will be a straight line through (3, 0) and (0, 6)

Possible pairs are: (1, 4) and (2, 2)

6

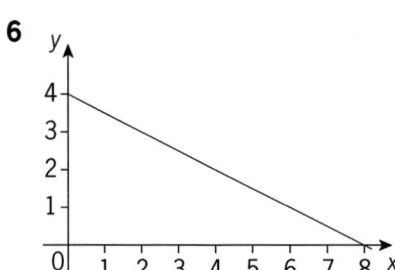

Possible combinations are (0, 4), (2, 3), (4, 2), (6, 1) and (8, 0)

4 Christmas cards and 2 birthday cards

B14.4 Rich task

Cab A Cost = $3x$
Cab B Cost = $x + 6$
For less than 3 mile journeys, Cab A would be cheaper and for journeys of more than 3 miles, Cab B would be cheaper.

Activity

The point is (4, 2).

Ex B14.4

1 a $x = 2$ $y = 5$

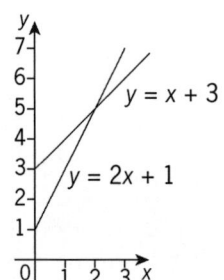

b $x = 2$ $y = 7$

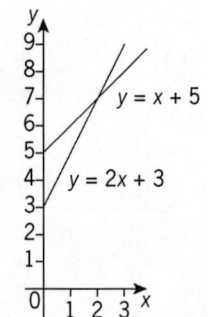

c $x = 3$ $y = 4$

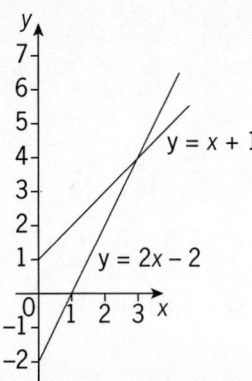

d $x = 3$ $y = 7$

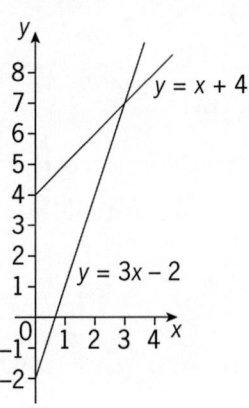

e $x = 2$ $y = 4$

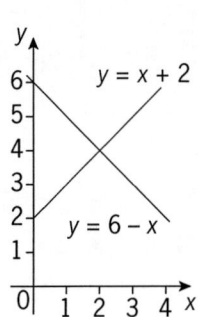

f $x = 4$ $y = 3$

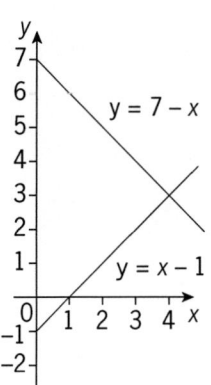

2 a $x = 2$ $y = 3$

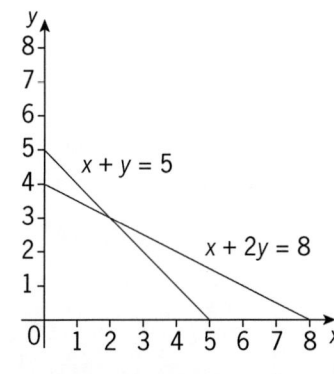

b $x = 3$ $y = 2$

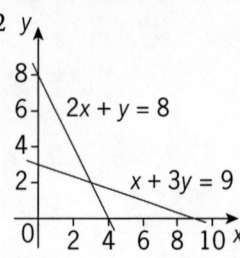

c $x = 3$ $y = 4$

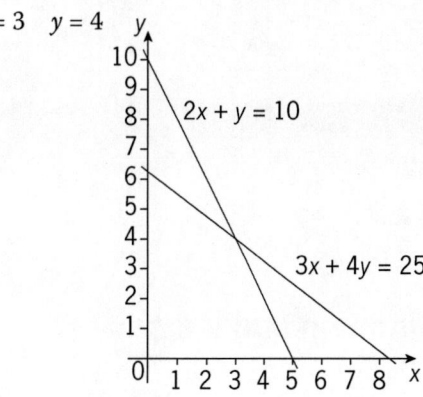

d $x = 3$ $y = 1.5$

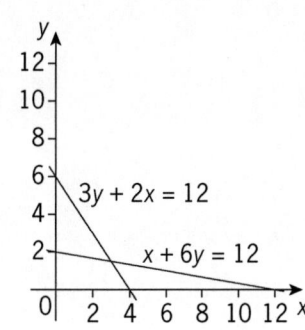

e $x = 6$ $y = 2$

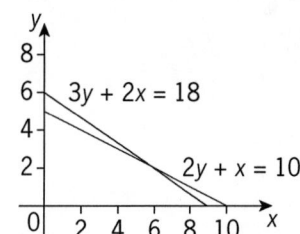

f $x = 2$ $y = 2$

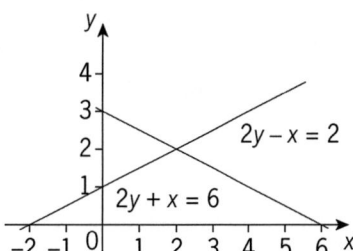

3

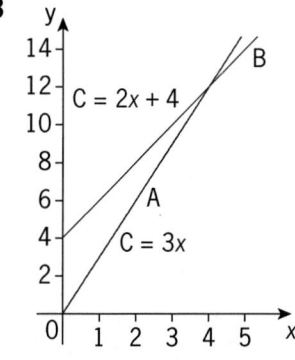

Firm A is cheaper for up to 4 spanners. For more than 4 spanners firm B is cheaper

Exam practice

1 a (2, 5)

b

2 a $\frac{1}{2}$

b

3 a $x = 1\frac{1}{3}$ $y = 3\frac{2}{3}$

B15 Estimation and indices

Check in

1 a 49   **b** 8   **c** 1000   **d** 0.32

2 5

3 yes

Ex B15.1

1 a 292   **b** 601   **c** 1739   **d** 273

  e 158   **f** 235   **g** 20250   **h** 96

  i 2496   **j** 3.3   **k** 86.17   **l** 36.25

2 a i 13.2 **ii** 0.87   **b i** 21.4   **ii** 19.902

  c i 7600 **ii** 0.045   **d i** 22.5   **ii** 7.2

3 a £2.76   **b** £7.77

4 a 33 mins **b** 35 mins

5 a 49, 51   **b** 77, 27 or 84, 34

  c 98 × 84 = 8232

B15.2 Activity 1

Students will find square numbers

Activity 2

Students will find ±6

Ex B15.2

1 a 343 **b** 400 **c** 225 **d** 216 **e** 125

2 a 7   **b** 100 **c** 5   **d** 4   **e** 9

3 a 10, −10 **b** 11, −11 **c** 3, −3   **d** 14, −14

4 a i 13 **ii** 10   **b**   1.3

5 a i 12 **ii** 1.2   **b i** 15 **ii** 1.5

6 a 10^3 **b** 10^6 **c** 10^6

7 a 27   **b** −198 **c** 15   **d** 56   **e** 7

8

9 From 1 + 8 2 + 7 3 + 6 4 + 5 1 + 15 2 + 14 3 +13
  4 + 12 5 + 11 6 + 10 7 + 9 7 + 18 8 + 17 9 + 16 10 +
  15 11 + 14 12 + 13 1 + 3

10 Rich task

The next number will be 25, these are square numbers.

B15.3 Activity

Students answers will vary, encourage class discussion.

This is also a potential opportunity for QWC practice.

Ex B15.3

1 a 600   **b** 8000   **c** 16 000   **d** 100

  e 100   **f** 13   **g** 8   **h** 50

2 a 5   **b** 11

3 a 9   **b** 10   **c** 25

  d 64   **e** 7

4 a 4   **b** 100   **c** 2   **d** 10

  e 7   **f** 0.5   **g** 12   **h** $\frac{1}{14}$

  i 2   **j** 15 000   **k** 1.3   **l** 100

  m 0   **n** 440

5 7

6 12

7 40

B15.4 Rich task

Dexter should accept the second option.

Rich task 2

  a i 32   **ii** 2^5

  b i 81   **ii** 3^4

  c Students should experiment with this and their
  answers will vary.

Ex B15.4

1 a 64   **b** 81   **c** 243   **d** 625

  e 72   **f** 256   **g** 16

2 i 8   **ii** 5

3 a i 5^3 **ii** 5^3 **iii** $2^6, 4^3$

b i $4^6 = 16^3$ **ii** all squares **iii** $4^6, 16^3$

4 a $2^4 \times 3$ **b** $2 \times 3 \times 7$ **c** $2^3 \times 3 \times 5^2$

d $2^8 \times 5$ **e** $3 \times 5 \times 7^2$

5 a 7^9 **b** 3^8 **c** 8^9 **d** 15^8

e 4^{12} **f** 3^6 **g** 8 **h** 9^5 **i** 6^4

6 2, 4

7 Problem
$x = 2, y = 4$

Exam practice

1 9 **2** odd (odd × odd = odd) **3** She has enough

Case study 5: Recycling

	Waste not recycled/ composted	Waste recycled/ composted	Total waste	Percentage recycled
1983/84	394	3	397	0.76
1984/85				
1985/86				
1986/87				
1987/88				
1988/89				
1989/90				
1990/91				
1991/92	417	11	427	2.57
1992/93				
1993/94	430	15	445	3.37
1994/95				
1995/96	423	27	450	6.00
1996/97	438	32	469	6.82
1997/98	441	36	477	7.55
1998/99	443	40	483	8.28
1999/00	457	48	505	9.50
2000/01	455	52	507	10.26
2001/02	456	60	516	11.63
2002/03	449	71	521	13.63
2003/04	425	87	512	16.99
2004/05	404	113	517	21.86
2005/06	376	135	511	26.42
2006/07	359	157	516	30.43
2007/08	334	173	507	34.12

a 27.7%

b 5 667%

New bottle 26 g; 7.7% reduction

Tray = 576 cm², lid = 375 cm², total = 951 cm²
39.4% lighter

B16 Similarity and enlargement

Check in

1

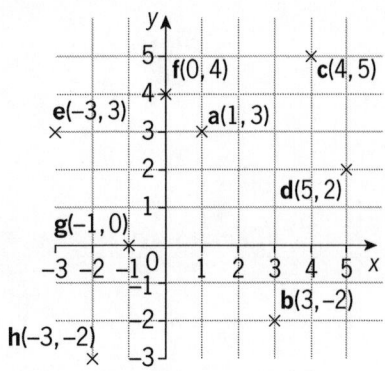

2 a 1 : 3 **b** 1 : 6 **c** 2 : 3 **d** 5 : 2

B16.1 Rich task

a and **j**, **c** and **I**, **f** and **g** are all congruent shapes.

b, **c** and **i**, **f**, **g**, and **h**, and **a**, **d**, **e**, **j** are all either congruent or similar.

Ex B16.1

1 a congruent

b not congruent

c congruent

2 a e.g

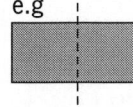 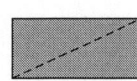 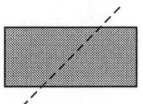

b The vertical line is; the other lines are not

3 a 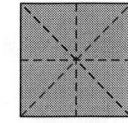 **b**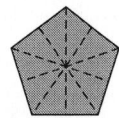

c 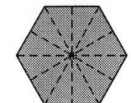 **d**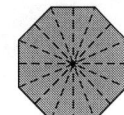

4 a similar

b not similar

c similar

5 a congruent **b** congruent **c** similar

d neither **e** similar **f** congruent

g neither

6 4.40 m long, 1.80 m high

Ex B16.2

1 a, b, d

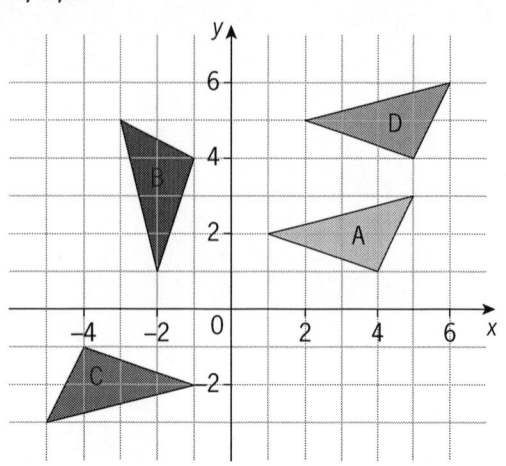

c Rotation of 180° about (0, 0) **e** Translation $\begin{pmatrix} 1 \\ 3 \end{pmatrix}$

2 a, b, d

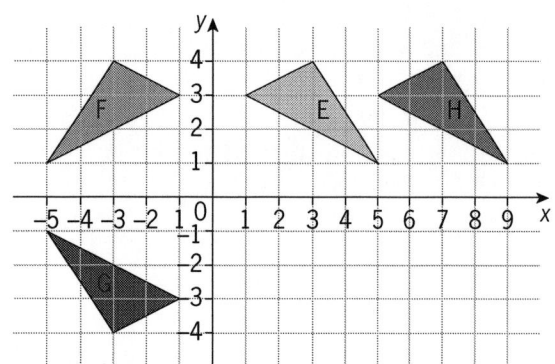

c Rotation of 180° about (0, 0) **e** Translation $\begin{pmatrix} 4 \\ 0 \end{pmatrix}$

3 Translation by the vector $\begin{pmatrix} 4 \\ -2 \end{pmatrix}$

4 a

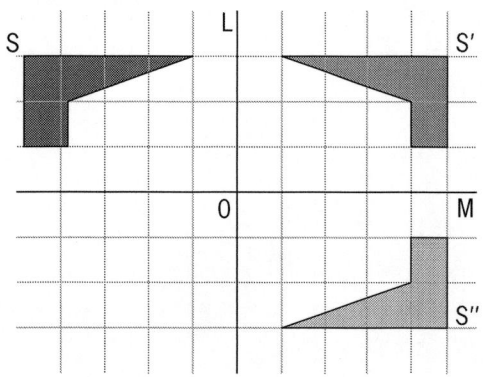

Rotation of 180° about point O

b

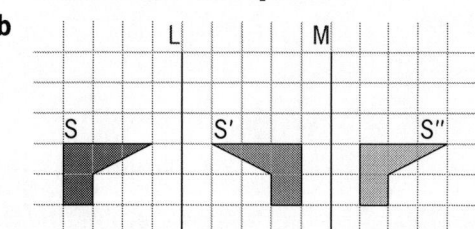

Translation of $\begin{pmatrix} 10 \\ 0 \end{pmatrix}$

5

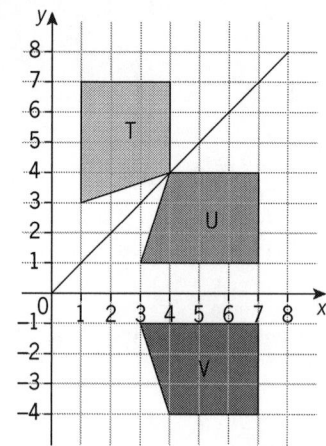

Rotation of 90° clockwise about the origin

6

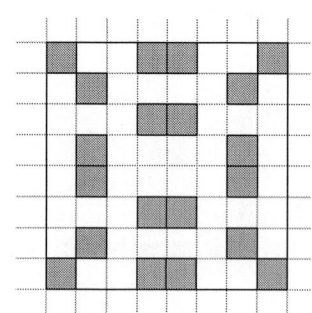

B16.3 Discussion

Class or group discussion indicating that the picture will get smaller the closer the projector is to the screen and larger the further away it is.

Ex B16.3

1

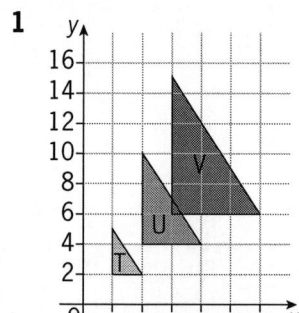

2

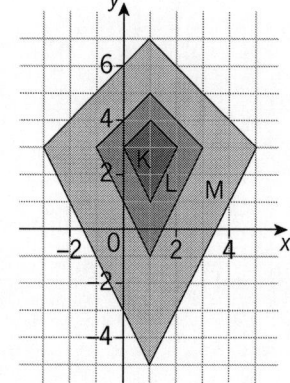

3

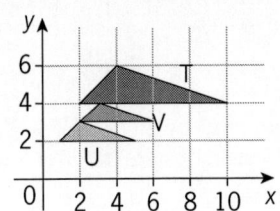

4

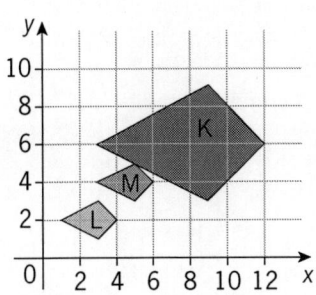

5 Vertices of images are

a (4, 6) (8, 6) (4, 12)   **b** (18, 0) (24, 6) (15, 9)

c (3, 16) (11, 16) (11, 20) (3, 22)   **d** (18, 17) (22, 17) (20, 15)

6 a

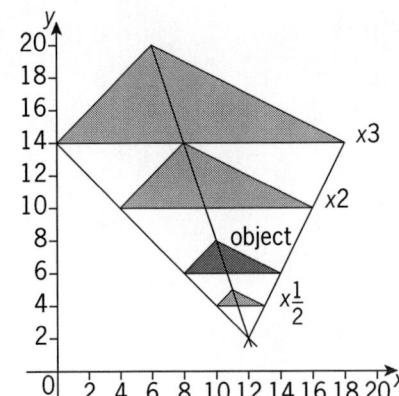

b

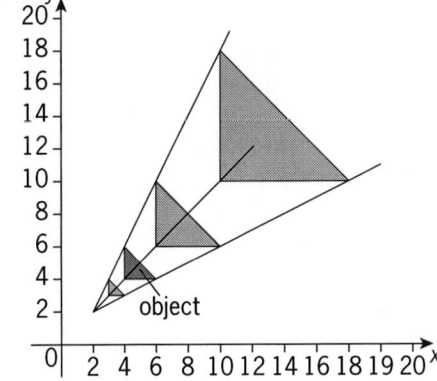

c

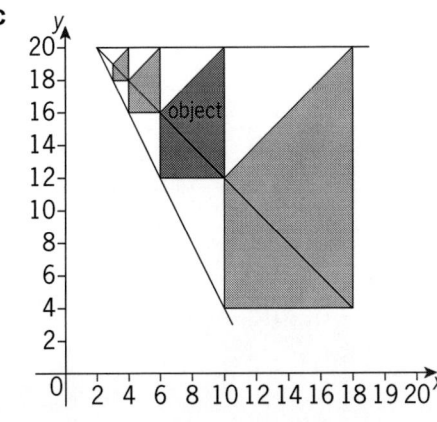

Ex B16.4

1 a (10, 1)

b R scale factor 2; S scale factor 3; Q scale factor $\frac{1}{2}$

2 3

3 a i (0, 3)   **ii** 2

b i (12, 1)   **ii** 3

c i (5, 7)   **ii** 4

d i (1, 24)   **ii** 5

4 a $\frac{1}{2}$ **b** $\frac{1}{3}$ **c** $\frac{1}{4}$

5 a (1, 7), $\frac{1}{2}$ **b** (4, 8), $\frac{1}{4}$

6 200

7 A4 to A3 has a scale factor 2

An enlargement (scale factor 2) is used for each successive paper size

8 180 × 130 mm

9 12 inches × 8 inches and 18 inches × 12 inches are enlargements.

10 inches × 8 inches and 7 inches × 5 inches will need to be cropped.

Exam practice

1

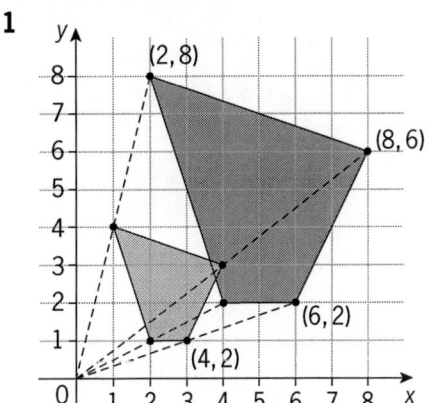

2 a, b

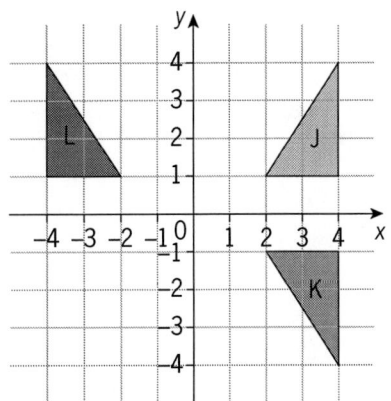

c reflection in y-axis

3 $\begin{pmatrix} 3 \\ -2 \end{pmatrix} \begin{pmatrix} 2 \\ 3 \end{pmatrix} \begin{pmatrix} -2 \\ 2 \end{pmatrix}$

C17 Percentages and proportional change

Check in

1 a 10   **b** 4

2 3

3 0.7   0.75   0.8   0.875

Ex C17.1

1 a £7   **b** £18   **c** £112

2 £58.24

3 a £1905   **b** £6705   **c** £502   **d** £29 130

4 a £74.25   **b** £6000   **c** £11 200

     d £10 500   **e** £120   **f** £3.30

C17.2 Problem

The trader made a £12.50 profit.

Rich task

0.65

Ex C17.2

1 a £374.40   **b** £48.95

2 a 35p   **b** £7.80

3 £82.68

4 £36 016.80

5 £124.67

6 Problem
They should reduce the price of the bar.

7 Rich task
Students should experiment with different numbers and methods to get a feel for how percentage increases and decreases work.

C17.3 Problem

Stan got the better deal.

Ex C17.3

1 a 13.7%   **b** 14.3%

2 73.3%

3 60%

4 5% profit

Ex C17.4

1 a £4800   **b** £19 800

2 a £36   **b** £136

3 a £1008   **b** 1008

4 £412.50

5 a £200   **b** £192 option   **c** by £8

C17.5 Rich task

Students should practice on paper and realise that the thickness doubles at every fold which quickly makes it impractical to keep folding in practice. They should think about what happens if you repeatedly double a number.

Ex C17.5

1 a £40   **b** £43.20   **c** £583.20

2 a i £4000   **ii** £36 000

    b i £7600   **ii** £32 400   **c** £29 160

3 a 5.4 m   **b** 4.86 m

4 a 1.68 million

    b 2.36 million (3 sig. figs.)

5 a 25 760   **b** 21 803

6 a £20 320.50   **b** £21 732.77   **c** £26 586.28

7 a £44 184   **b** £48 898.61   **c** £56 930.33

C17.6 Problem

If you work out the area of the photos, then the 30% bigger size is actually 39% bigger. The 100% bigger size is actually 99% bigger.

Problem 2

15 years.

12000 slaves.

Ex C17.6

1 a 76p   **b** 88p

2 a i 3 hours   **ii** 5 hours

        iii 7 hours 30 minutes

    b i 10.5 days   **ii** 16.8 days

3 a 5 litres for £1.29

    b 200 ml for £2.89

4 26p per biscuit

5 14

Exam practice

1 a 160ml

    b 17.5g

2 1.375%

3 6 eggs

C18 Area and perimeter

Check-in

1 a 600   **b** 71 000   **c** 48

   d 2630   **e** 4500   **f** 6

   g 75   **h** 6.5   **i** 3.2

2 a 9.6   **b** 22.5   **c** 10.5

3 a 7.8   **b** 15.5   **c** 9.0

Ex C18.1

1 a 9.6 cm   **b** 9.3 cm

2 a 15.3 cm   **b** 17.5 cm

3 a 19.2 metres **b** £13.00

4 a 5 cm^2 **b** 7 cm^2

5 3 cm^2 507 km^2

6 a 20 cm^2 **b** 6 cm^2 **c** 27 cm^2

   d 14 cm^2 **e** 14 cm^2 **f** 8.55 cm^2

7 a 4560 cm^2 **b** 2280 cm^2

8 Colorado, Wyoming
Multiplying length by width which is area is not equal to the actual area, because the shapes of the states are not true rectangles. The shapes are on the earth's sphere and are defined by the earth's meridian and so the shapes taper slightly towards their northern sides.

C18.2 Activity

You need pi squares to cover the circle.

Ex C18.2

1 a 16 cm   **b** 25 cm   **c** 19 cm   **d** 63 cm

2 a 89.2 mm   **b** 14.1 metres

   c 75.4 cm   **d** 21.4 cm

3 a 125.6 cm   **b** 125.6 metres

4 a 40 000 km (4 sig. figs.)

   b i 584 million miles   **ii** 1.6 million miles

      iii 67 000 miles

5 a 113 m^2 **b** 78.5 cm^2

   c 707 cm^2 **d** 5.31 cm^2

   e 1260 cm^2 **f** 7850 cm^2

   g 1810 cm^2 **h** 24.6 cm^2

6 452 m^2

7 16.6 m^2

8 a 615 m^2 **b** £52300

9 a 1.3 cm, 0.8 cm **b** 2.01 cm^2 **c** 3.30 cm^2

10 141 cm^2

C18.3 Rich task

   a 51 cm^2 **b** 17 cm^2 **c** 34 cm^2

Ex C18.3

1 a 56 cm^2 **b** 55 cm^2 **c** 48 cm^2 **d** 38 cm^2

   e 80 cm^2 **f** 36.5 cm^2 **g** 49 cm^2 **h** 36 cm^2

2 a 66 m^2 **b** £534.60

3 36 m^2

Ex C18.4

1 a 20 cm^2 **b** 30 cm^2 **c** 21 cm^2 **d** 15 cm^2

2 a 20 cm^2 **b** 15.6 cm^2

3 2400 cm^2

4 A square of side 2a

Trapeziums with parallel sides

   i a and 7a,   **ii** 2a and 6a.

Ex C18.5

1 a w = 5 cm   **b** h = 5 cm   **c** h = 7 cm

   d h = 6 cm   **e** r = 3.6 cm   **f** r = 3.0 cm

2 10 metres

3 2.5 metres

4 1.4 cm

5 a i 15.9 cm **ii** 31.8 cm   **iii** 207 mm

   b i 2.5 cm **ii** 5.2 m   **iii** 5.6 mm

6 333 cm

7 1 × 36, 2 × 18, 3 × 12, 4 × 9, and if you include a square, 6 × 6

The shape with the smallest perimeter would be a square of 6 × 6, with a perimeter of 24 cm.

Ex C18.6

1 a (2, 0)   2   4   **b** (1, 1)   3   9

2

	a	b	c	d
Length SF	2	3	4	2
Area SF	4	9	16	4

3 135 cm^2

4 a 9   **b** 3   **c** 21 cm

5 Yes, 2.5, 6.25

Exam practice

1 a 44 cm^2 36 cm

   b 72 cm^2 40 cm

2 a i C ii none

3 65.94 cm²

Case study: Holiday

1 £32.63 (assuming 13 weeks)

2 £4 per hour
£52 (assuming 13 weeks)

3 CDs £2.50 each; DVDs £3.50 each

4 a 219 euros

b £82.19 (2dp)
exchange rate £1 : 1.31 euros (2dp); 90.78 euros

Max temp in Rome = 37.2°C
Min temp in Rome = 17.2°C
Max temp in London = 77°F
Min temp in London = 60.8°F

C19 Algebraic manipulation

Check-in

1 a 4 **b** 5.061 **c** 26.368

2 a $x = 7$ **b** $x = 10$

Ex C19.1

1 a $2(x + y)$ **b** $2x + 3y$

2 a $5x + y$ **b** $7p + 10q + 2$ **c** $m - 1$

d $3(x - y + z)$ **e** $5t$ **f** $4 + 3p - 3q$

g 0 **h** $5t$

3 a $a = 10\ b = 10$ **b** $a = 5\ b = 3$ **c** $a = 7\ b = -5$

d $a = 2\ b = 6$ **e** $a = 3\ b = -1$ **f** $a = 3\ b = -2$

g $a = -5\ b = 8$ **h** $a = 0\ b = 2$

4 a $24x + 10$ **b** $14x + 9$ **c** $8p + 6$

d $11q + 17$ **e** $11r$ **f** $24n$

g $2x^2 + 6x$ **h** $2z^2 + 4z$

i $x^2 + 8x + 12$ **j** $y^2 - y + 6$

5 a $2(2x + 3)$ **b** $3(2y + 3)$ **c** $4(3z + 2)$

d $3(x + 5)$ **e** $5(x + 4)$ **f** $3(6z - 5)$

g $4(2 + 3y)$ **h** $5(3 - 2y)$ **i** $2(2 - t)$

j $x(x + 3)$ **k** $y(y - 5)$ **l** $z(4 - z)$

m $p(8 - p)$ **n** $3b(b + 2)$ **o** $4c(2c - 1)$

6 $4(6x + 3y)$

Any three from $24x + 12y$, $2(12x + 6y)$, $3(8x + 4y)$, $6(4x + 2y)$, $12(2x + y)$

C19.2 Rich task

Students should try trial and improvement methods.

Ex C19.2

1 a 8 **b** 9 **c** 7 **d** 8

e 6 **f** 8 **g** 7 **h** 9

2

x	x^3	Too high or two low?
2	8	too low
3	27	far too high
2.1	9.26	too low
2.2	10.64	too high
2.15	9.93	too low

Therefore the solution lies between 2.15 and 2.2.

The solution is 2.2 to 1 decimal place

3 8.3

4 a 4.3 **b** 6.3 **c** 5.4

d 20.5 **e** 26.4 **f** 0.6

Ex C19.3

1 a 8 **b** 8.1

2 $x(x + 4) = 70$

6.6

3 $30x - x^2 = 90$

3.4

4 $n^3 - n^2 = n$

1.6 (note that $n = 0$ and $n = -0.6$ are also solutions)

5 a 10 **b** 8.3

6 a 5 **b** 2.9 **c** 4.8

d 5.9 **e** 4.5 **f** −9.7

7 $n + 4$

35, 37, 39

Exam practice

1 if question is $x^3 - 3 = 17$, answer is 2.7

if question is $x^3 - 3x = 17$, answer is 3.0

if question is $x^3 - 3x^2 = 17$, answer is 4.0

2 7.7

C20 Measures and accuracy

Check-in

1 a a circle radius 6 cm

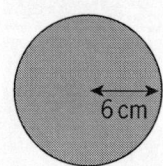

6 cm

b a circle radius 4.5 cm

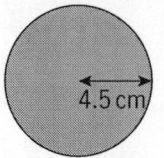
4.5 cm

2 a 28 cm² **b** 10 mm²

C20.1 Rich task

Cross section is E is a rectangle.

Ex C20.1

1 a i

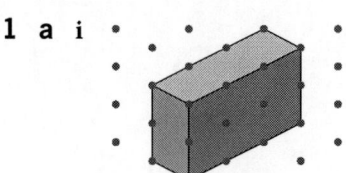

Six faces, twelve edges

ii

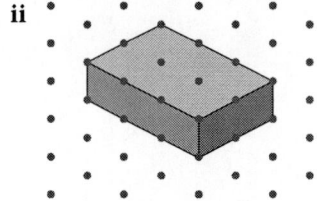

Six faces, twelve edges

iii

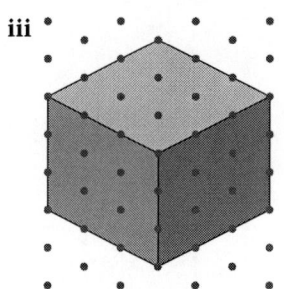

Six faces, 12 edges

iv

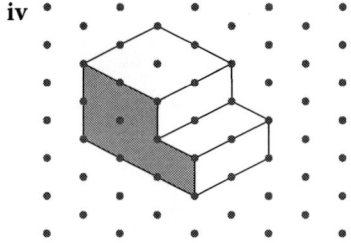

Eight faces, 18 edges

v

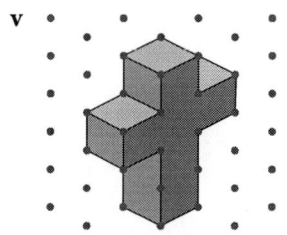

14 faces, 36 edges

vi

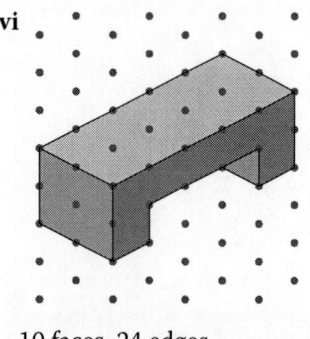

10 faces, 24 edges

2 a AA'

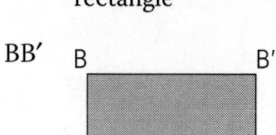

A   A'

rectangle

BB'

B   B'

rectangle

CC'   circle

C   C'

DD'   D   D'   square

EE'   E   E'   rectangle

FF'   circle

F   F'

3 a   **b**

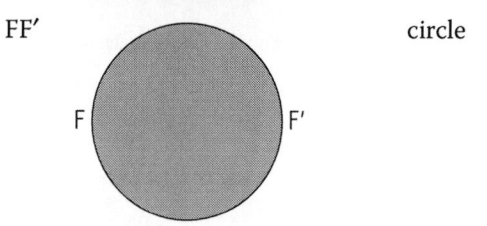

c

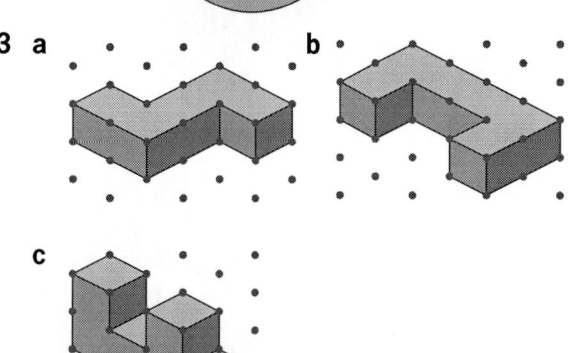

4 3 × 3 cube   26 small cubes have painted faces
      4 × 4 cube   56   -do-
      5 × 5 cube   98   -do-

Ex C20.2

1 A   view 2;   B   view 1;   C   view 3 for both buildings

2 a
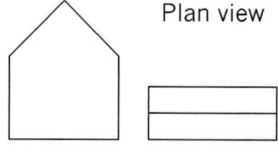
Plan view

b
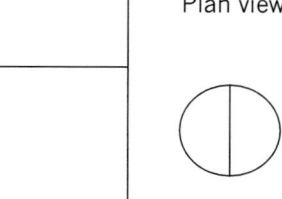
Plan view

c
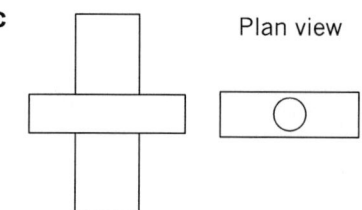
Plan view

d
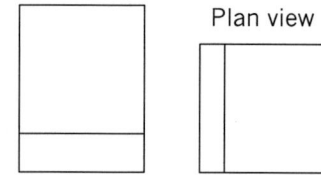
Plan view

3 a pyramid   **b** cone   **c** cylinder   **d** sphere

   e a half cylinder cut along its axis

   f a triangular prism

4 B;
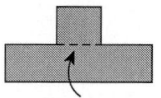
A and C have a line here
B does not.

5 a
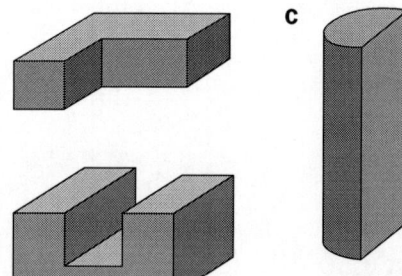

7 cube; sphere

C20.3 Rich task

Students should sketch out different possibilities of nets
thinking about how they will fit together.

Ex C20.3

1 a 1ˢᵗ and 3ʳᵈ   **b** pyramid

   c prism with a triangular cross-section

2 b The faces of a cuboid must be in pairs

3 For example,
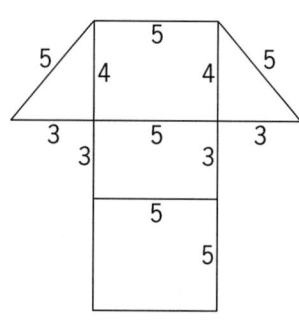

   prism with a triangular cross-section

4 Cube A: **a** t   **b** s   **c** u

   Cube B: **a** u   **b** s   **c** t

5 For example,
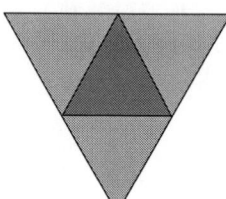 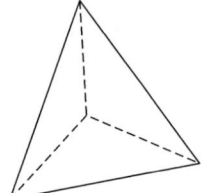

   Tetrahedron (pyramid with a triangular base)

6 a For example,
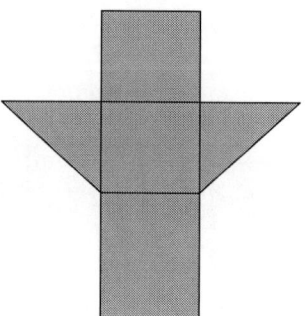

Ex C20.4

1 a 700 cm³   **b** 504 cm³   **c** 538 cm³

2 a 168 cm²   **b** 64 cm³

3 a 2.96 m²   **b** £36.85   **c** £6.50

4 For example,
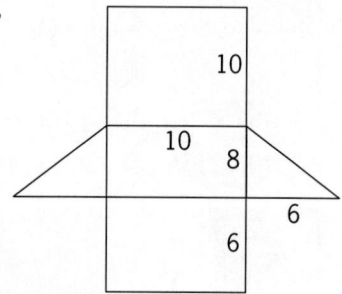

   surface area 288 cm²

For example,

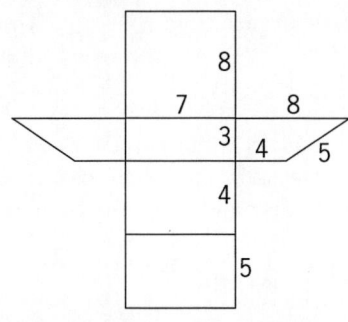

surface area 176 cm²

5 a 400 cm²; 25 cm × 20 cm   **b** 20%

Ex C20.5

1 a 188 cm² **b** 151 cm² **c** 126 cm² **d** 126 cm²

2 3140 cm² or 0.314 m²

3 a 251 cm² **b** 151 cm² **c** 151 cm² **d** 220 cm²

4 a 314 cm² **b** 603 cm²

5 848 cm²

6 50%

7 a has the smaller surface area of 603 cm².

b has surface area of 730 cm²

8 A sheet 52 cm × 15 cm (area 780 cm²)

Exam practice

1 for example

2 84 cm²

3 Join faces which are 5 cm × 4 cm   56 cm²

C21 Graphs

Check-in

1 a 9   **b** −2   **c** 12   **d** 2

2

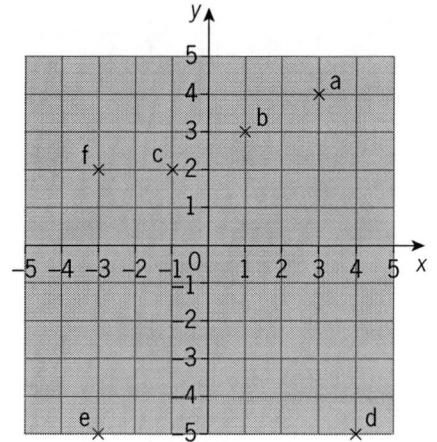

C21.1 Activity

a It's a straight line.   **b** Answer given.

c Because the line is flat at the top – their distance from London is unchanged for 3 hours.

d The line between b and c

e Their speed on the return journey was 50 mph.

Ex C21.1

1 a 200 m   **b** 4 mins   **c** 4 mins

d 100 m   **e** 12 mins

2 a Twice   **b** 300 m   **c** 2 mins   **d** 8 mins

3 a Y   **b** Z   **c** X

4 a A Aircraft   B Train   C Lorry
D Bicycle   E Pedestrian

b A 50 m/s   B 25 m/s   C 10 m/s
D 6 m/s   E 2 m/s

5 a 1 km   **b** A to B   **c** 4 km, 10 mins

d 24 km/h   **e** 6 km, 30 mins   **f** 12 km/h

6 a 150 m/min or 2.5 m/s   **b** 2 mins

c 500 m   **d** 5 min   **e** 100 m/min or 1.67 m/s

f 83 m/min or 1.4 m/s

7

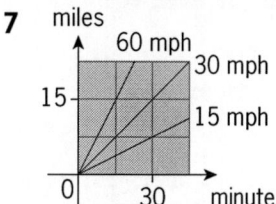

8 a Stephen, 20 mins   **b** 50 mins

c 30 km/h   **d** 30 km/h

9 a X Table tennis ball
Y Cricket ball

b The table tennis ball bounces 5 times, bouncing lower each time. The cricket ball bounces twice only.

10 The oil level decreases steadily for 3 weeks, then rapidly for 1 week. Then no oil is used for 2 weeks. Then, after 6 weeks, the oil is refilled to the original level. Then the level reduces steadily again.
The weather was probably a little cold until week 3, then very cold for week 3 to 4, warm for weeks 4 to 6 and then a little cold for weeks 6 to 8.

11 The jogger starts running at about 12 km/h. After 10 mins he turns and runs back at about the same speed. He slows and turns again after 20 mins. He then runs forward more slowly, stopping and turning after 30 mins. He then runs back to the starting point, arriving after 40 mins.

12 The machine moves quickly away for 2 secs, then turns and moves quickly back for 3 secs, then turns and moves away again more slowly. After 10 secs it has stopped moving.

13 a The coach leaves London, calling at Scalsby, Garthorpe, Skeltoft and Lincoln, It stops for 15 mins at Scalsby and Garthorpe, and it stops for 30 mins at Skeltoft. The whole journey takes $5\frac{1}{2}$ hours.

b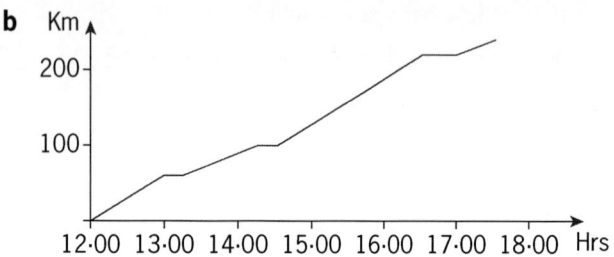

c 60 km/h, 40 km/h, 60 km/h, 50 km/h

d 44.5 km/h

C21.2 Rich task

Students should notice that the green line implies that the person's average heart rate is lower both before and after exercise perhaps implying that the person is fitter.

Ex C21.2

1 a i £15 **ii** £15 **iii** £65 **b** 23 kg

2 a L Firm B **b** Firm A charges £10

  M Firm A   Firm B charges £15

c Firm B is cheaper for longer journeys, 20 miles

3 a P Elex **b** Elex charges £60

  Q Trizity   Trizity charges £65

c 400 units **d** Trizity

4 a i The most economical speed is about 55 mph for petrol engines and 60mph for diesel engines.

  ii The miles travelled per gallon decreases.

  iii Diesel engines do more miles to the gallon than petrol engines at all speeds.

b

removing a bike rack	Increases fuel efficiency
accelerating fast	Decreases fuel efficiency
eating while you drive	No effect on fuel efficiency
tyres inflated at correct pressure	Increases fuel efficiency
having a clean air filter	Increases fuel efficiency
breaking hard and often	Decreases fuel efficiency

5 a 500 mins **b** £20 **c** 550 mins

d For less than 100 minutes per month.

6 a £80

b Over 6 m and less than or equal to 7 m **c** £150

7 a the distance travelled by a car driven at constant speed **Graph R**

b the temperature of a bowl of soup left uneaten **Graph P**

c the amount of money left in a purse on a shopping trip. **Graph S**

d the temperature outdoors on a cloudy day **Graph Q**

8 eg. on day 3 sheena uses half the oil for frying. When the remaining oil is cold she puts it back in the bottle. She uses more oil on day 6 and almost empties the bottle.

9 a all at one go **Graph Y**

  b in two gulps, half a cup each time **Graph Z**

  c sip by sip **Graph W**

  d not at all. **Graph X**

10 a The baby's weight reduces initially and after 10 days starts to increase again. By day 25 the baby has regained the weight it lost and continues to increase more rapidly.

  b 3.0 kg **c** Day 10

  d By day 25 **e** 400 g

11 A   Z   B   X   C   Y

The different shapes of the beakers give different graphs.

Beaker A is widest at the bottom and so initially the height increases slowly. Beaker B has a constant width, so the height increases uniformly with time. Beaker C is narrower at the bottom so initially the height increases more quickly.

C21.3 Rich task

Students might use Autograph or similar software to sketch graphs, this will help them to become familiar with the shapes of different graphs.

Ex C21.3

1 $y = x^2$

x	−4	−3	−2	−1	0	1	2	3	4
y	16	9	4	1	0	1	4	9	16

$y = x^2 + 3$

x	−4	−3	−2	−1	0	1	2	3	4
x²	16	9	4	1	0	1	4	9	16
+3	+3	+3	+3	+3	+3	+3	+3	+3	+3
y	19	12	7	4	3	4	7	12	19

$y = x^2 − 4$

x	−4	−3	−2	−1	0	1	2	3	4
x	16	9	4	1	0	1	4	9	16
−4	−4	−4	−4	−4	−4	−4	−4	−4	−4
y	12	5	0	−3	−4	−3	0	5	12

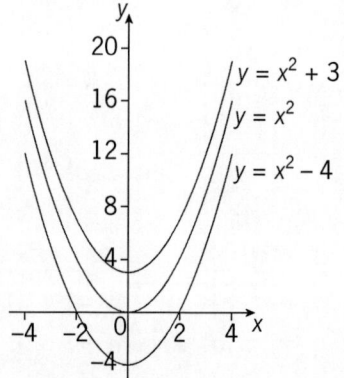

The curves can be transformed by translations:
+3 in the y direction, and −4 in the y direction

2 $y = x^2 - 2$

x	0	1	2	3	4
x^2	0	1	4	9	16
-2	-2	-2	-2	-2	-2
y	-2	-1	2	7	14

$y = (x - 2)^2$

x	0	1	2	3	4
$x - 2$	-2	-1	0	1	2
y	4	1	0	1	4

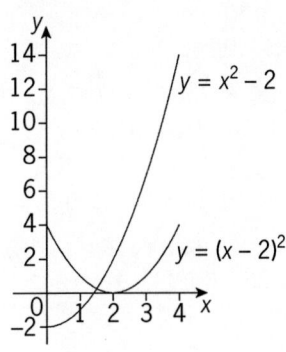

3 $y = x^2 - 5$

x	-3	-2	-1	0	1	2	3
x^2	9	4	1	0	1	4	9
-5	-5	-5	-5	-5	-5	-5	-5
y	4	-1	-4	-5	-4	-1	4

$y = 5 - x^2$

x	-3	-2	-1	0	1	2	3
5	5	5	5	5	5	5	5
$-x^2$	-9	-4	-1	0	-1	-4	-9
y	-4	1	4	5	4	1	-4

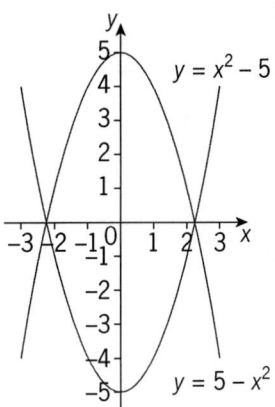

a Reflection in the x-axis **b** (2.2, 0) and (-2.2, 0)

4 $h = 6 - x^2$

x	0	1	2	3
h	6	5	2	-3

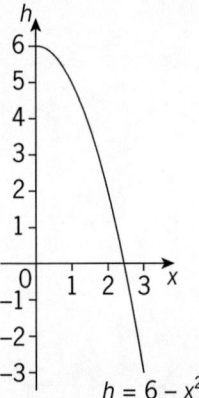

$h = 6 - x^2$

a 6 km **b** 2.4 km **c** 1.4 km

5 $y = 5 + t^2$

t	0	1	2	3
y	5	6	9	14

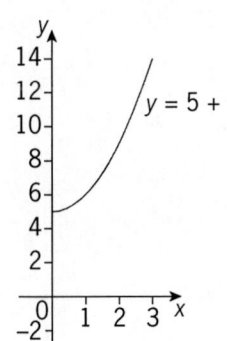

a i 5°C **ii** 14°C **b** 2.2 hours

6 $A = 2t^2 + 4$

t	0	1	2	3
$2t^2$	0	2	8	18
A	4	6	12	22

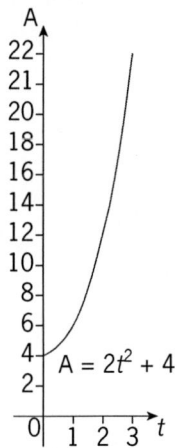

a 4 m² **b** 16.5 m² **c** 1.7 days

d No. This function shows the algae increasing rapidly, without a limit, but the lake must have a finite area.

7 $y = 3x^2 - 8$

x	0	1	2	3	4
$3x^2$	0	3	12	27	48
-8	-8	-8	-8	-8	-8
y	-8	-5	4	19	40

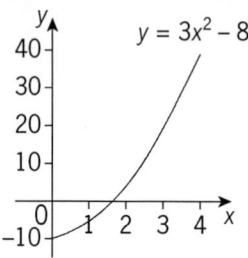

$y = 3x^2 - 8$

a 1.6 **b** 2.4 **c** 3.6 **d** $x \leq 1.6$

8 $y = 5x^2 - 10$

x	−3	−2	−1	0	1	2	3
5x²	45	20	5	0	5	20	45
−10	−10	−10	−10	−10	−10	−10	−10
y	35	10	−5	−10	−5	10	35

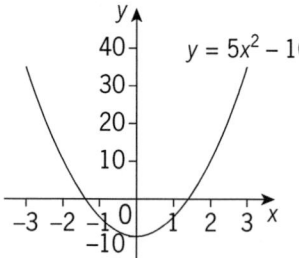

a 1.4, −1.4 **b** 0.6, −0.6 **c** 2.8, −2.8
d $-1.4 \leq x \leq 1.4$

9 $y = \frac{1}{2}x^2 - 3$

x	−6	−4	−2	0	2	4	6
½x²	18	8	2	0	2	8	18
−3	−3	−3	−3	−3	−3	−3	−3
y	15	5	−1	−3	−1	5	15

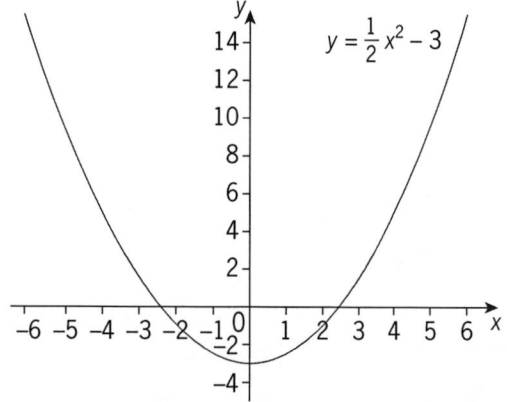

a 2.4, −2.4 **b** 5.1, −5.1

10

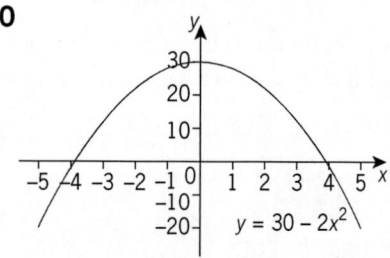

a i 3.9, −3.9 **ii** 2.2, −2.2 **b** $-2.2 \leq x \leq 2.2$

C21.4 Rich task

Position is fixed using coordinates. OS gives heights using contours.

Ex C21.4

1 A (300, 100, 30) B (200, 100, 50)
C (200, 300, 60) D (300, 200, 20)
E (300, 400, 75) F (100, 0, 40)

2 A (2, 5, 10) B (2, 3, 10)
C (4, 5, 20) D (5, 1, 20)
E (6, 3, 30) F (7, 4, 40)
G (6, 5.5, 30) H (1, 2, 0)
I (6.5, 1, 30) J (7.5, 3, 30)
K (3, 1, 10) L (4, 3.5, 20)

3 a A (20, 20, 50) B (40, 30, 50) C (30, 40, 100)
D (60, 50, 50) E (70, 40, 0) F (40, 15, 0)
G (20, 55, 100) H (60, 20, −50)
I (70, 10, −100) J (20, 40, 150)

b (40, 50, 50) (80, 20, −100) (20, 30, 100) (5, 40, 150)
(20, 5, 0) (40, 50, 50) (75, 30, −50) (50, 5, −50)

Exam practice

1 a 0 **b**

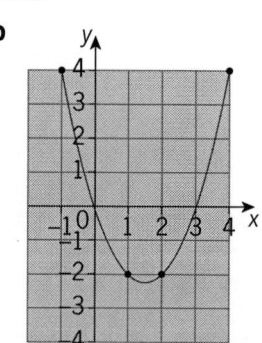

2 a Speedy by $\frac{1}{2}$ 1.60 **b** 6 miles

3 a

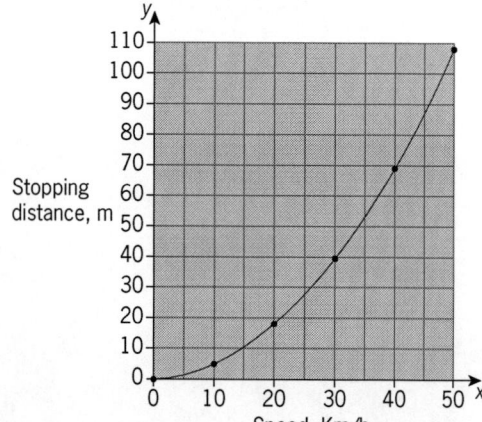

b 53 m,

c Driver's claim is not correct.
Stopping distance of 80 m implies speed of approx 44 km/h from graph, but skid marks are only from application of brakes which does not allow for reaction time. So skid marks of 80 m imply stopping distance greater than 80 m and therefore speed greater than 44 km/h.

Case study: Radio

a 2000Hz = 2kHz

b 2GHz = 2000 MHz

Waves a and c have same volume. Wave b is louder.

Waves a and b have same pitch. Wave c has higher pitch.

a 100.0 FM has frequency:
   i 100MHz   ii 100 000 000 Hz

b Speed = 100 000 × 3 = 300 000 m/s

c Frequency (kHz) = speed (m/s) / wavelength (m)

d Frequency = 300 000 /280 = 1 071.42 856 kHz = 1 071 428.5 Hz

e AM band

The Frequency is 1 071 kHz which is in the AM band and would be shown on the dial by 1071 AM

a 5 mins

b i 5 mins   ii 5 mins   iii 50 mins

c i 3:45pm   ii 3pm   iii 3:20pm

C22 Everyday arithmetic and bounds

Check in

1 27

2 a 1.3   b 0.3

3 a 3.56   b 8.04   c 0.06

Ex C22.1

1 a i 24°C   ii 74°F   b 55 m

2 a yes   b 55 mph

3 a i 127 miles   ii 203.2 km   b 92 miles

4 a 26 minutes

b i 2312, 2353   ii 28 minutes 23 minutes

c arrives earlier

Ex C22.2

1 a i 4.4°C   ii 36.9°C   iii −1.1°C

b i 71.6°F   ii 23°F   iii 28.4°F

2 John's estimate = 25, true value = 25.9

3 a 37 km/h   b 49 km/h

4 15.8 mg

Ex C22.3

1 £75.96, 3, £25.50

2 £1 = €1.41

3 Paris = £108.70, New York = £102.86, New York

4 9.25 BST next day

5 Students should think about flight times and time differences. If the flight time is less than the time difference then it is theoretically possible.

C22.4 Problem

Togo has roughly 310 people were square mile, Tuvalu has around 991 people per square mile. Tuvalu is more crowded.

Rich task

The one filled with sugar will be heavier.

Ex C22.4

1 a i 19.2 km/h   ii 17.1 km/h

b i 80 mph   ii 72 mph

2 a 7.43 mph   b 4.88 mph

3 40.6 km/h

4 4 km

5 a 3.1×10^{-5} m³ or 31 cm³   b 1.84 kg or 1840 g

6 258 per square mile

7 2500 sec = 41 minutes 40 seconds

Ex C22.5

1 a 67.5 68.5   b 3750 3850   c 725 735

d 4945 4955   e 17.55 17.65   f 23.35 23.45

2 a 27.5 – 28.5   b 47.5 – 48.5   c 111.5 – 112.5

d 555 – 565   e 9345 – 9355   f 9325 – 9375

g 510 – 530   h 415 – 425   i 43.55 – 43.65

j 5.15 – 5.25   k 7.25 – 7.35   l 39.5 – 40.5

m 99.5 – 100.5

3 a Yes, could be 154.5 cm   b 16.65 – 16.75 seconds

c Yes, could be 4.375 m

4 a 48.5%   b 78

Exam practice

1 3min 59.35sec   3min 59.45sec

2 a 60mph

b 40miles per gallon (using 4.5 litres = l gallon)

3 2.4 kg   +5.10

C23 Trigonometry

Check in

1 a 40 cm²   b 30 cm²

2 a 250   b 6300   c 41   d 250   e 3500

f 4   g 5.6   h 40   i 4.1   j 5.2

C23.1 Rich task

Oatiebisks have the most efficient packaging in terms of surface area of the packaging to the weight of the cereal.

Ex C23.1

1 **a i** 12   **ii** 24   **b i** 15   **ii** 45

   c i 30

     ii 60 (would overfill the box, but cannot fill exactly)
     45 (if cubes can be cut in half)

2 **a** 756 cm³   **b** 480 cm³   **c** 306 cm³

3 **a** 1083 cm³   **b** 1.083 litres

4 **a** 3 075 000 cm³   **b** 3075 litres

5 **a** 90 000 cm³   **b** 90 litres

6 **a** 452 cm³   **b** 61%

7 **a** 3 cm   **b** 6 cm   **c** 5 cm   **d** 9cm

8 20.4 cm

9 yes, it is 80 cm tall

10
	Length, cm	Width, cm	Height, cm
a	10	10	10
b	10	20	5
c	10	50	2
d	10	100	1
e	20	50	1

   The 10 cm × 10 cm × 10 cm pack is suitable.

11 The cube with dimensions 10 cm × 10 cm × 10 cm has the smallest surface area

C23.2 Rich task

The jumbo pack is the most efficient in terms of mass to surface area of packaging.

Ex C23.2

1 **a** 60 cm³   **b** 75 cm³

2 102 m³

3 350 cm³

4 A **a** 80 cm²   **b** 640 cm³
   B **a** 72 cm²   **b** 216 cm³
   C **a** 92 cm²   **b** 184 cm³

5 **a** 0.96 m²   **b** 2.4 m³

6 An infinite number of ways.
   The halves are cuboids or prisms with either triangular or trapezium cross-sections

7 **a** 10 cm² **b** 7 cm²   **c** 5 cm²   **d** 6 cm²

C23.3 Rich task

By measuring the volume of the water and then pouring it over the metal, subtracting the first measurement from the second, you should be able to find the volume of the metal.

Ex C23.3

1 **a** 314 cm³ **b** 170 cm³ **c** 100 cm³ **d** 126 cm³

2   Vegetable soup   470 ml
   Marmalade   360 ml
   Kidney beans   280 ml
   Tomatoes   840 ml

3 **a** 78 500 cm³   **b** 70 650 cm³

4 no, there is just over 1 litre in the bottle

5 2 litre engine

6 **a** 4 cm   **b** 6 cm   **c** 2 cm   **d** 12 cm

7 **a** 5.6 cm   **b** 2.6 cm   **c** 4.0 cm   **d** 5.9 cm

C23.4 Rich task

Length scale factor = 2

Area scale factor = 4

Volume scale factor = 8

Ex C23.4

1 **a** 3   **b** 9   **c** 27

2 **a i** 80 mm **ii** 600 mm² **iii** 2000 mm³

   b i 3.5 cm **ii** 1.4 cm²   **iii** 0.5 cm³

3 **a** 7400 metres **b** 2 100 000 m² **c** 0.005 km³

4 **a** 0.315 km   **b** 0.0445 km²   **c** 0.004 km³

5 Volume = 0.459 m³, diameter = 1 m, area = 0.133 m²

Exam practice

1 **a** 312 cm³   **b** 113 cm³

2 125 cm³

3 **a** 1600 cm²   **b** 12.5 cm³

C24 Graphs 2

Check in

1 **a** $\frac{2}{3}$ **b** $\frac{1}{2}$ **c** $\frac{3}{4}$ **d** $\frac{1}{4}$ **e** 1

2 **a** 1   **b** 1   **c** $\frac{3}{10}$ **d** $\frac{2}{5}$

3 **a** 0.9   **b** 0.4   **c** 0.85

4 **a** 0.01   **b** 0.25   **c** 0.35   **d** 0.05   **e** 0.36

Ex C24.1

1 **a** Unlikely **b** Evens **c** Unlikely **d** Impossible

2 **a** unlikely **b** evens

   c i unlikely **ii** highly unlikely **d** certain

3 **a** probability that X will happen is 0.6

   b probability that Y will happen is $\frac{1}{4}$

   c probability that Z will happen is 35% scale

4

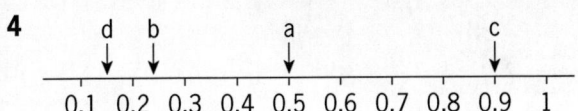

Ex C24.2

1 a $\frac{7}{25}$ **b** $\frac{18}{25}$ **c** $\frac{9}{25}$

   d $\frac{16}{25}$ **e** $\frac{10}{25}$ **f** $\frac{17}{25}$

2 a 0   **b** 1   **c** $\frac{18}{30}$ **d** $\frac{12}{30}$

3 0.2

4 a 3 is not a factor of 7   **b** 4

5 The second bag, because the fraction of green counters is higher

Ex C24.3

1 a 30

   b i $\frac{7}{30}$ **ii** $\frac{15}{30}$ **iii** $\frac{12}{30}$

     iv $\frac{9}{30}$ **v** $\frac{9}{30}$ **vi** $\frac{21}{30}$

2 a 0.45   **b** 0.25   **c** 0.3

3 a red and blue and orange   **b** yellow

   c i 0.2   **ii** 0.32   **iii** 0.23

4 a eg odd and even   **b** eg 1 or 2, 3 or 4, 5 or 6

   c eg even and prime, 2 is both

C24.4 Rich task

Students answers should address whether the spinner landed on any one particular colour more than you would expect and also whether this is sufficient evidence that the spinner is biased or not, and perhaps should suggest that further tests might be required to see if any noticeable trend continues.

Ex C24.4

1 140

2 120

3 0.625

4 a $22 \times 2 = 44$ **b** $\frac{34}{120}$ **c** 50

5 a i 0.11   **ii** 0.32   **iii** 0.27

    iv 0.41   **v** 0.87

   b i 80   **ii** 120

6 174

Ex C24.5

1 fair; would expect 140

2 fair; all frequencies between 31 and 35

3 a 0.4 0.35 0.37 0.33 0.36 0.37 0.37 0.36 0.36 0.35

   b 0.35   **c** biased; fair is 0.5

4 a $\frac{8}{36}$ $\frac{9}{36}$ $\frac{10}{36}$ $\frac{9}{36}$

   b fair; all approximately equal

5 a $\frac{11}{30}$

   b biased; other relative frequencies are $\frac{5}{30}$ or less

Ex C24.6

1 a table   **b i** $\frac{1}{12}$ **ii** $\frac{3}{12}$

2 a table   **b** $\frac{1}{4}$

3 a table   **b** $\frac{7}{12}$

   c 2 girls; P(2 boys) $= \frac{2}{12}$, P(2 girls) $= \frac{3}{12}$

4 a table

   b i $\frac{2}{36}$ **ii** 0   **iii** $\frac{6}{36}$

   c even; P(even) $= \frac{27}{36}$ P(odd) $= \frac{9}{30}$

5 a table   **b i** $\frac{1}{9}$ **ii** $\frac{3}{9}$

   c both have 2 out of 9 outcomes

Exam practice

1 a eg. 5, 6, 7, 8, 9

   b eg. 1, 3, 5, 7, 9

   c eg. 1, 2, 3, 5, 5

2 a $\frac{11}{44}$

   b $\frac{22}{44}$

3 $\frac{15}{36}$

Case study: Weather

   16°C; 2.5°C; -8.9°C

   Belfast 7°C

   Birmingham 6°C

   Cardiff 7°C

   Edinburgh 5°C

   London 7.5°C

   Newcastle 6°C

   South West England had the highest temperatures

   Scotland had the lowest temperatures

   Difference in temperature = 12.5°C

   Westerly wind (270°), 15 knots

   South Easterly wind (135°), 30 knots

   North Westerly wind (305°), 11.7 knots

Practice book answers

Practice 1a

1 **a** 20 **b** 900 **c** 2000, 500, 30

2 **a** Seven hundred and fifteen

b Eight thousand six hundred and ten

c Twenty six thousand and four hundred

3 **a** 49, 307, 311, 317, 416

b 9900, twelve thousand, 15 555, 25 000

c 79, 707, 719, 724, 763

4 **a** 415 **b** 8520 **c** 222

5 **a** 567 **b** 6414 **c** 8399

6 **a** 762 **b** 267 **c** 26

7 **a** 1614 **b** 3850 **c** 24 644

d 20 600

8 **a** 3794 **b** 4099 **c** 1121

d 304

9 210 610

10 **a** 8430 **b** 3048

Practice 1b

1 **a** $-8\,°C$, $-4\,°C$, $3\,°C$,

b $-5\,°C$, $-3\,°C$, $-1\,°C$, $0\,°C$

c $-11\,°C$, $-8\,°C$, $-2\,°C$, $22\,°C$

d $-5\,°C$, $-3\,°C$, $-2.5\,°C$, $-1\,°C$

2 **a** 9, 7, 5, 3, 1, -1 **b** 14, 10, 6, 2, -2, -6

c 10, 5, 0, -5, -10 **d** -6, -4, -2, 0, 2

e -8, -7, -6, -5, -4 **f** 11, 7, 3, -1, -5

3 **a** 3 **b** -3 **c** -6 **d** -8

e 2 **f** -10 **g** -16 **h** -7

i 5 **j** -7 **k** -18 **l** 0

m 7 **n** 2 **o** -12 **p** -5

q -7 **r** 0 **s** -9 **t** 15

u -22 **v** -2 **w** 2 **x** -11

4 **a**

+	5	2	−3	−7
−4	1	−2	−7	−11
0	5	2	−3	−7
−3	2	−1	−6	−10
6	11	8	3	−1

b

+	−3	−1	5	−2
6	3	5	11	4
−5	−8	−6	0	−7
−1	−4	−2	4	−3
3	0	2	8	1

5 **a** -10 **b** 6 **c** -32 **d** -6 **e** 5

f 36 **g** 1 **h** -16 **i** 2 **j** -4

k -6 **l** -7 **m** 56 **n** 294 **o** 30

p 72 **q** -600 **r** -32 **s** 0.25 **t** $-10\,000$

6 **a**

×	−3	−1	5	−2	3
2	−6	−2	10	−4	6
−4	12	4	−20	8	−12
1	−3	−1	5	−2	3
−5	15	5	−25	10	−15
−1	3	1	−5	2	−3

b

×	7	−1	0	−3	5
−5	−35	5	0	15	−25
1	7	−1	0	−3	5
3	21	−3	0	−9	15
−6	−42	6	0	18	−30
10	70	−10	0	−30	50

Practice 1c

1 **a** 19 **b** 242 **c** 12 **d** 3014 **e** 8

f 26 **g** 734 **h** 1

2 **a** 47 **b** 260 **c** 40 **d** 380 **e** 7800

f 86 000

3 **a** 800 **b** 80 **c** 50 000 **d** 2 **e** 0.08

f 0.03

4 **a** 11.3 **b** 8.8 **c** 211.7 **d** 0.9 **e** 0.3

f 16.0

5 **a** 1.67 **b** 8.76 **c** 0.45 **d** 0.07 **e** 85.22

f 16.96

6 a 36.6 **b** 5.86 **c** 38.8 **d** 71.0
e 9.6 **f** 1.0 **g** 12 **h** 2.6
i 9680 **j** 67 **k** 238

Practice 1d

1 a 1851 **b** 6.889 **c** 1.214 **d** 0.4189
e 7.889 **f** 19.35 **g** 0.049 47 **h** 221.5
i 24.37 **j** 6.619 **k** 3.306 **l** 2.303
2 a 41.73 **b** 8.163 **c** 0.1090 **d** 0.5001
e 20.63 **f** 10.09 **g** 6.191 **h** 10.27
i 8.627 **j** 22.02 **k** 1.093 **l** 44.72
m 45.66 **n** 52.86 **o** 22.51
3 a 5.479 **b** 5.272 **c** 0.2116 **d** 4.605
e 1.153 **f** 1.858 **g** 0.026 88 **h** 2.717
i 4.840 **j** 10.87 **k** 7.425 **l** 13.49
m 0.7392

Practice 2a

1 a

	Smoker	Non-smoker	Total
Male	190	210	400
Female	285	315	600
Total	475	525	1000

b 285

2 a

	Sky dive	Head shaved	Bathed in baked beans	Total
Loved doing it	171	64	33	268
Said afterwards, 'I must have been mad'	54	106	72	232
Total	225	170	105	500

b i $\frac{232}{500}$ **ii** $\frac{171}{500}$

3 a

	Argentina	England	Scotland	
Boy	4	0	10	14
Girl	1	2	7	10
	5	2	17	24

b 2 **c** 10% **d** Scotland

4

	Shaded	Unshaded
Squares	2	3
Circles	3	4

5 a

	Male	Female
Summer	4	2
Christmas	0	6
Autumn	2	2

b 10 **c** 60%

6 a

	Girls	Boys	Total
Can	70	80	150
Cannot	160	190	350
Total	230	270	500

b 29.6% **c** 45.7%

Practice 2b

1 a 5 **b** 4 **c** 3
2 a 4 **b** 4 **c** 1
3 a 6 **b** 6 **c** 5
4 a 9.6 **b** 11 **c** 12
5 a 5.1 **b** 6 **c** 7
6 a $6\frac{1}{4}$ **b** 6
7 a

No.	Tally	Frequency
1	IIII	5
2	IIII I	6
3	IIII IIII	10
4	IIII IIII	10
5	IIII I	6
6	IIII	5
7	IIII	4
8	III	3
9	I	1

b 2 modes: 3 and 4

8 a 2 **b** 11 **c** 15
9 a 3.5 kg **b** 5.08 kg **c** 4.29 kg

Practice 2c

1 a 18 **b** 37 **c** 57 **d** $\frac{7}{18}$
2 a 204 cm **b** 185 cm **c** 35 cm

3 a

Stem	Leaf
2	5 7
3	0 4 5 6
4	2 4 7 8 8
5	1 1 6 8 9
6	3 4 8
7	1 2

Key 2|5 means 25 marks

b 47 **c** 8

Practice 2d

1 For example **a** 1 3 9 12 15 **b** 2, 5, 7, 8, 11, 12
c 3 5 4 6 4 7 4 1 9 4

2 a 20 **b**

Goals	No.	Total
1	7	7
2	6	12
3	4	12
4	3	12

2.15 goals

Practice 2e

1 **a** 20 **b** 9

2 **a** 50 **b** 10.88 hours

   c Individual times for each battery are not given.

Practice 2f

2 **a** No chance for them to say so if they thought their meal was poor.

   b Allow options for poor opinions.

3 **a** Not all possible numbers are included.

   b The interval limits are not clear.

Practice 3a

1 **a** 0.6 **b** 10.3 **c** 3.8 **d** 6 **e** 20

   f 7.1 **g** 9.2 **h** 2.04 **i** 0.3

2 **a** 2.3 **b** 2.8 **c** 440 **d** 520 **e** 0.62

   f 0.66

Practice 3b

1 300 cm 2 2800 m 3 320 cm

4 3000 g 5 0.400 km 6 2.50 m

7 3000 kg 8 200 mm 9 5 litres

10 3.4 kg 11 1200 kg 12 0.260 kg

13 **a** gram **b** metre **c** kilometre

   d litre **e** centimetre

14 24 inches 15 2 yards 16 2 gallons

17 16 ounces 18 3 feet 19 32 ounces

20 36 inches 21 14 pounds 22 80 pints

23 **a** foot **b** pint **c** ton **d** inch

24 **a** True **b** True **c** True **d** False

25 **a** 4 inches **b** $4\frac{1}{2}$ gallons **c** 4 pounds

   d 100 litres **e** 80 km **f** 30 cm

26 **a** kilometre, mile **b** kilogram, pound

   c litre, gallon **d** metre, yard

   e centimetre, inch

27 **a** 0.57 **b** 17.5 pints **c** 1.7 litres

Practice 3c

1 **b** 42.5 m

Practice 3d

1 **b** Around 77° **c** Around 19.4 cm

2 ∠M = 64°

3 a = 6 cm

4 b = 6 cm

5 c = 9.7 cm

6 **b** 42.5 m

7 a = 82°

8 b = 78.5°

9 c = 41.5°

10

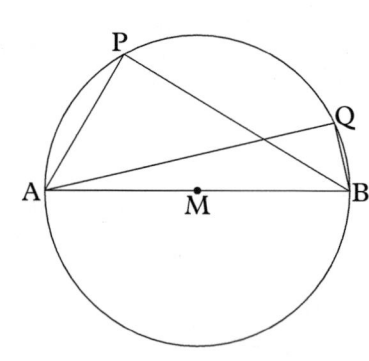

∠APB = ∠AQB = 90°

Practice 3e

1

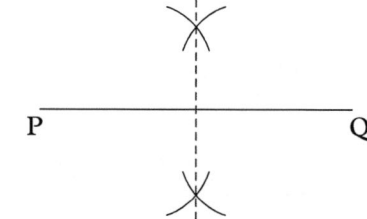

2

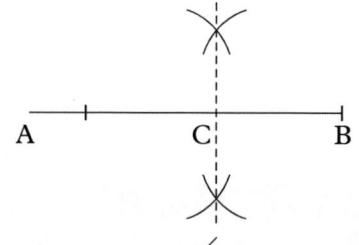

3

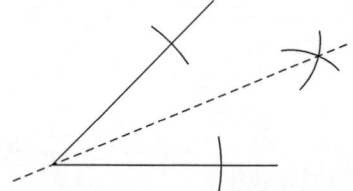

Practice 3f

1

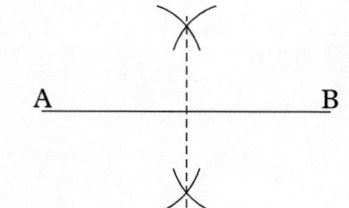

2

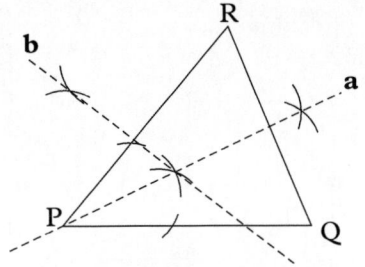

3

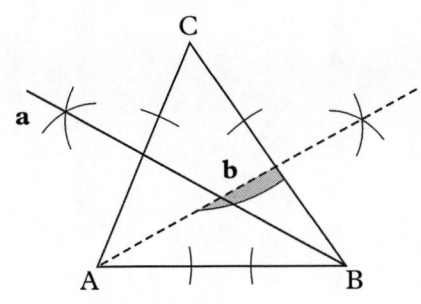

4

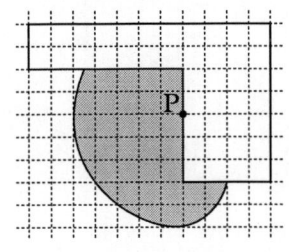

Practice 4a

1 a 1, 2, 3, 6   **b** 1, 3, 5, 15
   c 1, 3, 9   **d** 1, 2, 3, 6, 9, 18
   e 1, 3, 7, 21   **f** 1, 2, 3, 4, 6, 9, 12, 18, 36
   g 1, 2, 4, 7, 14, 28   **h** 1, 2, 4, 5, 8, 10, 20, 40

2 a 8 1, 2, 4, 8
     12 1, 2, 3, 4, 6, 12   1, 2, 4

   b 25 1, 5, 25
     40 1, 2, 4, 5, 8, 10, 20, 40   1, 5

3 a 2, 4, 6, 8   **b** 5, 10, 15, 20
   c 7, 14, 21, 28   **d** 11, 22, 33, 44

4 a 20   **b** 28   **c** 22

5 a 40   **b** 3, 6   **c** 40

Practice 4b

1 3, 5, 7, 19

2 True, there is only one even prime number, namely 2.

3 1, 4, 9, 16, 25, 36, 49

4 a 25   **b** 100   **c** 82   **d** 25

5 a 4   **b** 6   **c** 1   **d** 12

6 a 121   **b** No

7 a True   **b** False   **c** True   **d** False

8 a 15   **b** 27   **c** 49

9 a 17   **b** 63   **c** 4   **d** 27
10 a 8   **b** 8, 64   **c** 61   **d** 18
    e 61 and 64
11 a 3, 6, 9, 12, 15   **b** 4, 8, 12, 16, 20   **c** 12
12 a 4, 8, 12, 16, 20   **b** 10, 20, 30, 40 50   **c** 20
13 a 1, 3, 5, 15   **b** 1, 5, 25   **c** 5

Practice 4c

1 6 : 1   **2** 4 : 5

3 a 3 : 2   **b** 2 : 5   **c** 3 : 4   **d** 5 : 8

4 $\frac{7}{25}$

5 a 25 : 4   **b** 1 : 8   **c** 3 : 5

6 £30, £45   **7** £160, £640   **8** £125   **9** 180 g

10 25%

Practice 5a

1 a 7, 11, 15, 19, 23   **b** −2, 0, 2, 4
   c 3, 4, 6, 9, 13, 18   **d** 0.7, 0.8, 0.9, 1.0

Practice 5b

1 a 2, 5, 8, 11, 14   **b** 2, 7, 12, 17, 22
   c 24, 22, 20, 18, 16   **d** 25, 34, 43, 52, 61
   e −3, −1, 1, 3, 5   **f** 1, 2, 4, 8, 16
   g 80, 40, 20, 10, 5   **h** 1, 10, 100, 1000, 10 000

2 a 2, 8, 14, 20   **b** 2, 7, 12, 17   **c** 0, 3, 6, 9
   d 1, 3, 9, 27, 81 **e** 7, 4, 1, −2   **f** 1, 2, 4, 8, 16

3 a 7, 18, 29, 40   **b** 84, 64, 44, 24 **c** 3, 6, 12, 24
   d 200, 20, 2, 0.2

4 8 if the rule is "Double", or 7 if the rule is "The difference
   starts with 1 and constantly increases by 1."

Practice 5c

1 503

2 256, 1024

3 a 4 444 488 889   **b** 6 666 667

4 a • • • • •

     •   •

     •   •

     •   •

     •   •

     • • • • •

   b

n	1	2	3	4
no.	6	10	14	18

   c 50

5 **a** 1, 2, 4, 7, 11   **b** 10, 11, 9, 12, 8, 13

   c 1, 4, 9, 16, 25   **d** 1.4, 1.6, 1.8, 2.0

6 **a** $5 \times 6 = 5 + 25, 6 \times 7 = 6 + 36$

   b $10 \times 11 = 10 + 100$

Practice 5d

1 **a** $4n$ **b** $5n$ **c** $10n$

   d $7n$ **e** $5n + 1$ **f** $10n + 2$

2 $3n + 1$

3 **a** $2n + 2$ **b** $5n - 1$ **c** $9n + 2$

4 **a**

   b

n	1	2	3	4	5
no.	1	5	9	13	17

   c 77

   d $4n - 3$

5 27   **6** 19

Practice 5e

1 **a** 15   **b** $2n + 3$

2 **a** $17, 3n + 2$ **b** $35, 6n + 5$ **c** $33, 8n - 7$

3 $d = n - 3$

4 **a** $6^2 - 5^2 = 2 \times 6 - 1$ **b** $15^2 - 14^2 = 2 \times 15 - 1$

5 **a** 7   **b** 103

6 **a** 42   **b** 73

Practice 6a

1 **a** **i** 60%   **ii** 60%   **iii** 40%

   b Many more younger people chose skiing. Energetic holidays are more popular with younger people.

Practice 6b

1 **a** **i** $\frac{1}{4}$ **ii** $\frac{1}{6}$ **iii** $\frac{5}{12}$

   b **i** $\frac{1}{4}$ **ii** $\frac{1}{6}$ **iii** $\frac{5}{12}$

   c **i** 60   **ii** 100   **iii** 40

2 **a** **i** 25%   **ii** 20%   **b** **i** 60   **ii** 48

3 **a** Sector angles are 60°, 132°, 100°, 44°, 24°

   b 16

Practice 7a

1 **a** $11n$ **b** $5x$ **c** $6m$

   d $7c$ **e** $5m + 7n$ **f** $9n + 11$

   g $4a + 8$ **h** $8h - 11y$ **i** $9y + 6$

   j $2x - 7$ **k** $4x + 10y$ **l** $14y + 1$

   m $a + 3c$ **n** $10x - 5y$ **o** $d + 6$

2 **a** $5n$ **b** $m, 8n$ **c** $2a, 7b$

   d $3x, 7$ **e** $3x, 1$

3 **a** $4x + 8$ **b** $6x$ **c** $7x$

4 **a** $9a + 6b$ **b** $4c + 16x$ **c** $2y + 3$

   d $11b - 9c$ **e** $3a + 6$ **f** $6c + 14a$

   g $18c - 3y - 4$ **h** $11a + c - 10$ **i** $13d$

   j $4n^2 + 6n$ **k** $4n^2$ **l** $6n^2 + 70n + 6$

5 **a** True   **b** $6ab$

6 **a** $12ab$ **b** $12np$ **c** $30mn$

   d $3an$ **e** $6pq$ **f** $2n^2$

   g $12n^2$ **h** $18n^2$ **i** $49a^2$

7 **a** $7x, 2y$ **b** $x + 3, 2y + 3$

   c $2x + 1, 5y + 3$ **d** $4x - 2, 2y + 7$

8 **a** $2x + 6$ **b** $5b - 20$ **c** $8a - 16$

   d $3x + 3c$ **e** $7t - 7y$ **f** $10m + 10$

   g $6y + 12$ **h** $4u - 4x$ **i** $3x - 3y$

   j $9x - 18$ **k** $10a + 30$ **l** $2x + 2y$

   m $8c + 4d$ **n** $10y - 15$ **o** $44d - 33h$

   p $7n + 14t$ **q** $n^2 + 2n$ **r** $n^2 - 3n$

   s $n^2 - 10n$ **t** $2x^2 + x$ **u** $3x^2 - 2x$

   v $4x^2 + x$ **w** $6x^2 + 2x$ **x** $2x^2 - 6x$

9 **a** $7x + 6$ **b** $7y - 5$ **c** $8x - 5$

   d $17a - 21$ **e** $16x - 15$ **f** $10c + 33$

   g $20x - 10$ **h** 13   **i** $9a + 8$

   j $4y - 13$ **k** $5b + 18$ **l** $7a - 10$

10 **a** $x + x + x$ and $4x - x$

    b $x^2 + x$ and $x^2 + 2x - x$

    c $2x + 2$

Practice 7b

1 **a** 71   **b** 0   **c** 18   **d** 17

2 **a** 17   **b** 15   **c** -2 **d** 4

   e 4   **f** 10   **g** $3\frac{1}{2}$ **h** 2

   i 4   **j** -15 **k** 24   **l** 10

3 **a** $4p + 4q + 8$ **b** 40

Practice 7c

1 **a** 240 km   **b** 450 km

2 **a** 17 cm   **b** 20 cm

3 825

4 a 120 **b** 13 **c** 53

5 108

6 a 69 **b** −19 **c** 98 **d** 63

Practice 7d

1 a 3 **b** −11 **c** B and D

2 $4\frac{1}{2}$ **3** 7 cm **4** 5

5 £7.50

6 a $2\frac{1}{7}$ **b** $1\frac{2}{3}$

7 21 **8** $x = 5$ Perimeter $= 46$

Practice 7e

1 a 11 **b** 32 **c** 18 **d** 21 **e** 12

f 1 **g** 7 **h** 18 **i** 5

2 4, 11

3 a 2 **b** 5 **c** 7 **d** 5 **e** 0.25

f 0.4 **g** 3 **h** 18 **i** $\frac{1}{6}$ **j** 6

k 22 **l** −2

4 10, 5

5 7

Practice 7f

1 a −4 **b** 4 **c** 3 **d** $\frac{1}{9}$ **e** 2

f $\frac{3}{10}$ **g** 4 **h** 4 **i** 4

2 a $3x-3$ **b** $4x + 2$ **c** $5-10x$ **d** $9x + 6$

3 a 7 **b** $5\frac{1}{2}$ **c** 3 **d** −2 **e** $3\frac{1}{3}$

f 12 **g** 2 **h** 3 **i** 1

4 3, 5

Practice 7g

1 a 2 **b** 4 **c** $4\frac{1}{2}$ **d** $\frac{1}{2}$ **e** 14

f 99 **g** −200 **h** 14 **i** 10 **j** 12

k 28 **l** 16

2 1

3 a 5 **b** $\frac{1}{6}$ **c** 16 **d** 3 **e** −14

Practice 8a

1 a 055°, **b** 120°, **c** 200°, **d** 320°

2 a 076°, **b** 016°, **c** 098°, **d** 130° **e** 328°

3 b 11.5 km

4 1320 km

Practice 8b

1 a 5 cm **b** 7.81 cm **c** 10.6 cm **d** 5.66 cm

2 7.48 cm

3 a 4.58 cm **b** 5.20 cm **c** 6.24 cm **d** 4.47 cm

4 9.43 cm

5 19.2 km

Practice 8c

1 6.63 cm **2** 7.60 cm **3** 8.29 cm **4** 10.4 cm

5 10.9 cm

6 a 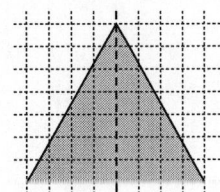 **b** 6.93 cm **c** 27.7 cm^2

$\left(\frac{1}{2} \text{ scale}\right)$

Practice 9a

1 $\frac{2}{5}$ **2** **3** $\frac{4}{5}, \frac{7}{10}, \frac{1}{4}$

4 a $\frac{2}{3}$ **b** $\frac{3}{5}$ **c** $\frac{2}{3}$ **d** $\frac{1}{4}$ **e** $\frac{3}{5}$

5 a $\frac{2}{6}$ **b** $\frac{4}{10}$ **c** $\frac{9}{12}$ **d** $\frac{7}{7}$ **e** $\frac{3}{18}$

f $\frac{21}{24}$

6 $\frac{2}{5}, \frac{9}{19}, \frac{1}{2}$

7 a $\frac{1}{3}$ **b** $\frac{4}{5}$ **c** $\frac{3}{12}$

Practice 9b

1 a $\frac{3}{10}$, 0.3 **b** $\frac{2}{5}$, 0.4 **c** $\frac{1}{10}$, 0.1

2 a 0.7 **b** 0.27 **c** 0.06 **d** 0.84 **e** 0.02

3 a 0.5, 0.6, 0.7, 0.8, 0.9 **b** 0.1, 0.3, 0.5, 0.7, 0.9, 1.1

c 1.1, 1.4, 1.7, 2.0, 2.3, 2.6

4 a 0.7, 0.71, 0.814 **b** 92.56, 94.9, 95

c 10.8, 10.85, 11, 11.02 **d** 0.402, 0.41, 3.95, 4.1

e 0.35, 0.36, 0.405, 0.5

5 a 17.34 **b** 8.12 **c** 124.0 **d** 11.771

6 a True **b** True **c** False **d** True

e False **f** True **g** True **h** True

7 A $\frac{3}{10}$, 30% B $\frac{1}{5}$, 20% C $\frac{1}{4}$, 25%

8 a 60% **b** 5% **c** 30% **d** 44% **e** 75%

9 70% **10** 92.5%

Practice 9c

1. **a** 4.8 **b** 10.1 **c** 3.94 **d** 4.22 **e** 39.5
   f 3.2 **g** 4.8 **h** 4.5 **i** 2.65 **j** 1.5
2. £8.95
3. £33.94
4. **a** £22.02 **b** £2.98
5. **a** 6.4 **b** 3.76 **c** 14.3 **d** 2.6 **e** 7.3
   f 2.3 **g** 3.75 **h** 7.23 **i** 9.34
6. **a** £3.55 **b** £4.93 **c** £18 **d** £5.20
   e £4.25 **f** £5.49
7. **a** 32.4 **b** 15.6 **c** 340 **d** 81.4 **e** 7.56
   f 90.74 **g** 8.6 **h** 0.4765 **i** 1700 **j** 130
   k 2.17 **l** 0.7 **m** 0.589 **n** 700 **o** 0.004
   p 2.008
8. £455
9. £365
10. **a** 22.2 **b** 41 **c** 39.02 **d** 146 **e** 157.6
    f 259.4 **g** 71 **h** 1976.8
11. £6.25
12. £14.50
13. **a** £6.35 **b** £7.41 **c** £3.34 **d** £8.16
14. **a** 0.14 **b** 0.3 **c** 4 **d** 1.68
    e 3.04 **f** 19.88 **g** 0.064 **h** 1.692
15. **a** 2.3 **b** 1.7 **c** 12.3 **d** 6.54
    e 0.124 **f** 0.168 **g** 1.11 **h** 6.5
16. 0.27 kg
17. £6.90
18. £13.84
19.

¹2	5		²5	7		³2
⁴4	4	⁵3		⁶2	4	6
0		⁷1	9		⁸8	8
	⁹1	6		¹⁰8		
¹¹2	5		¹²5	7		¹³9
¹⁴6	4		¹⁵1	3	¹⁶2	1
2		¹⁷9	9		8	

20. **a** 7.4 **b** 6.3 **c** 3.14 **d** 3.56
    e 3.42 **f** 5.61 **g** 8.3 **h** 7.2
    i 14 **j** 117 **k** 2.1 **l** 0.51
21. 12
22. 0.26 m
23. 17
24. 14
25. 0.382 kg
26. **a** 42.1 **b** 630 **c** 9.32 **d** 1.2
    e 1.2 **f** 7.36 **g** 2.13 **h** 0.086
    i 0.01 **j** 41.8 **k** 130 **l** 6.2
27. **a** £5.40 **b** £5.04
    c One thousand two hundred and seven point zero seven
28. 6, 50 cm
29. 0.45 cm
30. £236
31. **a** £252 **b** £ 106.50
32. 0.0174 cm
33. 23
34. £1.55

Practice 9d

1. 30%
2. **a** £11 **b** £20 **c** £42
3. 156

Practice 9e

1. **a** $\frac{5}{8}$ **b** $\frac{3}{5}$ **c** $\frac{7}{11}$ **d** $\frac{4}{9}$
2. **a** $\frac{3}{6} + \frac{2}{6} = \frac{5}{6}$ **b** $\frac{5}{20} + \frac{4}{20} = \frac{9}{20}$ **c** $\frac{5}{12}$
   d $\frac{5}{8}$ **e** $\frac{1}{12}$ **f** $\frac{1}{40}$
3. **a** $\frac{3}{20}$ **b** $\frac{3}{10}$ **c** $\frac{5}{18}$ **d** $\frac{33}{40}$
4. $\frac{10}{9} = 1\frac{1}{9}$
5. **a** $\frac{4}{5}$ **b** $2\frac{1}{4}$ **c** $\frac{5}{24}$ **d** $3\frac{1}{5}$
6. £216
7. **a** $\frac{17}{20}$ **b** $\frac{2}{5}$
8. Swimmers 40%, others 37.5%
9. $\frac{3}{4} - \frac{1}{2}, \frac{1}{12} + \frac{1}{6}, \frac{11}{12} - \frac{2}{3}, 7 \div 28$

Practice 9f

1. **a** $\frac{5}{4}$ **b** $\frac{8}{3}$ **c** $\frac{7}{2}$ **d** $\frac{27}{5}$ **e** $\frac{22}{7}$
2. **a** $2\frac{7}{12}$ **b** $3\frac{11}{12}$ **c** $8\frac{9}{10}$
3. **a** $2\frac{2}{3}$ **b** $2\frac{1}{4}$ **c** $2\frac{1}{5}$ **d** $2\frac{2}{5}$ **e** $3\frac{1}{2}$
4. **a** 2 **b** $2\frac{1}{2}$ **c** $5\frac{5}{8}$ **d** $3\frac{1}{12}$

Practice 10a

1 30° **2** 55° **3** 120° **4** 137°

5 a 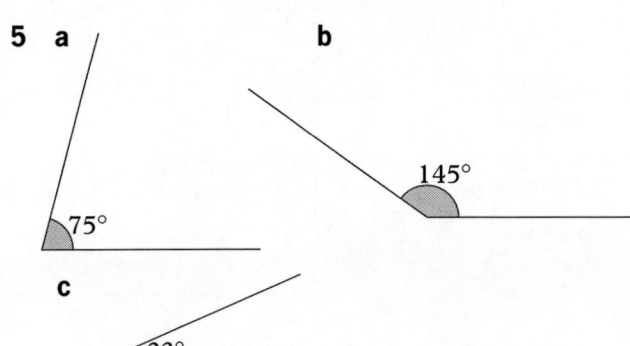 **b**

145°

75°

c

23°

6 66°, 48°, 66°   **7** 107°, 36°, 37°

8 40°, 97°, 43°   **9** 64°, 40°, 76°

10

11 y, x, z

a

c

b

Practice 10b

1 a $x = 48°$ **b** $y = 134°$ **c** $x = 39°$

  d $a = 65°$ **e** $x = 31°$ **f** $x = 44°$

  g $a = 36°$ **h** $x = 51°$

2 a $x = 100°$ **b** $y = 80°$ **c** $e = 60°$

  d $x = 30°$ **e** $x = 44°, y = 136°$

  f $x = 75°, y = 105°, z = 75°$

  g $x = 60°, x + 60° = 120°, y = 60°$ **h** $a = 72°$

Practice 10c

1 a $a = 73°$ **b** $b = 59°$ **c** $c = 103°$

  d $d = 135°$ **e** $e = 70°$ **f** $x = 80°, y = 75°$

2 a $a = 95°, b = 115°$

  b $a = 60°, b = 50°, c = 70°$

  c $x = 68°, y = 112°$

  d $x = 60°, 2x = 120°$

  e $y = 45°, 3y = 135°$

  f $y = 65°, y + 50° = 115°, x = 75°, x + 30° = 105°$

3 a $a = 50°$ **b** $x = 40°, b = 60°, 2b = 120°$

  c $c = 80°, c + 20° = 100°$

  d $d = 105°, d - 30° = 75°$

Practice 10d

1 a $a = 70°$ **b** $b = 73°$ **c** $c = 55°$

  d $d = 37°$ **e** $e = 23°$ **f** $x = 74°$

2 a $x = 66°$ **b** $y = 40°$ **c** $z = 38°$

  d $a = 48°$ **e** $z = 112°$ **f** $e = 68°$

3 a $a = 110°, b = 55°$

  b $z = 23°$ **c** $x = 34°$ **d** $x = 39°$

Practice 10e

1 a i Trapezium   **ii** Parallelogram

   iii Square   **iv** Kite   **v** Rhombus

  b Square, Rhombus, Kite

2 a $x = 108°$ **b** $y = 50°$ **c** $z = 76°$

  d $p = 270°$ **e** $d = 110°$ **f** $e = 102°$

3 a $f = 98°$ **b** $x = 60°, 2x = 120°, y = 48°$

  c $a = 65°, b = 40°$ **d** $c = 46°, d = 54°$

  e $a = 60°, b = 40°$

Practice 11a

1 a A(4, 1) B(5, −3) C(−2, 2) D(−4, −3) E(2, −4) F(0, 4)

   G(−3, 4) H(−2, −4) **b** $x = -2$ **c** $y = -3$

2

a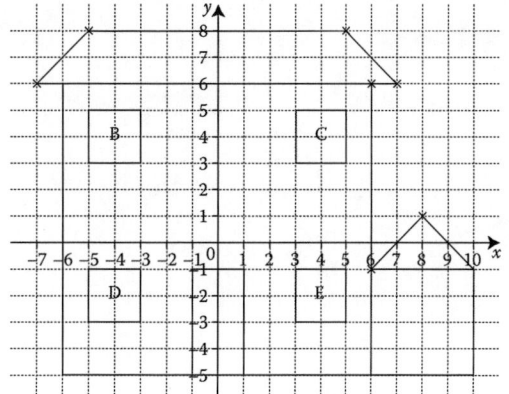

b kite - (4, 11)
   rectangle - (9, 11)
   parallelogram - (6, 4)
   square - (8, 6)

Practice 11b

1 a $n > -2$ **b** $n < 1$ **c** $n \leqslant 3$
d $n \geqslant 0$ **e** $-5 \leqslant n < 2$ **f** $-4 < n < 0$
g $-1 \leqslant n < 5$ **h** $-4 < n \leqslant 2$

2 a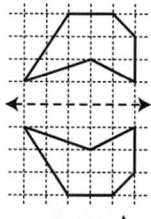

b

c

d

e

f

3 a 2, 3, 4   **b** 1, 2, 3, 4, 5   **c** $-2, -1, 0, 1$
4 a $x > 4$ **b** $x < 3$ **c** $x > 4$
d $x > 3$ **e** $x \geqslant 2$ **f** $x < 4$
5 $11 < x < 24$
6 $-1 < x < 4$

Practice 12a

1 a 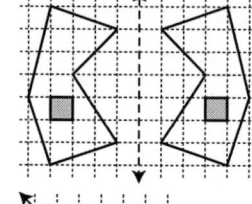   **b**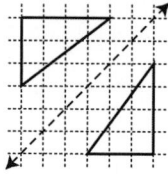

c   **d**

e

2 a 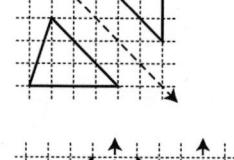   **b**

c   **d**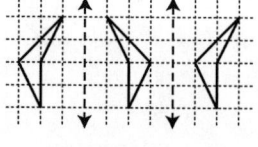

3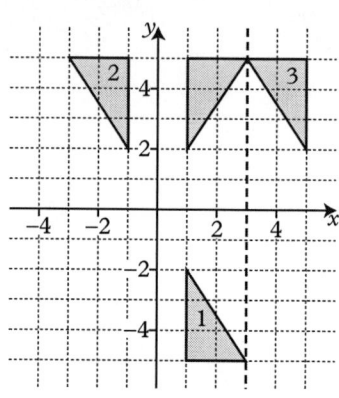

Practice 12b

1 a 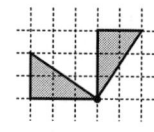   **b**   **c**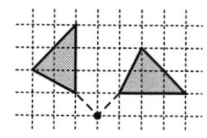

2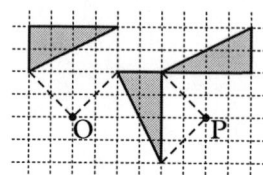

3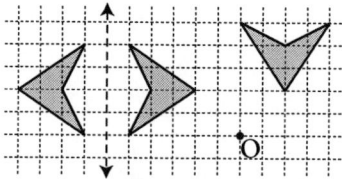

4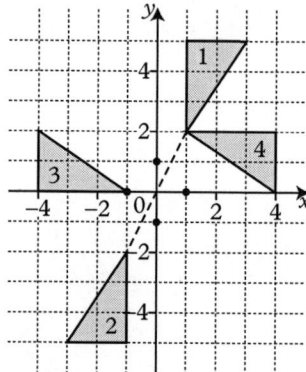

d Rotation of 90° anticlockwise about $(1, 2)$

5 a Rotation of 90°, clockwise, about $(0, 0)$ **b** Rotation of 90°, anticlockwise, about $(1, 1)$

c Rotation of 180° about $(0, 0)$ **d** Rotation of 90°, clockwise, about $(-2, 1)$

Practice 12c

1 a $\begin{pmatrix} 4 \\ 3 \end{pmatrix}$ b $\begin{pmatrix} 1 \\ 2 \end{pmatrix}$ c $\begin{pmatrix} 1 \\ 3 \end{pmatrix}$ d $\begin{pmatrix} 5 \\ 0 \end{pmatrix}$

   e $\begin{pmatrix} 4 \\ -2 \end{pmatrix}$ f $\begin{pmatrix} -7 \\ 3 \end{pmatrix}$ g $\begin{pmatrix} 5 \\ 6 \end{pmatrix}$ h $\begin{pmatrix} 0 \\ 5 \end{pmatrix}$

Practice 12d

1 a   Reflection in $y = -1$ b   Rotation of 90°, anticlockwise about $(0, 0)$.

   c   Translation $\begin{pmatrix} -3 \\ 3 \end{pmatrix}$

Practice 13a

1 b   Positive

2 a   Negative (strong)

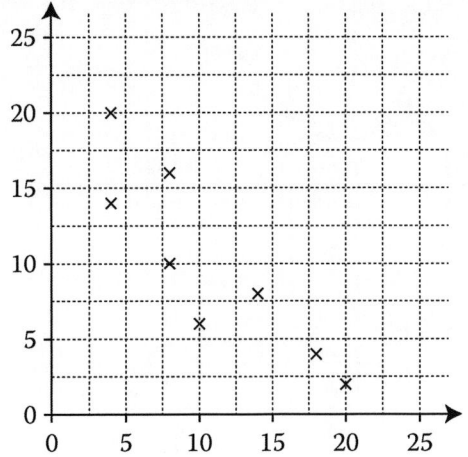

  × Series1

   b   Positive (quite strong)

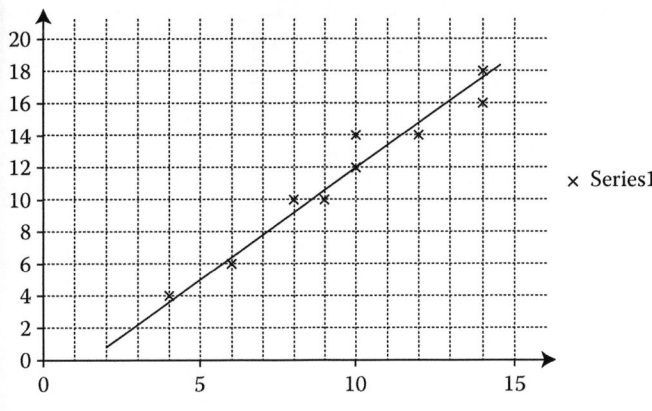

  × Series1

Practice 13b

1 a   B and D   b   A and F   c   C and E

Practice 13c

1 a

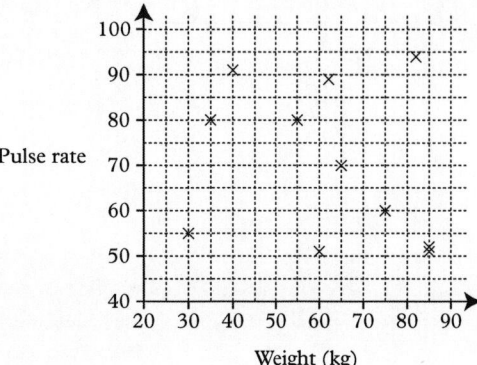

   b   no correlation

2 a, c

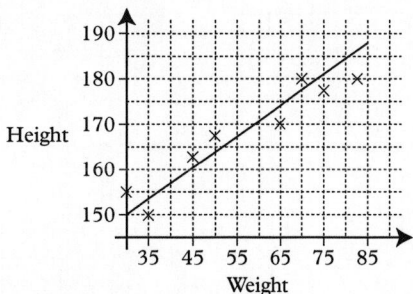

   b   strong positive correlation   c   ≈55 kg

3 a   no correlation   b   weak negative

   c   strong positive

Practice 14a

1   $(1, 4), (5, 6), (6, 3), (2, 2), (7, 1), (8, 4), (4, 4), (2, 7), (7, 6)$

2 a $y = 4$ b $y = 6$ c $x = 2$

   d $x = 7$ e $y = x$

3 a

x	0	1	3	5
y	3	4	6	8

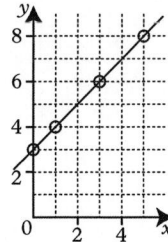

   b

x	0	1	2	3	4	5
y	1	3	5	7	9	11

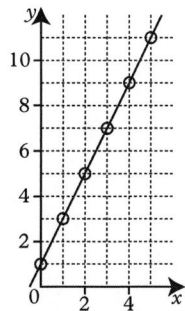

c

x	0	1	2	3	4	5
y	−3	−1	1	3	5	7

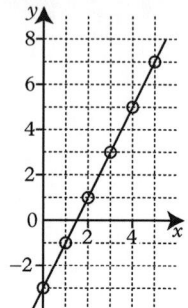

1 a (8, 3)   **b** (2, 9)   **c** (4, 1)

2 a 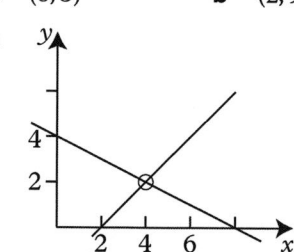   **b** (4, 2)

   b x = 4

   y = 2

d

x	0	1	2	3	4
y	4	6	8	10	12

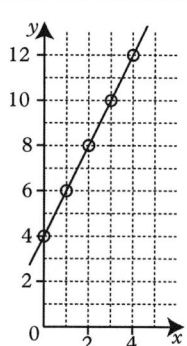

e

x	−2	−1	0	1	2
y	−4	−1	2	5	8

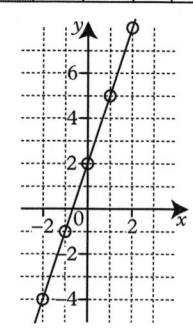

Practice 15a

A

1: 2	6	▓	2: 8	4	▓	3: 6
4: 4	4	5: 8	▓	6: 3	5	2
0	▓	7: 4	9	▓	8: 6	2
▓	9: 9	5	▓	10: 1	▓	▓
11: 1	1	▓	12: 4	2	▓	13: 6
14: 3	6	▓	15: 8	1	16: 3	6
2	▓	17: 6	0	▓	9	▓

B

1: 2	5	▓	2: 8	9	▓	3: 5
4: 4	2	5: 7	▓	6: 4	2	7
3	▓	7: 5	9	▓	8: 9	2
▓	9: 2	0	▓	10: 3	▓	▓
11: 8	1	▓	12: 8	4	▓	13: 7
14: 6	6	▓	15: 2	3	16: 1	5
9	▓	17: 5	7	▓	7	▓

f

x	−2	−1	0	1	2	3
y	−5	−3	−1	1	3	5

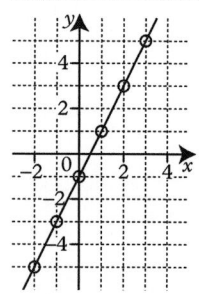

4 a

x	0	1	2	3	4
y	−1	1	3	5	7

b

x	0	1	2	3	4
y	3	4	5	6	7

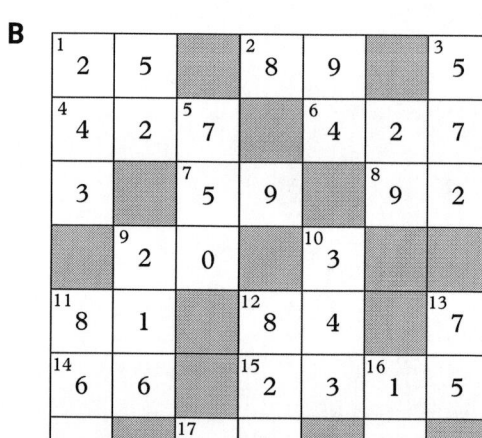

c (4, 7)

Practice 14b

1 $\frac{1}{4}$, −1, 4

2 $\frac{5}{4}$, $\frac{1}{5}$, −4

3 a $y = 3x + 2$ **b** $y = 4x - 1$ **c** $y = 6 - 2x$

   d $y = 2x$ **e** $y = 8 - \frac{1}{2}x$ **f** $y = 5 - x$

4 a 3   **b** 5

5 $y = 2x + 3$

Practice 15b

1 a 9   **b** 16   **c** 49   **d** 1   **e** 27

2 a 5^5 **b** 6^3 **c** 7^6 **d** 10^8 **e** 100 000 000

3 a 13   **b** 36   **c** 19

4 a 6   **b** 8   **c** 9

5 a 5   **b** 7   **c** 1   **d** 100

6 4.5 cm

Practice 15c

1 **a** 20(C) **b** 200(B) **c** 300(C) **d** 80(A) **e** 5000(C)
  f 2(C) **g** 7(A) **h** 100(B) **i** 0.1(C) **j** 500(A)

2 **a** 49.98 **b** 65.27 **c** 25.44 **d** 81.37 **e** 2.97
  f 11.52

3 **a** 81.78 **b** 4.15 **c** 13.68 **d** 38.94 **e** 56.16
  f 29.24

4 **a** 18.72 **b** 89.18 **c** 63.99 **d** 7.638 **e** 31.16
  f 48.248

Practice 15d

1 **a** $\frac{1}{2}$ **b** $\frac{1}{4}$ **c** $\frac{1}{9}$ **d** $\frac{1}{10}$ **e** $\frac{1}{36}$

2 **a** 3^5 **b** 5^7 **c** 6^7 **d** 2^{11} **e** 2^8 **f** 3^4

  g 5^6 **h** 6^7 **i** 4^4 **j** 7^2 **k** 8 **l** 9^{-4}

3 **a** False **b** True **c** True **d** True
  e True **f** False **g** False **h** True

4 **a** 3 **b** 2 **c** 4 **d** −2 **5** 141

Practice 16a

1 A and H, D and E, F and I

2 B, C and G

Practice 16b

1 **a** 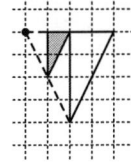 **b**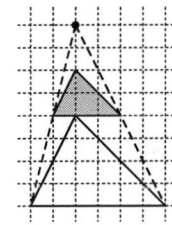

  c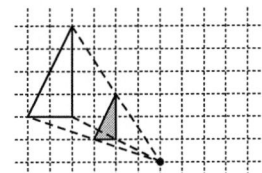

2 **a** 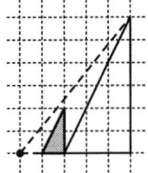 **b**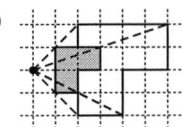

  c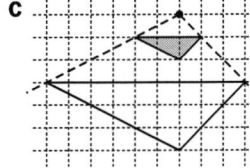

3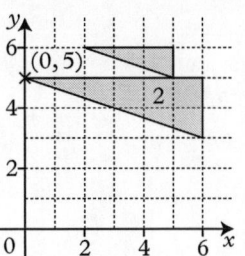

4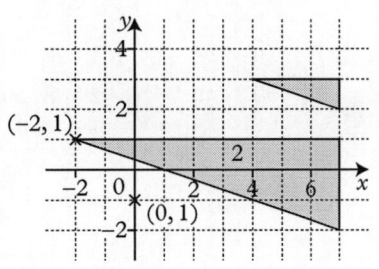

Practice 17a

1 £231

2 **a** £83.20 **b** £266.40 **c** £644

3 **a** $\frac{2}{3}\left(66\frac{2}{3}\%\right)$ **b** $\frac{3}{4}$(75%)

4 £66

5 £25.38

6 A(£135) B(£141) ∴ Difference = £6

7 £1463

Practice 17b

1 4% **2** **a** 6% **b** 2% **c** 10%
3 5% **4** 62.5% **5** 14% **6** 6

Practice 17c

1 **a** £5250 **b** £5512.50 **2** £3374.59
3 £3573.05 **4** £4800, £4750.75 **5** 432

Practice 18a

1 **a** $17\,\text{cm}^2$ **b** 20 cm

2 **a** $42\,\text{cm}^2$ **b** $121\,\text{cm}^2$ **c** $84\,\text{cm}^2$

3 **a** 28.4 cm **b** 44 cm **c** 38 cm

4 **a** $12\,\text{cm}^2$ **b** $30\,\text{cm}^2$ **c** $35\,\text{cm}^2$

5 10.5 cm

6 5 cm

Practice 18b

1 **a** $60\,\text{cm}^2$ **b** $54\,\text{cm}^2$ **c** $26\,\text{cm}^2$

2 **a** 38 cm **b** 42 cm **c** 30 cm

3 7.5 square units

4 $1000\,\text{cm}^2$

5 60

6 $48.75\,\text{m}^2$

7 a $25\,000\,\text{m}^2$ **b** 2.5 hectares

8 9 square units

Practice 18c

1 a 22.0 cm **b** 25.1 cm **c** 32.7 cm

2 a $38.5\,\text{cm}^2$ **b** $50.3\,\text{cm}^2$ **c** $84.9\,\text{cm}^2$

3 34.6 cm

4 $78.1\,\text{m}^2$

5 $85.8\,\text{cm}^2$

Practice 19a

1 a $3x + 6$ **b** $4x-12$ **c** $10x + 5$
   d $21x-7$ **e** $x^2 + x$ **f** $x^2 + 4x$
   g $2x^2 + x$ **h** x^2-2x **i** $3x^2 + 10x$

2 a $13x + 8$ **b** $7x-8$ **c** $7x + 7$
   d $11x + 10$ **e** $2x^2 + 3x$ **f** $3x^2 + 5x$

3 $x^2 + 7x + 10$

4 a $x^2 + 5x + 4$ **b** $x^2 + 8x + 7$ **c** $x^2 + 6x + 9$
   d $x^2 + x-6$ **e** x^2-x-20 **f** $2x^2 + 7x + 3$
   g $x^2 + 8x + 16$ **h** $x^2 + 2x + 1$ **i** x^2-16

5 a $4(2a + b)$ **b** $5(a + 3b)$ **c** $5(3a + 4b)$
   d $7(a + 3b)$ **e** $9(3a-4b)$ **f** $4(a + 2b + c)$

6 a $4(5x + 3y)$ **b** $6(5x-2y)$ **c** $9(3x + y)$
   d $7(5x-2y)$ **e** $20(2x + y)$ **f** $5(2x + y + 2z)$
   g $x(3x + 2)$ **h** $2x(2x + 1)$ **i** $x(5x + 1)$
   j $x(x-2)$ **k** $y(2y + 5)$ **l** $3x(4x + 7)$

Practice 19b

1 a 7 cm **b** 14 cm **c** 2.2

2 9.6

3 a 3.7 **b** 5.9

4 19.1 cm

Practice 20a

1

Shape	Edges	Faces	Vertices
A	12	6	8
B	9	5	6
C	18	8	12
D	8	5	5

2 a Cylinder **b** Cone **c** Sphere

3 a Isosceles **b** Square **c** Octagon **d** Polygon

Practice 20b

1 b F

Practice 20c

1 a $72\,\text{cm}^2$ **b** $150\,\text{cm}^2$

2 1.75 m, 1.05 m, 1.05 m

Practice 20d

1 a $125.7\,\text{cm}^2$ **b** $292.2\,\text{cm}^2$ **c** $276.5\,\text{cm}^2$

2 $311.6\,\text{cm}^2$

Practice 21a

1 a 30 km **b** 12:00
   c i 30 km/h **ii** 60 km/h **iii** 60 km/h

2 a 25 km **b** 14:45
   c 40 km/h, 20 km/h, 0 km/h, 10 km/h, 80 km/h

3 She sets off, but after a time slows down. She visits
   her parents, and returns home at a speed which is
   somewhere between her two outward speeds.

Practice 21b

1 a i £50 **ii** £30 **iii** £35.70
   b i $56 **ii** $140 **iii** $168

2

Practice 22a

1 a 129 miles **b** 87 miles **c** 241 miles

2 £7.25

3 a 520 000 **b** £208 000

4 £2.47

Practice 22b

1 **a** $n + 10$ **b** $3n$ **c** $5n + 10$
2 **a** $52\,°F$ **b** $2\,°F$ **c** $6\,°C$

Practice 22c

1 283.5 miles
2 73 cm
3 £625
4 £3120
5 ┌───────────────┐
   │ •   •   •   • │
   └───────────────┘

Practice 22d

1 100 pounds
2 2.2 miles

Practice 22e

1 120 km
2 10 m/s
3 4 h
4 600 km
5 12 km/h
6 45 m
7 86.15 mi/h
8 94 mi/h
9 180 mi, 247 mi, therefore 67 mi

Practice 23a

1 **a** $10\,cm^3$ **b** $12\,cm^3$ **c** $18\,cm^3$ **d** $22\,cm^3$
2 **a** $30\,cm^3$ **b** $72\,cm^3$
3   4   200

	l	b	h	V
a	4 cm	3 cm	2 cm	$24\,cm^3$
b	2.2 cm	5 cm	4 cm	$44\,cm^3$
c	1.5 m	2 m	5 m	$15\,m^3$
d	4 cm	2 cm	3 cm	$24\,cm^3$
e	3 cm	4 cm	5 cm	$60\,cm^3$
f	10 m	2.5 m	4 m	$100\,m^3$

5 72 minutes

Practice 23b

1 $240\,cm^3$
2 $280\,cm^3$
3 $357\,cm^3$
4 $144\,cm^3$

Practice 23c

1 $6158\,cm^3$
2 $1005\,cm^3$
3 $243\,cm^3$
4 A, $188.5\,cm^3$; B, $240\,cm^3$. Therefore B.

Practice 23d

1 **a** 2:3   **b** 4:9
2 **a** 21 cm   **b** $2430\,cm^3$

Practice 24a

1 **a** $\frac{1}{4}$ **b** $\frac{1}{4}$ **c** $\frac{1}{4}$
2 **a** $\frac{1}{6}$ **b** $\frac{1}{6}$ **c** $\frac{1}{2}$
3 **a** $\frac{1}{9}$ **b** $\frac{2}{9}$ **c** $\frac{1}{9}$ **d** $\frac{4}{9}$
4 **a** $\frac{1}{6}$ **b** $\frac{1}{2}$ **c** $\frac{1}{3}$
5 **a** $\frac{1}{12}$ **b** $\frac{1}{2}$ **c** $\frac{1}{2}$ **d** $\frac{1}{6}$ **e** $\frac{1}{2}$ **f** 1
6 **a** $\frac{1}{11}$ **b** $\frac{2}{11}$ **c** $\frac{3}{11}$ **d** $\frac{8}{11}$
7 **a** $\frac{1}{4}$ **b** $\frac{1}{8}$ **c** $\frac{3}{8}$ **d** $\frac{1}{4}$

Practice 24b

1 **a** $\frac{1}{6}$ **b** $\frac{2}{3}$
2 **a** $\frac{1}{3}$ **b** $\frac{4}{9}$ **c** $\frac{2}{9}$
3 **a** i $\frac{5}{11}$ ii $\frac{2}{11}$
   b i $\frac{5}{11}$ ii $\frac{1}{11}$ iii $\frac{5}{11}$ iv 0
4 **a** $\frac{2}{7}$ **b** Three fives
5 **a** $\frac{1}{4}$ **b** $\frac{1}{7}$ **c** $\frac{1}{28}$ **d** $\frac{3}{14}$ **e** $\frac{9}{28}$
6 **a** $\frac{1}{4}$ **b** $\frac{1}{6}$ **c** $\frac{1}{4}$ **d** $\frac{1}{3}$ **e** $\frac{1}{2}$

Practice 24c

1 **a** $\frac{1}{6}$ **b** False, it is only probable that you will.
2 **a** $\frac{3}{13}$ **b** $\frac{1}{13}$ **c** $\frac{5}{13}$ **d** $\frac{8}{13}$
3 **a** $\frac{1}{30}$ **b** $\frac{1}{5}$ **c** $\frac{3}{10}$ **d** $\frac{1}{3}$ **e** $\frac{1}{6}$ **f** 0
4 5

5 a 10 **b** 30

6 a 5 **b** 10

7 a $\frac{1}{2}$ **b** $\frac{1}{4}$ **c** $\frac{1}{8}$ **d** $\frac{1}{8}$ **e** $\frac{3}{4}$

Practice 24d

1 a HHH, HHT, HTH, THH, HTT, THT, TTH, TTT **b** $\frac{1}{8}$

2

Myself	Brother	Myself	Brother
Tea	Tea	Orange	Tea
Tea	**Coffee**	**Orange**	**Coffee**
Tea	Orange	Orange	Orange
Tea	Water	Orange	Water
Coffee	Tea	Water	Tea
Coffee	Coffee	Water	Coffee
Coffee	Orange	Water	Orange
Coffee	Water	Water	Water

3 a

+	4	5	6
1	5	6	7
2	6	7	8
3	7	8	9

b $\frac{2}{9}$

4 a

+	1	2	3	4	5	6
1	2	3	4	5	6	7
2	3	4	5	6	7	8
3	4	5	6	7	8	9
4	5	6	7	8	9	10
5	6	7	8	9	10	11
6	7	8	9	10	11	12

b $\frac{1}{12}$ **c** $\frac{5}{36}$